THE 'MARKET PANACEA'

Dedicated to
Francisca, Saskia and Friso

THE 'MARKET PANACEA'

Agrarian transformation in developing countries and former socialist economies

Edited by
MAX SPOOR
Institute of Social Studies

INTERMEDIATE TECHNOLOGY PUBLICATIONS 1997

Intermediate Technology Publications Ltd
103–105 Southampton Row, London WC1B 4HH, UK

© this selection, Max Spoor 1997

A CIP catalogue record for this book is available from the
British Library

ISBN 1 85339 414 9

Typeset by J&L Composition Ltd, Filey, North Yorkshire
Printed in the UK by BPC Wheaton Exeter

Contents

Preface

THIS BOOK IS about agrarian transformations, comparing the experience of structural adjustment in developing countries and the transition from centrally planned to market economies in the former socialist countries. The genesis of the project can be traced to two panels at the May 1995 Wageningen International Conference on 'Agrarian questions' in which I was fortunate enough to participate. Subsequently, the organizers of the event approached me with a view to editing a volume of selected conference papers.

The study of agrarian transformations, in particular in relation to processes of market liberalization and privatization has, in fact, been the focus of my research during the past decade. Working at the UNAN university in Nicaragua for four years during the second half of the Sandinista era, it was possible to closely monitor the effects of state interventionism, and the first steps towards structural adjustment. Since my return to the Institute of Social Studies, teaching in the post-graduate programme of Agricultural and Rural Development, my thinking on these issues has benefited from the thorough discussions on agrarian policies and adjustment processes with participants of LDCs (and gradually also from former socialist countries). Therefore, given my particular interest in the relationship between 'market-oriented' economic reforms (under 'structural adjustment' and 'transition') and the agrarian sector in developing countries (LDCs) and the former Soviet Union (FSU) respectively, the idea to compare some of these experiences was a logical – and challenging – step.

Nevertheless, only some of the papers presented at the two conference panels have been included in this book. This is due to a combination of my own preferences, because some were to be published elsewhere, or simply the operational difficulties of editing a book which seeks to bring together contributing authors who reside in so many different places, despite the great improvements that cyberspace has brought researchers. In the final 'harvest' of ten chapters, five originate from the original conference, one in part, while four others were specially written to complement the volume or were intercepted at other conferences, in Moscow and Reading. The particular attractiveness of this project – apart from its fascinating content – was to enjoy regular contact with scholars in a rather 'exotic' combination of places, such as Sofia, Bucharest, Kiel, Hanoi, Copenhagen, Tashkent, Bishkek, Portsmouth, Keele and Norwich. These highly productive collaborations finally led to this book which hopefully reflects the wide experience and insights of my respected co-authors. Nevertheless, the usual disclaimers apply.

Max Spoor, The Hague, April 1997

List of contributors

Andy Thorpe, Department of Economics, University of Portsmouth, UK.

Max Spoor, Institute of Social Studies, The Hague, The Netherlands

Philip Raikes, Centre for Development Research, Copenhagen, Denmark.

Deryke Belshaw, School of Developmental Studies/Overseas Development Group, University of East Anglia, Norwich, UK.

Peter Lawrence, Department of Economics, Keele University, Staffordshire, UK.

Michael Hubbard, Development Administration Group, School of Public Policy, University of Birmingham, UK.

Diana Kopeva, Department of Agricultural Economics, University of National and World Economics, and Policy Advisory Unit, Ministry of Agriculture and Food, Sofia, Bulgaria.

Mihail Dumitru, Institute of Agricultural Economics, and TACIS/EU Delegation, Bucharest, Romania.

Peter Wehrheim, Institute for Food Economics and Food Policy, University of Kiel, Germany.

Dao The Tuan, Vietnam Agricultural Science Institute, Hanoi, Vietnam.

Introduction

THE OVERARCHING IDEA of the 'market panacea' has been the main force behind structural adjustment programmes (SAP) in developing countries during the 1980s and 1990s while, in an entirely different context, the sudden collapse of the Soviet Union has been followed by a transition from planned to market economies in the eastern bloc. Here, too, the key policies of SAP, namely market liberalization, privatization and state withdrawal have formed the main 'agenda for reform'. The binding idea behind this book, as illustrated by its title, is to query whether this general cocktail of market medicine is likely to alleviate the stagnation caused by 'interventionism'. It focuses primarily on the dynamics between the agrarian sector and the market-oriented reforms introduced by structural adjustment and transition, comparing policy analysis and performance in the context of the developing countries (LDCs) and former socialist economies.

Furthermore, it illustrates the unintended or unexpected outcomes of these programmes of economic adjustment. The contributions to this book identify some important missing links in mainstream analysis of SAP and the transition from planned to market economies. In particular, the crucial linkage between the macro (stabilization-oriented) reforms and the sectoral, meso and micro transformations that are taking place. It is evident that most adjustment and transition policies have been implemented – under entirely different scenarios and in countries with widely varying resource endowments – in a rather strait-jacketed way. With the exception of sectoral adjustment programmes (or loans), the agrarian sector – a critical sector in terms of employment, food production and export generation capacity – has rated surprisingly low on the reform agendas.

The term 'market panacea' might strike the reader as provocative, as it has become commonplace in international forums – especially those in which economists call the tune – to stress over and over again the necessity of 'less state' and 'more market'. We have reached the point where anyone who seeks to identify weaknesses or failures of the market mechanism (at both a theoretical and operational level) is branded as being analytically 'unsound'. Neo-classical economics (and the related, but certainly not identical, ideas of 'neo-liberalism') is now accepted as 'mainstream thought'. This means that in former socialist countries economics teaching is dominated by a new discipline, crudely, but quite symbolically, called 'market economics'. Some analysts query whether we need any theory of the transition from planned to market economies at all. A well-known scholar of the (former) Soviet Union recently raised this question, noting that some authors respond negatively on the basis that, as we already have a theory of 'the market', the transition towards the market simply boils down to a policy debate about the pace and sequencing of reforms (Lavigne, 1995). Furthermore, although there is still a debate about SAP and its impact, and some scholars, such as Engberg-Pedersen *et al.* (1996) for Africa, or Weeks (1995b) and Bulmer-Thomas (1996) for Latin America, clearly show its limitations (and limited success), much of the current debate seems to be about modalities, accepting the boundaries of mainstream thought about economic development and not contradicting its essence.

There is also a 'triumphal' tendency expressed by the International Financial Institutions (IFIs), which insist that the main pillars of structural adjustment and market transition strategies (market liberalization, privatization and state withdrawal) have restored growth in the LDCs and the former socialist economies. Some of the chapters in this book focus upon the composite measures of success, such as GDP and agricultural output growth rates, that are currently utilized, pointing to the weaknesses of such 'success indicators' and the need to be much more critical and less self-complacent in analysing the effects of such major transformations, in particular as regards the agrarian sector. With possible exceptions, such as the cases of Uganda and Vietnam in this book, we conclude that there are no irrefutable data that indicate whether SAP or market transition strategies (MTS) have produced a sustained, across the board, recovery or not. More importantly, a number of critical issues in this process of 'assessing the adjustment' and 'assessing the transition' (borrowing the title from the *World Development Report*, (World Bank, 1996) are advanced in the following chapters. These include; (i) the long-term limitations to the agro-export model, (ii) the highly imperfect nature of agrarian (including land) markets, (iii) the complex effects of privatization and market liberalization on peasant farmers in terms of income distribution, poverty and access to land and other assets and (iv) the limited institutional change and the poorly defined (new) role for the state in supporting the new policy frameworks – often seen as the Achilles' heel of the SAPs and MTSs.

Market liberalization within the context of LDCs has been particularly directed towards ending the dominance of parastatal – often highly inefficient and corrupt – institutions, that have been monopolizing agricultural production and marketing for a number of decades (sometimes since the colonial epoch onwards). There is no doubt that many of these highly interventionist strategies designed to replace the market simply served to drain resources from the agricultural sector, with its well-known negative consequences. This policy can be traced to the early 1980s, SAP advocates insisting that agrarian markets could be relatively efficient and integrated, as long as state intervention was withdrawn. Although as the decade wore on there was a growing recognition of the problems of imperfect or even 'missing markets', at a policy level (and in particular, within the policy advice extended by the IFIs on SAP or MTS), the complexities of this were either not granted proper attention or were ignored.

At a global level, with the new (often agro-) export-led growth model stressing the importance of free trade policies (GATT, NAFTA and WTO), adjustment of the agrarian sector focused on two, sometimes contradictory, policy directives. First, to improve the traditionally strong export crop (or livestock) sectors, notwithstanding the 'fallacy of composition' critique. Second, to diversify into non-traditional exports, although the main limitation here is they are small niche markets. Privatization, most notably through the introduction of private land property rights and the promotion of land markets – seen as the main guarantor of efficient resource allocation – is another important foundation of SAP, becoming the near sacrosanct pillar of the agrarian transition in the former socialist countries. Distributionist land reform has now been removed from the policy agenda, and land markets have taken its place. The 'tragedy of the commons' argument is applied with equal 'rigour' to communal lands in Africa, indigenous communities in Latin America, or collectives in the former Soviet Union, with private property rights now being seen as the preventive mechanism that will deliver the long-term policy objectives of modernization and sustainability. The insecurity of land markets in LDCs, segmented, inefficient, and monopolistic as they often are, is however in sharp contrast with the 'security' these new property titles are supposed to provide, in particular for the still-significant strata of peasant farmers. Institution-building, along with policies directed towards the formation and the strengthening of (in particular, rural) markets, seldom accompanies these reforms.

This book is not proposing 'more state' and 'less market' as a reaction to the mainstream, market-oriented, message of the 1980s and 1990s. Rather, it attempts to show both the limitations of mainstream thought-inspired analysis on economic adjustment and agrarian transformation, and the equally simplistic message that hails from the opposite corner. Instead, it identifies and analyses the complexities of policy impact, pleading for more emphasis on institution building, a policy area that has become threatened in an era in which state withdrawal is still at the top of the policy reform agenda. The most recent call for good governance (more efficient, less corrupt and more democratic governments) which accompanies market-oriented reform, however necessary and important, ignores the growing schism between 'market reforms' in LDCs and former socialist economies and the central economic issues of growth and income distribution, poverty, social exclusion and sustainability.

The book consists of 10 chapters, and is divided into two parts, dealing with agrarian transition in LDCs and in the former socialist economies respectively. Part I is dedicated to evaluating the impact of structural adjustment programmes (SAP) on the agrarian sector in less developed countries, drawing on regional overviews and specific case studies from Latin America and Africa. In Chapter 1 Thorpe presents a résumé of structural adjustment and its impact within the Latin American continent. Three particular areas of reform are discussed which closely align with the main issues of the book: (i) the liberalization of prices and markets; (ii) institutional reforms; and (iii) the privatization of land (and property rights) and the emergence of land markets. While expressing general doubts about the supposed uniform (and positive) outcomes of these reforms, more specifically he points to some quite contradictory effects of certain policies. In the case of price liberalization, for example, exchange rate devaluation indeed provided a positive stimulus for export production (as well as spin-offs to domestic food producers), but low demand elasticities in the world market (the 'fallacy of composition'), increased input prices (which negatively affect technified production) and the reduced internal demand for food (as inflationary pressures raise food prices), make the impact not altogether straightforward. While domestic food prices were liberalized, the introduction of price band systems (such as in Chile and some countries in Central America) has led to domestic prices tracking severely distorted – as a consequence of protected, monopsonistic markets and large-scale subsidies in industrialized countries – world grain prices. Furthermore, it is questionable whether the macro-level 'credit squeeze' (due to positive real exchange rates and reduced credit allocation) will actually improve small-scale producers' access to financial markets. In relation to institutional reform and the privatization of parastatals, he points to two phenomena: a severe drop in state expenditure on agriculture (research, extension etc.), while the privatization (sometimes, liquidation) of state companies in the agrarian field has not always led to the entry of efficient private enterprises. On the theme of land markets, Thorpe – while acknowledging the positive advantages that SAP brings in the form of improved access to land and the opportunity of using formal land titles as collateral – argues that those who have little (the land-scarce and resource-poor peasant farmer) are more likely to lose out, increasing the problem of rural unemployment and poverty. Three major concerns over SAP in Latin America remain: the (positive) output versus the (negative) distributional effects; the long-term (positive) growth potential versus the short-term (negative) impact on rural poverty; and the need for a greater flexibility and country specificity of reforms, something which Thorpe suggests is absent in current IFI practice.

Following this overview, Spoor and Thorpe respectively present case-studies from the Latin American continent, analysing SAP and food market liberalization (Nicaragua) and land-titling and land markets (Honduras). In Chapter 2 Spoor analyses agrarian food markets in Nicaragua, comparing peasant behaviour in 'basic grain' (in particular, maize) production during the late 1980s and early 1990s. This period, characterized by various stabilization and adjustment programmes and the radical change to a neo-liberal political regime, had 'a profound impact on agrarian markets'. Spoor shows that markets in which there was a history of state intervention were actually inefficient, and that production decisions (in terms of crop-mix and input use) had no correlation whatsoever with real relative prices. This conclusion is based on a farm survey in an important (and equally war-torn) agricultural region in the north of Nicaragua, which was originally carried out in early 1989 (at the beginning of the Sandinista reform programme), and four years (and agricultural seasons) later in early 1993, halfway through the Chamorro period. Food market liberalization had already become part of the policy agenda during the final years of the Sandinista regime. Nevertheless, relative prices in the 1988/9 agricultural season (the base year of the study) were still heavily distorted, with a 'two tier' price system and various parallel market systems operating. The UNO-government went much further in market liberalization, implementing an across the board privatization of the large production, agro-processing, marketing and input parastatals, while freeing prices (only an irregularly functioning price-band system was left in operation) in the early 1990s. By 1993 the comparative farm survey indicated that peasant farmers were closely associating their production decisions to relative market prices, while the capital/labour price ratio had, after an initial upward explosion and subsequent gradual decline, stabilized. A substantial drop in the use of fertilizers (and a strong decrease in pesticide use) underlined this development, with a drop in yields partly reflecting this reduced use of external inputs. Spoor concludes that while markets have become more efficient, price liberalization has been a necessary but not sufficient condition for the development of agrarian markets. The main problem is the lack of existing rural market structures and, in particular, institutions. New 'high profit, low volume' markets have emerged, but these hardly correspond to those envisaged by the designers of structural adjustment.

One of the other pillars of structural adjustment in Latin America (and elsewhere in LDCs) is analysed by Thorpe in Chapter 3. As an empirical elaboration of his opening essay, he examines the issue of land property rights and emerging land markets in Honduras. The policies and legislation promoting land titling and land markets are based on the proposition that 'customary' and 'informal' land rights (or usufruct rights) were an obstacle to modernization. While Honduras has a history of land reform, in particular due to the influence of the USA's Alliance for Progress initiative in 1961, it is also representative of the typical bi-modal (large-scale haciendas and small-scale minifundios) agrarian structure of many Latin American countries. Widespread land-titling was initiated during the 1980s, the idea (in line with neoliberal mainstream thought) being that formalized private land property rights would promote investment and encourage preventive measures to be taken against endemic coffee diseases. In the early 1990s new legislation was introduced to promote formal land markets, seen as a main instrument for efficient allocation of resources, and hence agricultural modernization. Thorpe notes that in the co-operative sector, which had developed strongly in the 1970s and 1980s, substantial sales took place now that legal restrictions over selling had been removed. The main beneficiaries of this emerging market in agrarian reform land were the multinational fruit companies, powerful domestic agro-industrial groups in addition to high military and civil officials who, in another context within this book, would be described as *nomenklatura* (see Chapter 6). Thorpe further argues that private land markets provide few benefits to small farmers. In a detailed regional study on the relation between land titling and (a) access to formal credit and (b) technical assistance, he finds little statistical justification for the SAP claim that formal titling mechanisms increase access to such inputs. In fact, Thorpe and other authors on Honduran agrarian problems go as far as to suggest that private land titles have amplified the formal base for ongoing land disputes, thereby 'modernizing insecurity' – a provocative position which is in sharp contradiction to the mainstream message of 'secure property rights'.

Raikes, in Chapter 4, provides a comparative analysis of structural adjustment and its impact in sub-Saharan Africa. SAP has led to a much-needed reduction of inefficient, and often corrupt, parastatals. But the overall emphasis on macro-reforms, on simply 'getting the prices right' and on state withdrawal – letting the market allocate resources – have underestimated the complexities of reforms at meso- and micro-levels. Raikes therefore notes that, apart from a few exceptions, the architects of structural adjustment in Africa have 'little reason for self-satisfaction'. Although the previous interventionist approach to 'modernization' has failed, the promised fruits of structural adjustment for peasant farmers specifically, and rural dwellers in general, are equally sour. The major beneficiaries of SAP have been larger commercial, export-oriented, farmers.

Nevertheless, the main focus of Raikes' essay relates to the use and significance of composite measures of success, such as GDP and agricultural output growth rates, or indebtedness. The World Bank and the IMF are the main proponents of these success indicators, using them in order to show that 'reformers do better' and 'non-reformers do worse'. Raikes commences with the proposed World Bank group stratification for Africa (based on a sliding scale of policy reform implementation) and carefully extracts the data for indebtedness and agricultural growth, comparing the pre- and post-SAP periods. His conclusions differ from those of the World Bank. First, even in the case of a success story such as Uganda (see Chapter 5), indebtedness has increased. Second, and even more importantly, indebtedness (as a percentage of GDP) and agricultural growth do not correlate in any simple positive way with 'policy reform implementation'. Furthermore, when one takes into account the unreliability of agricultural output data (due, in large part, to the production of 'unregistered' smallholders), and the substantial discrepancy between figures quoted by sources such as the World Bank and the FAO, the value of such composite success indicators becomes, according to Raikes, rather doubtful. The chapter ends with a brief but interesting discussion of five African cases, Burkina Faso, Ghana, Tanzania, Uganda and Zimbabwe, all, with the exception of Zimbabwe, members of the World Bank's 'A-team' of reformers. The discussion shows that even in this – assumed – homogeneous group of reformers, the change (post-reform in comparison with pre-reform) in agricultural growth figures is quite diverse, hiding the greatly complex and differential impact of adjustment (and non-adjustment).

A case that is generally seen as providing a model of successful adjustment in Africa is discussed in Chapter 5 by Belshaw, Lawrence and Hubbard. They analyse in detail one of the main SAP policy items, exchange rate 'alignment'. While real exchange rate appreciation can actually occur as long as sufficient aid is flowing in (and is partly caused by it), there is widespread agreement regarding its negative effects on trade and growth. This was the case in Uganda where aid flows led to indebtedness increasing rapidly in the mid-1990s. The economic recovery and subsequent growth rates recorded following the 1986 crisis have generally been hailed as a success although, as the authors note, in comparison with an extrapolated 'normal growth rate' for an African economy over the same period, the composite measure of GDP growth tends to overstate the success. Inflation has been curtailed, real interest rates are positive and money supply growth has been reined in. After acknowledging the success of Ugandan stabilization, Belshaw, Lawrence and Hubbard then turn to the problem of the real exchange rate and producer price stimuli, in relation to agro-exports. Structural adjustment did promote a limited diversification, but exchange rate appreciation and, in particular, the low share of the producer price in the export parity price of coffee, the main export crop, has not encouraged producers to renovate their coffee holdings. Consequently, the output of traditional (tradable) crops like coffee, tobacco, tea and cotton have generally not recovered to pre-1986 levels. The authors attribute this to the main bottleneck in the otherwise successful Ugandan adjustment: the relative slow change in institutions, such as in the marketing chains – previously monopolized by the state. Finally, in the complex environment of increasing aid levels and appreciating real exchange rates, Belshaw, Lawrence and Hubbard argue that the government should intervene to stabilize the exchange rate indirectly, targeting government funds for employment creation, and possibly offering subsidies that induce investments in exportable commodities. The latter sector is also in need of substantial rehabilitation programmes for the traditional (but highly rewarding) export crops, in particular, coffee. Apart from managing the exchange rate, institutional change should be a priority in the further process of adjustment.

In Part II of this book, five cases of agrarian transition in former socialist economies are analysed. The same pillars upon which SAP in LDCs was based, such as price liberalization, privatization and state-withdrawal (deregulation), are also fundamental in the IFI's 'agenda for reform' for the countries in transition. While in the early stages of transition there was debate over whether reform should be 'gradualist' or of a 'shock-therapy' type, by the mid-1990s mainstream thought now accepts deviations only in terms of the sequencing of reforms, hammering home the message that 'stronger, more sustained, liberalization spells a smaller output decline – and a stronger recovery' (World Bank, 1996:28). To date, little attention has been paid to the agrarian sector in this transitional period, an oversight which the following five chapters attempt to rectify. Although there are clearly differences of opinion about the outcomes of transition, these authors by and large conclude that the necessity for fundamental institutional change in this process is underestimated, while the process of privatization of land (or land use rights) and the impact of market liberalization is more complex and contradictory than mainstream thought seems to be willing to accept – conclusions that are quite in line with the analysis of SAP and agrarian transformation in LDCs, presented in the first half of this book.

In Chapter 6, Spoor looks at agrarian transition in the former Soviet Union (FSU) Central Asian states, focusing in particular on Kazakhstan, Kyrgyzstan and Uzbekistan. First, he acknowledges that those Central Asian States (CAS) with large-scale agro or mineral export sectors were cushioned somewhat from the general contraction after the collapse of the USSR. Overall, the agricultural sector was less affected than the industrial (more integrated and dependent) sectors. Hence, 'initial conditions' count for a lot in explaining the impact of reforms (or non-reforms). Second, agrarian sector reforms are discussed. In the CAS, as in Russia, land (or usufruct right) privatization advanced slowly, with Kyrgyzstan and Kazakhstan the front-runners. There are very diverse (and sometimes dynamic) developments, from land fragmentation in Kyrgyzstan, to the recent take-over of huge (and possibly highly inefficient) *kolkhozi* in the north of Kazakhstan by private investors. In Uzbekistan (generally seen as a slow reformer on the World Bank's 'Reform Progress Index'), the emergence of a variety of family sub-contracting forms of usufruct rights can be observed, although the *kolkhozi* still dominate. Agricultural output of the main commodities seems, in Uzbekistan, to have either stabilized or improved (in the case of grains), while the share of agricultural output (potatoes, vegetables and grains) produced by private family farms in Kyrgyzstan has recently increased substantially. Spoor suggests that the reasons behind the 'slow' land reform are diverse, ranging from (a) the still-hostile market environment ('missing markets' and existing monopsonies, inefficiencies etc.), (b) the sensitivity of land as an ethnic issue (there is a history of violent land disputes) and (c) rural dwellers' fears of losing access to existing social services if the collectives are abandoned in favour of private production. Third, the other fundamental pillar of economic transition, market liberalization, has seen the breakdown of the existing 'state order system', through which the state procured agricultural commodities at fixed prices, while providing finance and inputs to the *sovkhozi* and *kolkhozi*. This has been – as in privatizing the parastatals and deregulation in LDCs – a gradual and complex process in the countries involved (whether identified as 'slow' or 'fast' reformer). Spoor warns that it is very difficult to uncover any simple positive correlation between the pace and extent of land privatization and market liberalization in the CAS and the degree (and speed) of economic recovery, as is argued by the *World Development Report* (1996) for the whole set of 28 countries in transition. He states that the complex relationship between the initial conditions and country-specific idiosyncrasies, the existing structural dependencies and macro-developments lead to a variety of results (often unintended), concluding with one of the principal messages of this book: 'in these transitional processes there are no simple recipes nor ideal outcomes, but mainly complex dynamics and unexpected, or sometimes unintended results of adjustment policies'.

In the Central and Eastern European countries (CEEC) Bulgaria is an interesting case, as agrarian transition here has been dominated by a widespread land reform. In Chapter 7, Kopeva studies the disarticulation of the previously dominant 'bi-modal' land structure, dominated by large state and collective enterprises – known as the TKZS – and the highly productive, but extremely small, household plots. Land reform included: (a) the restoration of land property rights to former owners; (b) the dismantling of the TKZS and the distribution of their assets; (c) the creation of 'enabling conditions' in order to promote the emergence of new farm types, such as private family farms and new forms of co-operatives. Currently, however, the Bulgarian agricultural sector is in severe crisis (a situation already evident before the 'transition'), while the agrarian reform seems to have stagnated. Newly created private farms have great difficulties surviving in the rather hostile market environment (with 'missing', incomplete and inefficient rural markets). The macroeconomic 'money squeeze', that was introduced to stabilize the economy, has caused a severe shortage of finance for agricultural enterprises. This has been aggravated by uncertainty over property rights, slow institutional change in the banking sector and the absence of foreign investment in the agricultural and food industry sector. The land reform has been based on land restitution using a combination of old boundaries and land reallocation plans laid down by Municipal Land Commissions. Policy implementation, as well as outcome, is highly complex. While land consolidation is necessary, it is seemingly not on the farmers' (or owners') agenda. Around 20 million parcels of less than one hectare of land have been allocated to an estimated five million smallholders, a process of extreme land fragmentation. Still, a great variety of new farms have emerged, and the sector is best typified as being still in a state of flux, with a great number of farms only informally established. While only a small private farm sector has accumulated land, thereby becoming economically viable enterprises, the majority remain minifundia. Kopeva's main conclusion therefore is that farm policies should be primarily flexible and adapted to Bulgarian reality, while based on a clear assessment of the emerging farm structure.

According to Dumitru, in Chapter 8, the agrarian reform in Romania has also focused on the change in land ownership, omitting the structural and institutional reforms that could have improved sectoral performance. The reforms returned land to former owners and distributed collectively-owned land to farm members. The dominant sector of Agricultural Production Co-operatives (comparable with the Russian *kolkhozi*), has been partly privatized, and partly transformed into shareholder associations. State farms remain untouched, undergoing only a cosmetic change in the sense that they are now referred to as 'commercial companies' in the current environment. A multitude of small farms has emerged, fragmented and mostly in a 'deplorable state'. The author stresses that only one-fifth of the new landowners are 'peasants of working age'; most are elderly people, and two out of five are city-dwellers. Within the small-farm sector new types of co-operation – in the form of 'family associations' – have emerged, but they lack any institutional support from the government. Dumitru states that although the parastatals responsible for inputs, marketing and finance most recently became part of the privatization move, these enterprises remain heavily state controlled and monopsonistic. The dichotomy of oversized, technologically well-equipped, state farms and new agricultural associations (the heirs of the APCs), versus the small family farms with archaic technology levels, leaves the latter in a hostile market environment, with little chance of survival, let alone possibilities to expand or accumulate. Dumitru concludes that the agricultural sector in Romania is in profound crisis, while the new 'market' system is yet to function. Nevertheless, on an optimistic note, he states that agriculture in the transitional period functioned as a buffer, and agricultural reform contributed greatly to social stability (in particular, by temporarily absorbing unemployed labour). He considers that the emergence of efficient land markets, in order to promote land consolidation backed by a mortgage-based credit system, are essential in Romania, but this must be undertaken jointly with structural and institutional reforms that support and stimulate the newly established farm-types. Within Romania the search for a new agrarian model (or 'pattern') continues, and the outcome is still not entirely predictable.

Agrarian transition in Russia is analysed by Wehrheim in Chapter 9, in the context of the simultaneous process of decentralization (regionalization) that has been implemented since the early 1990s. He raises the issue of whether regionalization is increasing inefficiency as, while the previously established division of labour between regions was a 'planned' or 'forced' one and certainly not always congruent with existing resource endowments and comparative advantages, in the current climate regions are attempting to increase their income at the expense of others and/or the centre. Wehrheim then focuses upon three geographically rather distant regions in the Russian Federation, Pskov, Orel and Roskov, an interesting choice as these regions featured in an earlier World Bank research project on farm restructuring. Wehrheim's research, based on survey work with Russian scholars in the field, updates part of this analysis. Following the agrarian reform, the *sovkhozi* were transformed into joint-stock companies, the *kolkhozi* were reconstituted in a variety of new enterprise forms and family farms were permitted to emerge. Nevertheless, by the end of 1994 the collective sector was still predominant in all three oblasts, although a growing share of production (in particular, vegetables) was produced by household plots and *dacha*-gardens. In analysing the market environment in which these new farm-types operate, Wehrheim finds that the collapse of regional processing and marketing parastatals has led to the emergence of informal trading channels and even barter trade. The evolving nature of demand there has caused a clear switch in agricultural production towards low income elasticity commodities (potatoes, cereals, vegetables) and away from meat, a factor which explains part of the dramatic overall drop in livestock numbers. While observing that regional governments have an overt tendency for protectionism, using subsidies to satisfy certain vested interests, Wehrheim makes a plea for the retention of sufficient federal powers in agricultural policy making, so as to guarantee both the openness of regional markets and a regionally balanced public investment policy. He finally points to the necessity of institution building (supporting financial, input and output markets) and a rapid improvement of managerial (and entrepreneurial) capacity of farm enterprises, in order to speed up the agrarian transition which, to date, has been much slower than was originally envisaged.

In the final Chapter 10, Tuan analyses the transition in Vietnam primarily as a process of continuous institutional change. Vietnam, with the possible exception of the FSU economies of Central Asia, is the only developing country for which the agrarian transition from planned to market economy is discussed in this book. As such, it provides an interesting counterpoint to those cases detailed in Part I. Vietnam's reforms date from the early 1980s when, following reunification and a first wave of collectivization attempts in the South, the first market-oriented reforms were introduced in agriculture. Most important, perhaps, was the legislation that gave co-operatives the possibility of contracting out parts of rice production to member households. After 1986, when the well-known *doi moi* (renovation) reform was decreed, land legislation was changed and contracts with households could now take the form of fully fledged land leases. The response to this change was very positive as, by the late 1980s, Vietnam had become self-sufficient in rice and could export substantial quantities. In the early 1990s leases became tradable and transferable (although formally all land still remained the property of the state) and long-term usufruct rights over land were established. Tuan looks into the outcome of these successive land reforms at local and regional levels, using a simple typology of peasant households ranging from food-deficient to exclusively market-oriented. While there were substantial average income increases (and a comparable reduction in the percentage of rural dwellers living under the poverty line), the gap between the lowest incomes (food-deficient peasants) and the highest (exclusively market-oriented) grew substantially. He also shows differences in the regional impact of these reforms (part of which is due to different initial conditions), in particular when one compares the densely populated deltas of the northern Red River and the southern Mekong. In calculating (from repetitive peasant household surveys) Gini-coefficients for income distribution, Tuan finds that although they still remain relatively low, the Red River delta Ginis have increased while those computed for the Mekong delta suggest only a slight growth in inequality. Tuan predicts increasing social differentiation now that property (usufruct) rights are well defined and 'marketable'. Like other authors in this book he also stresses the existence of an institutional crisis in transition period. This is particularly serious when markets are highly imperfect. He also suggests that the state should be responsible for aiding the development of new forms of peasant co-operation, rural organization and grassroot market development.

The contributions in this book on economic adjustment and agrarian transformation in LDCs and former socialist economies, while having obvious differences in analysis and judgements regarding the policy impact of reforms, point in quite similar directions. First, the country and regional studies, presented in Parts I and II, show that the 'agenda for action' (of structural adjustment programmes) or the 'agenda for reform' (of market transition strategies), have been largely dominated by three elements: market liberalization, privatization and state-withdrawal (known as deregulation). Second, the impact of these policies and the dynamic relation of economic adjustment and agrarian transformation have been quite complex in nature, and much less linear and straightforward than originally predicted by their designers and advocates. The results cannot be grasped by focusing on composite 'indicators of success', nor can any simple positive correlation be convincingly shown between the 'degree of policy implementation' and sectoral performance. Third, the Achilles' heel of many of these processes of economic adjustment and agrarian transformation is the lack of institutional change and 'initiative' state action, in particular directed towards improved structures and functioning of rural input, land, financial and output markets. Fourth, while in many countries that are going through these transformations the population dependent on agriculture (and rural dwellers in general) is still large, measures to improve their livelihood remain rather low-placed on the policy agenda. This is the more surprising as, in particular for them, the 'market panacea' has more often than not delivered the promised benefits.

PART I

STRUCTURAL ADJUSTMENT AND THE AGRARIAN SECTOR IN DEVELOPING COUNTRIES

1 Structural adjustment and the agrarian sector in Latin America[1]

ANDY THORPE

From ISI to export-led growth model

THE POST-WAR strategy of import substituting industrialization (ISI) that was adopted across the Latin American region sought to promote the rapid development of the industrial sector through a combination of overvalued exchange rates, high tariff walls and/or quotas, specialist industrial development banks and a wide range of fiscal incentives and inducements. Industrial wage costs, contained by cheap food policies, offered Latin American entrepreneurs a comparative production advantage over their extra-regional counterparts. As domestic markets became satiated with home-produced manufactured goods, and ISI gave way to an export-led growth (XLG) model, this competitive edge was to be critical in the international marketplace. However, agriculture was very much the 'Cinderella' within this strategy. Export-oriented agriculture had been penalized by the prevailing exchange rate policy of overvaluation, while producers for the internal market suffered from both the plethora of domestic food price controls and 'cheap' food imports. Economic policies would continue to favour industrial development, to the detriment of agriculture, in particular of food production, until the early 1980s (IICA, 1989: 29).

Despite this bias, agricultural output increased at a respectable rate in the immediate post-war period, consistently outstripping population growth (Weeks, 1995a: 1). The explanation can be traced to a combination of factors. On the supply side of the equation there was a sharp increase in the area cultivated as the agricultural frontier was pushed back. Thorpe (1995b: 7) calculated that forested area in Central America shrank from 58 per cent to only 31 per cent of the surface area over the period 1961–91, while in the rest of Latin America deforestation continues at very high rates (Kirmse, Constantino and Guess, 1993:1). Another contributing factor on the supply side was the intensification of the production process, as agricultural yields per land unit increased. Part of this development was endogenous, springing from peasant experimentation and innovation[2], and part exogenous. Exogenous influences on Latin land productivities have been characterized by Piñeiro (1985) as a series of technological waves, commencing with the diffusion of improved agronomic practices in the 1940s. This has been superseded by the introduction of mechanized techniques (mid-1950s to mid-1960s), improved seeds (mid-1960s to mid-1970s), the agro-chemical 'fix' (mid-1970s to mid-1980s) with applied biotechnological techniques likely to be next on the agenda (de Janvry, Runsten and Sadoulet, 1987). To these two factors we must add a third, demand-side stimulus. A massive growth in international demand for agricultural commodities in the post-war period helped boost output growth. Nowhere was this more evident than in the case of Central America. Here, the cotton bonanza (late-1940s onwards) saw Central American production volumes expand more than twentyfold by the early 1960s (Williams, 1986: 16–17). This was succeeded by a cattle boom (late-1950s onwards), such as in Nicaragua, which saw meat exports, mostly directed to the US market, increase dramatically.

The respectable aggregate growth rates registered by agriculture in this period helped to obscure the dramatic changes that these three factors were having on national agrarian structures. In Nicaragua, for example, the land given over to pasture rose sharply from 1.9 to 4.6 million hectares between 1960 and 1978 (Clemens, 1993: 3). Census figures from Costa Rica indicate that pastureland increased from 0.6 to 1.6 million hectares over the period 1950 to 1973 (González, 1993: 36), while in El Salvador the number of hectares under cotton grew from 21 100 in 1953–54 to around 114 000 ten years later (Arias Peñate, 1988:219). The scale economies these production systems offered favoured the concentration of landholdings. The result was increased landlessness.

As the stirrings of rural unrest gathered momentum, Castro came to power in Cuba. Conscious of the lead this could give to the rest of Latin America, the Kennedy administration launched the Alliance for Progress in 1961. Agrarian reform figured highly within the Alliance's agenda and, in a number of cases, access to funds was conditional upon satisfactory reform programmes being undertaken.[3] However, agrarian reform failed to live up to expectations[4] and, with landlessness growing, by 1980 an estimated 73 million of Latin America's rural dwellers (21 per cent of total population) fell below the poverty line (CEPAL, 1990: 2). The situation was most acute in Haiti, Guatemala, Nicaragua and Honduras, where over 80 per cent of the rural population were classified as poor (FAO, 1988: 39).

The demise of the ISI strategy

While ISI remained the dominant development strategy throughout the 1960s and 1970s, the recognition that agriculture also faced structural bottlenecks (apart from the issue of access to land) led to increased state intervention. State development banks such as Banrural (Mexico), Banco Agrícola (Bolivia), BANDESA (Guatemala), Banco Agrario (Peru) and the *Juntas Rurales* of the Banco Nacional (Costa Rica) were set up to alleviate credit constraints. These were supported by state enterprises such as Fertimex and Pronase (Mexico) and Promech (Honduras) which facilitated and/or subsidized the distribution of fertilizers, machinery and improved seeds. Institutions such as IHMA (Honduras), ECI and ECASA (Peru) and IRA (El

Salvador) sought to rectify imperfections in commodity commercialization, while others like EMBRAPA and EMBRATER (Brazil) provided either free or subsidized research and extension services. In some instances, INASA (Chile), CATSA (Costa Rica) and Productos Lácteos Sula (Honduras), state intervention led to direct control over commodity processing. Macroeconomic policy was also modified. The disincentive effect that overvalued exchange rates had on agro-exporters, for example, was reduced through schemes such as CATS (Costa Rica), CERT (Colombia) and CETRAS (Honduras).

By the 1980s, however, the Latin American inability to transform ISI into XLG had resulted in growing internal and external imbalances – imbalances that were funded by external borrowing. Thus, when Bolivia became the first Latin American nation to declare a unilateral moratorium on its debt servicing in 1980 it merely heralded a wave of subsequent regional defaults as inflows of foreign capital dried up. With external indebtedness (in 1980) averaging 54 per cent of GDP,[5] a search for an alternative, outward looking strategy began, strongly influenced by economists at the World Bank, the International Monetary Fund and other multilateral institutions. In practice this new vision has entailed the implementation of 'neo-liberal' policy measures via the adoption of national structural adjustment programmes (SAPs).

Agriculture and agricultural policy were not immune to these pressures for change. Despite the sector reporting higher rates of growth than any other during the 1980s (Kay, 1995: 15), these nevertheless fell short of population growth rates. By 1989 rural poverty had swollen by an additional 1.5 million households (Herrero and Trejos, 1992: 405) and over half the Latin American countries had seen their level of food dependency increase (PNUD, 1994: 170–71).[6] SAPs were therefore buttressed by sectoral adjustment packages designed to reactivate and modernize agriculture. The impact of adjustment on the rural sector is complex, however, (Demery, 1994: 46) and so, given the constraints of space, we shall concentrate on surveying the analytical issues and evidence relating to just three aspects of 'agrarian neo-liberalism': (i) the liberalization of prices, (ii) institutional reform and privatization and (iii) the shift from land redistribution towards land market promotion as a resource-allocation mechanism. Of these, price reform, being the fundamental neo-liberal imperative in the quest for agricultural development, consequently receives most attention in the rest of this chapter.

Getting prices right for Latin American agriculture

While certain crops have always been seen as 'tradable', food staple (often referred to as 'basic grains') output has usually been characterized as being solely for internal household consumption. Nevertheless, the proportion of basic grains destined for the market has increased considerably in recent years.[7] This growing commercialization of agriculture translates into an increased responsiveness to price changes, whether occasioned by international price movements, trade or fiscal policies, domestic price realignments (both output and input) or simply weather conditions. Price reforms are best addressed on three levels. First, by analysing the impact of SAP exchange rate policy on output. Second, through a discussion of the relaxation of domestic price controls. Third, how liberalization and deregulation in the capital market feeds through to affect credit provision in the rural marketplace.

Overvalued exchange rates: a tax on agricultural exports
Exchange rate overvaluation is seen by SAP acolytes to have penalized agricultural production through reducing price incentives. A reversal of this policy (currency devaluation being the chosen instrument of the majority of SAPs), while likely to encounter strong opposition, increases the price of tradables relative to non-tradables thereby benefiting exporters while stimulating import substitution. The impact of such trade policies will, furthermore, be greater for small open economies reliant upon an agricultural sector in which the majority of commodities are tradable.[8] In practice, the evaluation of production-stimulating effects of devaluation packages is fraught with difficulty. As de Rezende (1989: 210) notes in the case of Brazil, there is a difficulty in isolating policy effects. Brazilian domestic crop production performed much better than expected in the devaluation period but this he attributes to climatic conditions and international commodity price trends, rather than to any inherent feature of the devaluation programme.

While it is undeniable that the weather will always be an important element in agricultural output levels, the impact of a SAP-induced devaluation will depend upon a number of further factors. First, the impetus that such a policy gives to exporters will be realized only if access to external markets is unimpeded. In instances where exports are constrained by quotas (as in the case of the US sugar market or the now defunct International Coffee Agreement) then exchange rate translation gains are on offer, but positive output responses are unlikely. Second, demand elasticities for primary agricultural exports are low and increased production on an aggregate level will cause a disproportionate fall in price, thereby proving a disincentive to producers. A newer variant of this is the 'fallacy of composition' argument advanced by some critics of SAP in recent years.[9] Finally, unexpected fluctuations in international commodity prices can accentuate or dampen the revenues resulting from trade policy decisions. The strong and sustained fall in international commodity prices in the recessionary 1980s, for example, severely reduced the expected benefits of devaluation for the Latin economies (López Cordovez, 1990: 363). Reca and Garramon (1989: 809) go further, illustrating how this commodity price collapse, in conjunction with unfavourable weather conditions, were key factors in the substantial decline of Argentine grain output during the period 1984–5 and 1986–7, despite the substantive devaluation implemented within the 1985 Austral Plan.

There is also doubt about how responsive to devaluation production is at the farm-gate level. First, as permanent crops such as coffee have a three- to five-year lagged response to the type of incentive devaluation may offer, supply responses in the short term are likely to be low. Second, risk-averse smallholders may actually reduce the acreage of a certain crop if devaluation and market liberalization increase the variance of the producer price. The third influential factor relates to the degree of insulation between producer and market. In Brazil, for example, the distance between international and farmgate coffee prices has insulated farmers from market signals, with consequent negative effects on both productive efficiency and export responsiveness (Goldin and de Rezende, 1990). Insulation varies between crops. While increased border prices (in domestic currency terms) generally filter back – at least in part – to the export producer, marked imperfections in domestic distribution channels negate most of the potential devaluationary benefits for non-exporting producers. This is important, for while conventional wisdom tends to suggest that SAP stimuli for non-tradable production arrives through the medium of domestic grain price, liberalization and devaluation may also benefit producers for the internal market through a substitution effect.[10]

Nevertheless, devaluation is a two-edged sword: although export prices rise there is a concomitant increase in the price of imported agricultural inputs.[11] The effect of this is greatest for those producers whose crops have low international values (such as yuca, potatoes or white maize) and yet have a degree of dependence on imported inputs. In the absence of compensating measures these producers will be among the first to reduce the use of such inputs, turning instead to other more locally available technologies and techniques. The effect is both immediate and pronounced, as De Janvry and Sadoulet (1989: 1206) make clear. Latin American tractor and fertilizer imports dropped 40 per cent and 15 per cent respectively as a consequence of the devaluations of the 1980s.

It is equally probable that devaluation may trigger cost-push inflation. In real terms then, the higher producer prices that devaluation appears to offer the exporter are not quite so attractive, and the desired incentive effect is partially circumscribed. For this reason Green (1989: 38) argues that a real devaluation needs to be sustained for at least 18 months to prevent the incentive effect from being stillborn – better still, for 36 months or more if its full benefits are to be realized. In Brazil recognition of this saw early-1980s exchange rate policy being tied to record inflation levels. In El Salvador it was not, and the 33 per cent devaluation of the colón produced an almost mirror-like response in the inflation rate, which in rising to 32 per cent in 1986, largely wiped out the benefits of the devaluation.

On the whole, exchange rate policy remains a key component of SAP and evidence can be offered to suggest that such a strategy has proved highly successful in stimulating fruit production in Chile (exports up from $20 million in 1974 to $747 million in 1990), soya in Brazil and flowers in Colombia. On the other hand, Ecuadorian production remained buoyant in the 1980s by retaining overvalued exchange rates and promoting exports through a system of subsidies and tax exemptions (Pomareda *et al.*, 1989:42), while in Argentina Menem's removal of farm export taxes had a greater impact on output than did the accompanying devaluation (Maletta, 1995:132). Morales (1991a:65), however, notes that market liberalization has produced no clear short-term improvement in either the terms of trade or peasant output levels in Bolivia. Finally, exchange rate policies can have a profound distributional impact too – one that is often forgotten, played down or left unanswered (Ferroni and Valdés, 1991:7, Valdés, 1993:274). This is because agriculture's dual role as a source of both foreign exchange and domestic nutrition allows for a degree of 'market-switching' in the case of tradable food staples. If commodities are diverted from domestic to international markets, the resulting scarcity worsens living standards for consumers of domestically produced tradables whose incomes are not derived from the sale of such crops. In countries where domestic food crops form a substantial part of the basic food basket it can also increase inflation.

Liberalization of the internal market

Historically, the belief that the agricultural sector would continue to produce regardless of price had led to rigid forms of price control designed to transfer agricultural produce to the cities at minimum cost. Nevertheless, the overvaluation of exchange rates, the taxation of agriculture and the installation of state channels for the procurement, storage and distribution of basic grains at controlled prices led to a progressive deterioration in real producer prices. Reduced producer prices caused production to stagnate or even decline, thereby accentuating the problems of food insecurity in Latin and Central America and prompting a number of policy reforms which pre-dated SAP.

Generally, however, these price-support schemes raised the levels of government subsidy required. Buainain and de Rezende (1995: 164) note how the coverage of the Minimum Price Programme in Brazil was ultimately truncated due to the government's inability to finance the programme. In Venezuela, the food deficits that emerged from exchange rate overvaluation in the 1980s were tackled from 1986 onwards by tough import controls. These were designed to expand output by letting domestic producer prices rise above world market levels. Corn imports were prohibited, rice imports were sharply curbed and sorghum import restrictions were tied to domestic production shortfalls. At the same time, low consumer prices were guaranteed by price controls and subsidies at the point of sale. These policies, however, required the government to devote an increasing proportion of its budget to agricultural support (Krissoff and Trapido, 1991: 142). In Mexico, since the mid-1970s, the huge state distributor CONASUPO purchased about 20 per cent of domestic grain at premium prices, before selling it on to *tortilla* producers at subsidized prices. While this served to pacify the urban population by keeping the real cost of *tortillas* low, it burdened the state with additional outgoings (Appendini and Liverman, 1994: 154). In Nicaragua, ENABAS was set up by the Sandinistas to stimulate grain production and marketing through the medium of guaranteed prices to producers and low-priced supplies to urban consumers. As the sphere of operations expanded, so did its operational costs and the gap between producer and consumer prices (Spoor, 1995b: 73).

Under structural adjustment the emphasis changed. Domestic agricultural prices were liberalized and controls and regulations eliminated, leaving only price support for a limited number of 'strategic' commodities through a price band mechanism (López Cordovez, 1990: 385). Nevertheless, such policies have not gone uncriticized. First, the benefits (and technical and financial support) were monopolized by these 'strategic' commodity producers (Paz-Cafferata and Larios, 1988:14). Second, in those instances when domestic prices lie below international prices, the aggregate response of staple (tradable) commodity producers in the new liberalized environment is not altogether clear. The international price premium calls into play two contradictory tendencies. On the one hand, the higher price provokes a desire to increase the crop percentage marketed (analogous to a substitution effect between production for sale and consumption). Yet on the other hand, improvements in relative prices means that less grain now needs to be produced and sold in order to generate the same level of income as previously (the income effect). Which of these tendencies is the dominant one remains unclear. Third, the price band system takes prevailing (and past) international prices as a yardstick when these are themselves heavily distorted (especially for cereals) due to the size of subsidies offered to producers in the principal surplus-producing countries.

The Agricultural Credit Squeeze under SAP
The majority of the Latin American countries have historically accepted the need for subsidized credit programmes as a compensatory measure to redress adverse domestic agricultural terms of trade. Yet for the World Bank (1986: 112–3) such a credit policy is inappropriate, as subsidized credit is seen to have prejudicial ramifications on optimal resource allocation for financial institutions, the rural credit market and the economy alike. The widespread adoption of SAPs in the region has seen the majority of countries accepting mainstream wisdom and eliminating subsidized credit programmes, re-capitalizing their rural credit institutions and reducing credit allocations which are unsupported by risk evaluations.

In Costa Rica, differential rates which had been set for small producers, traditional agricultural product producers, and medium producers respectively, were seen as distortionary and were eliminated as part of the early 1980s adjustment programmes (Fallas Venegas, *et al.*, 1988: 40). This, plus a concomitant tightening of the money supply so as to squeeze aggregate demand, saw the supply of agricultural credit (measured with respect to agricultural GDP) fall from 40 per cent in the 1970s to between 15 and 20 per cent in the adjustment years of the 1980s. A similar development emerged in Argentina. Monetary policy under the heterodox Austral plan saw agricultural credit fall sharply from 26 per cent of agricultural GDP in 1985 to just 15 per cent in 1987 (BCRA, 1988). In Chile, too, the credit liberalization of the 1970s was followed by a severe monetary contraction under the adjustment programme of the early 1980s. The resulting rise in real interest rates led to bankruptcy and forced land sales in the agricultural sector (Muñoz and Ortega, 1991: 176). Rationing credit by price, however, can have undesirable effects upon the distribution of credit. Whereas in Nicaragua a *'lluvia'* (rain) of cheap credit had followed the Sandinista's assumption of power at the start of the 1980s (Spoor, 1995b: 127), ten years later the sectoral adjustment programme introduced by the UNO government led to nominal interest rates set by BANADES, the Nicaraguan state bank, being the highest in Central America. As the price of credit rose, so did the portion secured by the large-farm sector, from 31 per cent in 1990 to 71 per cent just two years later (Jonakin, 1995: 12). As a consequence, countries that have introduced SAP-influenced macro-policies during the course of the last decade (Brazil, Colombia, El Salvador, Ecuador, Honduras and Peru), continue to justify the retention of preferential interest rates on the grounds that it extends credit to a wider group of producers[12] (López Cordovez, 1990: 368–9).

Finally, the policy of introducing positive real interest rates through increases in the nominal rate has a further cutting edge. The new (higher) cost of credit provides an additional burden for the producer until the harvest is sold. Higher prices might compensate only partially for this. Even among strong SAP advocates such as Norton (1987: 59), there is a concern that conventional adjustment policies might reduce output growth and producer incomes through higher financing costs, or cause reduced input usage (with ultimately the same effect).

Institutional reform and privatization

Structural adjustment programmes and their sectoral components affect state agrarian institutions in two fundamental ways. First, the emphasis on reduced public expenditure impinges upon operational capacity, the agricultural sector being one of the biggest losers in the budget-trimming exercise. De Janvry and Sadoulet (1989: 1208) indicate that Latin American governments' agriculture expenditure declined by a third to just 4.5 per cent during the early adjustment period (1980–4). Baumeister (1991b: 209) has noted how Guatemalan public sector agricultural spending was reduced from 7.1 per cent to 4.1 per cent during the 1980s. Further evidence is provided by Calva (1991: 108) who has commented on the contractionary Mexican policy that sliced 58.5 per cent in real terms off Mexican state expenditures on agriculture between 1981 and 1987 – compared to a more 'modest' cut of 31.8 per cent for total public expenditure. This drastic decline in state support for agriculture during the 1980s has seen agrarian institutions experience problems in the new environment as they discover that reduced or fluctuating budgets impede their historically determined *modus operandi*. Institutional overhaul is thus the second element of the neo-liberal agenda, neo-liberal strategists taking a great interest in the operational efficiency of the agrarian institutions (Valdés, 1992: 302).

In the case of public credit institutions, Clemens (1993: 26) has pointed out how in Nicaragua revenue cutbacks had seen BANADES sharply reduce both its financing of maize and beans in 1992-93 to a level of about 14 per cent compared with the previous year, and the number of BANADES branches and personnel. For BANADES 'legally-accepted land titles, financial solvency and sufficient productive potential' were the new minimum lending criteria, while 'the bank actually started foreclosing on properties' (Spoor, 1995b:206). In Mexico Banrural saw its rural credit portfolio reduced by almost a third between 1980 and 1988, the impact being even more pronounced in Chihuahua where financing fell by 37 per cent, and land sown by courtesy of Banrural funding declined by 75 per cent over the period 1989 to 1992. Now, those with the potential to compete in international markets are rewarded with Banrural credits while other rural producers are obliged to rely upon the limited funds disbursed by PRONASOL[13] (Heredia and Purcell, 1994: 14).

Synthesizing the neo-liberal reforms implemented across the region leads us to the conclusion that the future for agrarian development banks is bleak – as they come more and more to mimic commercial lenders there remains little rationale for them to remain in state hands. In their place, sectoral adjustment programmes often propose the introduction of parallel credit mechanisms – PRONASOL in Mexico, and the Cajas de Crédito Rural in Honduras are just two examples – yet whether this new *modus operandi* will be any more successful in reaching those historically precluded from obtaining credit remains in doubt (Thorpe, 1992: 171).

Substituting for the market?

Most of the SAP criticism of institutional involvement, however, has been directed at the market intervention institutions whose aims were to implement pricing policy while facilitating the collection and distribution of designated commodities through the elimination of the intermediary. In El Salvador, the Instituto Regulador de Abastecimientos (IRA) was to regulate prices, purchase grains from small and medium producers and provide 'permanent and opportune' grain storage services. Aragón (1994: 136ff), however, notes that in practice IRA's guaranteed prices were often below production costs, while it frequently chose to purchase grain from intermediaries rather than directly from the producers. The Instituto Nacional de Café (INCAFE) held monopoly rights over the internal and external commercialization of coffee, but this did not prevent it being criticized both for its slowness in paying producers and for accumulating sizeable annual deficits. Now, with structural adjustment, grain and coffee markets have been liberalized, IRA storage centres have been sold off and the remit of both IRA and INCAFE have been sharply reduced. In Mexico, as fiscal constraints became progressively tighter in the 1980s, CONASUPO first halved its grain purchases and then, following the deregulation and liberalization of grain import procedures, has gradually withdrawn from commercialization activities (Luiselli, 1988: 32; Matus and Vega, 1992: 322). The recommendations in the instance of market intervention institutions are clear. Deregulation and liberalization are seen as essential if producer incentives are to be restored. Consequently, state intervention in the commercialization sphere must be scaled back, or even completely eliminated. The principal problem is, however, as López and Spoor (1992) have pinpointed, the presumption that the space left by the state's withdrawal will be filled by an efficient network of private market agents.

State distribution institutions come under fire too, the critique being that they historically provided generalized food subsidies to the population at large – often at the expense of the most needy. Instead, more cost-effective methods are suggested which target vulnerable groups explicitly. These include:

- the relocation of state shops selling subsidized necessities to marginal *barrios* (as currently recommended in the case of the BANASUPROs in Honduras)
- food coupons issued through health centres to those with symptoms of malnutrition (as is currently being done in Recife, Brazil, for example)
- the leasing of previously state-owned shops to local households (as private operation is seen to be more cost effective), who then retail designated goods at designated prices (Grupo Esquel, 1989: 75).

Other state institutions are not immune to the reformist zeal of neo-liberalism. In Honduras, agro-processing companies such as Productos Lácteos Sula and ACENSA, along with the forestry enterprise CORFINO and various technical and extension services, have been privatised. A similar fate befell a large number of agrarian institutions in Nicaragua in the aftermath of the Sandinistas' electoral defeat; HATONIC, CAFENIC and AGROEXCO being the first of many to pass into private hands (CENPAP, 1993: 77). In Argentina, however, the Menem government has chosen to modernize and/or decentralize rather than privatize the federal provision of agricultural services. The *Programa de Modernización de Servicios Agropecuarios* (PROMASA) is directed towards reorientating service provision at the federal level, while PROSAP – *Programa de Servicios Agropecuarios Provinciales* – is intended to expedite service provision at the local level (Maletta, 1995: 147). Finally, agrarian reform institutions are also overhauled and their objectives redefined. In Nicaragua there is an acceptance within the Instituto de la Reforma Agraria

(INRA) that its role as a redistributive agency has largely ceased. Now, under the SAP regime, it delineates its tasks as being to restore 'stability' in the rural areas through a process of legalizing the tenure situation (INRA, 1993: 49). Similar reorientations can be identified in the rest of the Latin American region, most particularly in the Central American isthmus (Noé Pino, Jímenez and Thorpe, 1994). However, as Thorpe shows in a later, more detailed, chapter of this book (Chapter 3), the SAP approach to land tenure might not be quite the panacea it is painted when viewed from the perspective of those whose access to the soil is limited or restricted.

As is apparent then, neo-liberal policy prescriptions are varied (due in part to the plethora of rural institutions and their respective objectives) and this element is probably the most heterogeneous of the SAP package. Preferred options, in addition to those noted above, include increased institutional co-ordination, more cost-effective research and training facilities along with the pruning of administrative expenditures generally.

Land distribution and land markets

In the context of land policy, SAP theorists are at a marked disadvantage to the more radical Latin theorists, as their reform platform is unable to 'capture the political power evoked by calls for "Land to the Tiller!" with a battlecry like "Tax the Oligarchs!" – not to mention "Equilibrium Exchange Rates!" ' (Tomich, 1991: 177). Nevertheless, land reform in Latin America, with few exceptions, is held by most students to have failed. Instead, given the climate of instability and insecurity that talk of land reform can engender in the countryside, many look beyond direct expropriation and redistribution as the most feasible policy options.

Within structural adjustment a market-driven solution backed by appropriate fiscal policy is held to be the answer. Underutilized land is to be taxed and, if the tax is levied progressively, sub-division is encouraged, thereby offering improved access to land-hungry peasants. But up-to-date official land registers are needed for this to work. The existence and effective functioning of such registers, besides permitting the tax base to be consolidated, allows concrete titles to be granted. Titles thus issued are perceived as offering security, helping to reduce the probability of land invasions and litigation, quickening the process of land transfer and promoting both agricultural investment and soil conservation practices. This process has a secondary pay-off: titles provide an acceptable form of collateral, thereby helping to resolve the traditional problem of restricted access to formal credit channels for small and medium producers. At the same time, titling allows the first tentative steps to be taken towards the establishment of a formalized land market, such titles providing the necessary currency.

In the course of the Salvadorean land reforms (1978–87) for instance, title provision allowed nearly 40 000 proprietors to sell their land (Goitia, 1991:

182–4). The more recent creation, under the 1991 Law for the Financing of Small Rural Properties, of a Salvadorean land bank has provided financial backing to peasants seeking to enter the land market.[14] Nevertheless, title provision not only provides the opportunity to enter the land market but also offers the option to exit, albeit unwillingly. The work of Carter and associates (1990a, 1990b, 1991) in Peru and Paraguay, for example, suggests that titling in fact makes the smallholder more liable to withdraw to a 'poverty refuge' through the sale of land. In a Chilean case, Muñoz and Ortega (1991:175) note that studies have indicated that 37 per cent of the lands assigned under the 1973 parcelization scheme changed hands within five years. Politically, too, the rewriting of Agrarian Reform Laws may be an option best avoided (Morales, 1991a: 66).

Agriculture and adjustment: an evaluation

It is apparent from the preceding discussion that neo-liberal adjustment packages adopted throughout the Latin American region share a similarity in both their design and their desired objectives. They are designed not only to remove past price distortions but also to promote and improve resource allocation so as to 'modernize' agriculture. However, the uniformity of policy at the design stage has not resulted in identical outcomes, and the decision to tailor programmes to national needs and conditions is evident as a consequence.[15] Despite this tailoring of programmes to individual national realities there remain three genuine concerns about the general effects of structural adjustment on the agricultural sector. First, one can differentiate between positive aggregate (production) effects and the negative distributional ones (Norton, 1987: 42). Thus it is paramount to identify the rural groups most adversely affected by SAP policies and question the nature and effectiveness of compensation mechanisms. As Timmer (1986: 114) points out, although it is generally the wealthier who suffer most in terms of real income loss, their wealth cushions them and (unlike the poor) they suffer little or no nutritional consequences. Second, most often 'the negative effects on the poor are certain and immediate, while the positive effects are uncertain and only gestate over the long term' (FAO, 1990: 3).

Ideally, compensation mechanisms should be established early on in the adjustment process to ameliorate the transition costs caused by the sea change in economic policies (Glewwe and De Tray, 1991: 29). A multitude of countries have attempted to make this transition less painful through improved targeting and delivery of compensation programmes. This has proved problematic as the institutions charged with the responsibility are new and generally ill-equipped to cope with the burden of the 'adjustment' poor. Finally, given that the present SAPs do not envisage turnrounds overnight in Latin American agricultural performance, policy must above all be flexible. While 'prices remain paramount' for its advocates, the impact of the structural adjustment strategy will depend on the point to which the incentives offered through the functioning of the price mechanism filter down to the producers, and thence either their capacity to respond, and/or the rapidity with which they do so. In a region which has spawned a whole school of economic thought based on the identification of structural bottlenecks in the developing economy, it cannot be assumed that the 'correct' prices will, by themselves, induce the right response (FAO, 1989: 8, Thorpe, 1991: 6). To this end it is critical that the SAPs adopted to restore agrarian growth paths are closely monitored and modified as the need arises.

Notes to Chapter 1

1. An earlier version of this chapter entitled 'Structural Adjustment Programmes and the Agricultural Sector in Latin America' appeared in the June 1995 edition of the *British Review of Economic Issues*, Vol. 17 (42), pp. 97–124. BREI and Dr Peter Reynolds are gratefully acknowledged for waiving copyright in this instance.
2. Some of the best examples drawn from the Latin field relate to basic grain production and are found in the works of Bentley (1990, 1991) and Bentley and Andrews (1991).
3. The Alliance of Progress has been cited as the key factor responsible for the adoption of agrarian reform legislation in both Chile (Furtado, 1981: 273) and throughout Central America (Bulmer-Thomas, 1989: 249). It also influenced agrarian policies in other Latin economies (Dorner, 1972: 136).
4. Kay (1995: 21) offers three reasons for the failure of rural reform processes; (i) the lack of either power or a political will to enforce them, (ii) mistakes in design and implementation and (iii) the opposition encountered from landlord or other groupings.
5. Debt/GDP ratios varied quite sharply within the region. At one extreme stood Guatemala, Colombia and Paraguay [under 30 per cent] while at the other end of the spectrum were Chile [91 per cent], Costa Rica [133 per cent] and Bolivia [140 per cent].
6. By food dependency we are referring to the gap between consumption and food production per capita. While eight countries reduced their levels of food dependency, 12 suffered increases.
7. In the Central American case, marketed output now encompasses 52 per cent of the maize, 58 per cent of the beans and 87 per cent of the rice production (Baumeister, 1991a: 7, 1991b: 198).
8. In the case of agricultural commodities, basic staples such as wheat and rice are considered to be tradable – whereas crops such as cassava, beans, potatoes and variants of Andean maize are generally designated as non-tradables (see for example Byerlee and Sain, 1991: 74). Mundlak *et al.* (1991: 12) suggest that in the Argentine case (1913–89) around 67 per cent of agricultural production can be construed to be tradable.
9. Nevertheless, from the perspective of an individual country which has a small market share, output expansion is both possible and profitable for exporters. An example of such has been the growth of Central American coffee and non-traditional exports in recent years.
10. For example, devaluation raises local prices of imported commodities, including food. It could well be the case, then, that imported wheat is 'priced out of the

market' and replaced by domestically produced white maize, cassava, rice or beans. This represents a reversal of the 1970s scenario, when overvalued exchange rates increased urban consumption of imported wheat in Brazil, Peru, Ecuador and Venezuela (Byerlee and Sain, 1991: 78), thereby discouraging domestic production.

11. As there is not likely to be an immediate output response given the lagged nature of agricultural production, input price rises can strongly inhibit productive activity, as Luiselli (1988: 35) discovered in Mexico. Maletta (1995: 135) notes the same phenomenon in Argentina during the first phase of Menem's economic reform programme (1989–92).

12. There is some dispute, however, about the extent of smallholder access to formal credit channels (see Thorpe and Restrepo, 1995a: 37ff).

13. PRONASOL, the national solidarity programme aims to alleviate poverty through three main strategies, the provision of (i) welfare benefits, (ii) production benefits (these include rural credit) and (iii) regional development programmes. A concise summary of the programme is provided by Pánuco-Laguette and Székely (1996: 206ff).

14. The chief constraint to peasant land access is the 'speculative premium' that is generally incorporated into land prices. While the majority of SAP remove one source for such a premium – the availability of subsidized credit – it can also create others. Brazilian stabilization measures, for example, provoked an increase in the premia for reasons of exemption. Under the Cruzado Plan (1986), controls had been introduced which affected the holding of specified financial assets. This caused investment portfolios to shift in favour of non-specified, exempt, assets such as land – whose price rose accordingly (Brandao and De Rezende, 1989: 720).

15. While this should be evident from the preceding discussion, a further example may prove salutary at this point. SAP-dictated internal market liberalization is accompanied by the introduction of price-band systems, the price-band system being seen as state-directed in the standard package. In the Chilean case however, a private marketing agency COPAGRO was initially entrusted with the job (1984), although its subsequent collapse led to the state assuming the reins two years later (Cox, 1988: 10, Muchnik and Allue, 1991: 69).

2 Agrarian transformation in Nicaragua: Market liberalization and peasant rationality

MAX SPOOR

Introduction

THIS CHAPTER ANALYSES the effects of market liberalization on peasant rationality and choice of techniques in Nicaragua.[1] The analysis is focused on the period between 1988 and 1993, during which – in an atmosphere of relative peace which had been rare in the 1980s in Nicaragua – various stabilization programmes, wide-scale market liberalization and the radical change in political regimes had a profound impact on agrarian markets. At a sectoral level production and marketed output contracted; however, if one studies the changing forms of market integration during this period at micro-levels, there are indications that peasant farmers have responded to the radically changing market conditions, such as relative prices. The different responses of grain-producing peasant farmers and production co-operatives are then explored, relating them to peasant rationality and efficiency, while critically reflecting whether the outcomes corroborate the underlying ideas of the structural adjustment that was initiated by the Sandinistas in the late 1980s and further pushed by the Chamorro government since 1990.

The question is raised whether peasant farmers and co-operatives in Nicaragua were inefficient and suddenly became efficient, rational, or even 'profit maximizing' producers after the market reforms.[2] Were they all entrepreneurs who reacted swiftly on signals of the market and the changing set of relative prices, following a 'poor but efficient' thesis (Schultz, 1964) combined with the supposed allocative panacea of the market after liberalization? Or can their behaviour be better explained by a 'survival algorithm' (Lipton, 1968; Ellis, 1988)? Arguments are presented that in the pre-reform situation peasant farmers and co-operatives were in fact rational, although on the surface they might have first looked inefficient. It was, however, not the peasant producer but the set of agrarian policies, the structure and functioning of agrarian markets (and the particular conditions that the war produced) that were to blame. Markets have indeed become more efficient after the reforms, although the restructuring of relative prices was a necessary, but certainly not a sufficient, condition for the development of agrarian markets. In order to discuss peasant rationality and producers' response on reforms a case study of Nicaragua is used to show the effects of political and economic macro-events on agrarian markets, presenting a detailed empirical analysis of two farm surveys that were done in 1989 and 1993 in the northern municipalities of Jalapa, Jicaro and

Quilalí. The first moment of measurement was at the end of the 1988/89 maize harvest (February 1989), when peace negotiations and a truce with the *contra* created conditions for researchers to penetrate these war-stricken zones. It was a crucial moment, as a full year had passed since the monetary reform implemented by the Sandinista government. The second moment was exactly four agricultural seasons (and years) later, in February 1993.[3] By then, the UNO government (Unión Nacional Opositora) had been nearly three years in power, and most of its programme of market liberalization, deregulation and privatization was well advanced. In this chapter the discussion will be focused on the maize sub-sector, using detailed survey data of input and output, in order to understand the impact of the market reforms on the choice of techniques and the development of peasant rationality.

The following analysis starts from two propositions. First, in the highly state interventionist agrarian markets in Nicaragua during most of the 1980s, co-operatives as well as private producers were involved in a number of individualized transactions with different actors. The outcomes of these transactions often depended on the willingness of an official to deliver a service, the relationship (whether or not a close relative, friend or political ally) to the client, and the time involved in queuing and attending to the bureaucracy. Therefore, agrarian market transactions, while on the surface seemingly uniform and bureaucratized, were taking place in segmented, heterogeneous and non-transparent markets.[4] Overuse of chemical inputs and machinery services became a widespread phenomenon, but this was a rational reaction rather than indicating inefficient behaviour of peasant producers in this set of individualized market and non-market transactions. When analysing the data on the physical amounts of chemical inputs, one has also to understand that part was used to hoard, to speculate or trade, with substantial gains (in spite of storage losses). Production systems appear to be inefficient when costs are measured at 'real' market price levels, as no sanction for such behaviour existed and for a long time most inputs were financed by subsidized credit through the impact of inflation on fixed nominal interest rates. However, decisions on input purchases and the use of technology were made within an environment of deficient marketing and pricing policies, and the 'speculative paradise' conditions created by war.[5]

Second, in a highly inflationary situation credit loses its intermediary function and becomes purely an instrument of income transfer. The real interest rate, as the price of credit, therefore outweighs in importance the crop price for producers (Spoor, 1995b). Medium and large private producers and production co-operatives (CAS or Cooperativas Agropecuarias Sandinistas) received during the 1980s greater credit subsidies for their mostly capital intensive production of grains than did the peasant producers. They were better off, while appearing to be more inefficient. Those with less access to credit were also less subsidized. Hence, private medium and large farmers used inflation in their favour. When hyper-inflation developed, they increased their dependency on bank credit, while the more risk-averse peasant farmers had no access or did not manage these erratic market conditions in such a way. The CAS production co-operatives were also subsidized because they were entangled in several state circuits, benefiting from infrastructural investments, but also squeezed because of obligatory sales at low official prices to the parastatal purchasing network.

Economic and institutional adjustment in post-war Nicaragua

During the 1979–87 period in Nicaragua state intervention predominated and shaped agrarian markets, particularly those for grains and traditional exports such as cotton and coffee. In the domestic grain market this meant that parastatal input suppliers, crop agencies and the national development bank, in conjunction with economic policies of overvalued exchange rates, consumer subsidies and administered producer prices contributed to the creation of a segmented and artificial set of market and non-market relations in which agricultural producers were operating. The partial liberalization of grain markets since early 1985, when the economy was in a virtual state of seige, led to increasing inflationary pressures. Market transactions became even more heterogeneous and forms of barter trade or the use of a dollar standard in informal price formation became commonplace. Although since that time some economic reforms started to develop, they were only seriously implemented in the post-war period in Nicaragua that started in early 1988 (when most hostilities in fact ended, although large-scale disarmament followed only under the post-1990 UNO government). While differentiating these changes between the 1988-90 Sandinista period and the post-1990 years under UNO rule, there is a certain continuity in the process of economic adjustment, in terms of market liberalization, privatization and state compression. The main tracks of the adjustment process, with its effects for the agrarian sector, in particular for the northern part of Nicaragua where the farm survey was carried out, are the following.

Changing role of the state

The process of institutional change since 1988 was dominated by the withdrawal of the state from many social and economic spheres. State compression was already introduced as an instrument to cut government expenditure during the last two years of the Sandinista regime. However, this had a substantial impact on the agricultural sector through a strong reduction of extension services and agricultural research. Although it did indeed reduce substantially the government bureaucracy (such as internal trade inspectors) the process was accompanied by continuous reorganizations that hampered economic policy formulation and implementation. Directly after the UNO government took power, the state apparatus even showed signs of general paralysis. For political (or personal) reasons Sandinista cadres were purged, while others preferred a transfer to the private sector, often taking with them the knowledge as well as the material infrastructure.[6] Therefore, while this continued process of state compression was in line with the general neo-liberal principles of the UNO programme, the state was increasingly less capable of providing even 'facilitative' support to the agrarian sector.[7] Only during 1993, under pressure from, and with the financial aid of, large donors, a greater streamlining of the state's future role towards the agricultural sector came to the drawing board, in which a new land register and a National Institute for Agricultural Technology were the focal points.

At a regional and local level these global changes were felt as an endless stream of institutional reforms, often implemented overnight. Nevertheless, deregulation and liberalization did restructure the markets for grain, inputs and machinery services. As an example, we may take the valley of Jalapa (which was part of the survey area), where under the Sandinista government, apart from the regional office of the Ministry of Rural Development and Agrarian Reform (MIDINRA) the state was strongly present with a parastatal enterprise. This company, ELMA, not only had large areas of rice, beans and tobacco under cultivation, but also monopolized the local market for machinery services. Furthermore, chemical inputs were mostly sold by the parastatal PROAGRO, while the rest of the market was in co-operative or private hands. By the end of the 1980s, the machinery of ELMA was to be 'privatized' and transferred to a so-called producers' controlled CDC (Centro de Desarrollo Campesino), but private interests in the parastatal, and insufficient peasant pressure, halted this process. When the UNO came to power, the position of the ELMA was rapidly weakened, land was sold or given back to former owners, or leased to investors from the Pacific regions. However, part of the enterprise's assets were left to its workers who have regained some of the market in machinery services, using the enormous quantity of tractors and additional machines the ELMA had in stock.[8] In both machinery services and chemical inputs the state has practically withdrawn from the market, causing new forms of articulation to arise around the use of machinery, providing new 'market opportunities', particularly for those CAS co-operatives that had a surplus in capital assets. The private sector in Jalapa filled much of the gap in the chemical input market, competing with the association of co-operatives (UCA or Unión de Cooperativas Agropecuarias) and the peasant store of the co-operative enterprise ECODEPA.

Agricultural markets in transition
Domestic agricultural markets have greatly changed over the period under study, influenced by market liberalization and deregulation, and with the opening towards external markets. Already during the Sandinista adjustment programme the grain procurement and distribution parastatal ENABAS lost much of its market position, when the domestic grain market was practically liberalized. However, import and export monopolies and control over food

donations were left untouched. This changed further during the first years of the UNO regime, when after the 1991/92 agricultural season the state withdrew from domestic procurement and ENABAS was used only for the distribution and sales of food donations. The only remains of its initial price stabilization role was a new price band system in which a buffer was formed that had to protect the domestic market from sharp fluctuations in foreign market prices. In practice, importers found ways to avoid customs controls and the system did not work very well.

New (and old) market agents have (re)appeared, but the agrarian markets (in particular for grains) became 'low volumes, high profit' markets (Spoor, 1994). The influx of food aid, cheap imports, and particularly the uncertainty for the private sector, prevented investment in infrastructure, while capital flight continued. Furthermore, public investment in agriculture was strongly curtailed as part of the stabilization effort that squeezed the budget. Therefore, in spite of market liberalization, rural markets remain underdeveloped and a hampering factor in agricultural modernization, rather than being the 'midwives of agrarian change' (Harris, 1990). Indeed, some new marketing agents have entered the grain market in the zones where the case study was undertaken, like those coming from Honduras or even El Salvador, but also from domestic urban centres such as Estelí and Managua. However, as transport subsidies (which were implicit in the pan-territorial pricing policy of ENABAS) have been eliminated, the region – in spite of its enormous productive capacity – has comparative disadvantages in terms of accessibility and distance to nearby market centres. The main access roads are in a very bad state during the rainy season and many feeder roads are not all-season roads. Transport costs (and post-harvest losses) during the 1992/93 season were therefore substantial.

Resettlement and land disputes
The agrarian sector has felt the influence of the post-war reconstruction programme directed to the resettlement of former *contra* guerrillas and the land disputes between beneficiaries of the Sandinista land reform and former land owners. In particular, in the north of Nicaragua (as in the areas of the survey such as Jalapa and Quilalí) these processes caused great tensions that even led to armed occupations of several towns, such as Ocotal and Estelí. The economic pressure put on producers (in terms of low output prices, higher input prices and much reduced access to credit) also contributed to a month-long armed occupation of the local Development Bank (BND) office and the closing of the route to Jalapa during 1992.

In spite of a large-scale UN-sponsored resettlement programme intended to integrate thousands of *contras*, the post-war period has produced a fragile form of peace, in which only very limited stability can currently be maintained. There exist grave security problems, with a number of rural gangs terrorizing the peasantry. Land disputes have also led to the return to former land owners of land owned by the state and increased pressure on co-operatives that lacked proper land titles, a problem that did not receive sufficient attention during the Sandinista agrarian reform. Co-operatives and private farmers were also forced to sell land in a process of decapitalization or to improve their cost structure. Consequently an incipient land market has developed, although still in a very segmented forum. Although most of the co-operatives of Jalapa have remained undivided, in other parts of the country many were parcelized.

Structure of relative prices (factors of production, credit and output)
Relative prices of inputs, credit and crops changed rapidly during the post-1988 period. Agricultural credit, which during the years of high inflation had become a reliable income transfer for the peasantry, was already partially indexed to devaluations and consumer inflation after the Sandinista money reform. However, when the UNO second stabilization programme of March 1991 was launched, credit policy – within the course of one season – was stripped from its previous image. By the 1992/3 agricultural season only a very limited number of clients were still financed, a drop which was particularly felt by the large stratum of the peasantry producing maize and beans. Between the 1989/90 and 1992/3 agricultural seasons the National Development Bank (BANADES) reduced its finance for corn from 186 700 to only 19 800 *manzanas* and for beans from 79 100 to only 5 600 *manzanas*.[9] At regional level in Jalapa, Jicaro and Quilalí, some of this gap was filled by credit funds that were available for resettlement programmes such as the UN programme PRODERE (Programa de Desarrollo para Desplazados, Refugiados y Repatriados). This programme also provided credit to peasant associations in order to be able to buy the harvest and sell it to ENABAS or private traders. Furthermore, as a relatively new phenomenon, private input suppliers are providing some short-term credit to a selected group of customers, and even substitute for some of the vanished technical assistance (that was previously provided by the Ministry of Agriculture and the Bank).

Exchange rate policy already changed drastically with the money reform of the Sandinistas in February 1988, when the long time fixed official exchange rate was devalued from 70 (old) Córdobas to 10 (new), Córdobas, equivalent to 10 000 (old) Córdobas. During two years of following hyper-inflation, the government would try unsuccessfully with regular devaluations of the Córdoba to 'catch up' with this whirlwind of price increases, a policy which was also continued during the first stabilization programme of the UNO government. Monetary stability was reached only after the introduction of the second stabilization round, introduced in March 1991, which combined an economy-wide money squeeze with sufficient foreign resources to close the existing macro-economic gaps. Finally, under the influence of monetary policies and the withdrawal of subsidies, the artificial relative price structure of chemical inputs and machinery services was completely overhauled, also meaning the reconstitution of the distorted (according to market prices) capital/labour price ratios. In Table 2.1 the price changes for a standard package of chemical inputs used in maize production is shown, compared with the development of official and market prices of maize.

What, however, should not be ignored is that the real recovery rate of agricultural credit during 1988 was only just over 10 per cent (!), because of the large gap between nominal interest rates and inflation, while in 1989 (with bank finance still covering 80–100 per cent of chemical inputs) this was still only 60 per cent. Although much of the restructuring in relative input prices took place during the Sandinista adjustment programme, the effect of the extreme rise in nominal input prices, which can be seen in Table 2.1 was therefore considerably softened. By not adjusting credit policy, the extreme adjustment of relative prices – unintendedly – was less felt by producers. What is not shown here, but equally important, is that rice and beans, because of their much higher parallel market prices in the late 1980s, became an attractive complementary product for maize producers. Only a dip in domestic beans prices (caused by an export ban) in 1992 caused producers to look for other alternatives. In Jalapa and Quilalí, where early in 1993 a reduction in beans production was noticeable in the survey, there was a shift towards vegetable production, such as tomatoes.

Table 2.1: Relative prices of chemical inputs for maize (1987/8–1992/3)

Current prices/December						
Input	*UM*	*Units*	*1987/8*♥ *C$UM*	*1988/9*♦ *C$UM*	*1989/90*♣ *C$UM*	*1992/3*▲ *C$UM*
NPK	QQ	2.0	1128	13280	400700	51.2
Urea 46%	QQ	2.0	7750	10159	244200	73.0
Decis	Lt	0.5	22033	24700	659554	82.0
Filitox	Lt	1.0	8750	9575	291689	46.4
Atrazine	Lb	2.0	286	2454	83620	13.0
Gramoxone	Lt	2.0	835	5834	260440	25.0
Prowl	Lt	1.0	4400	11165	380470	66.0
Input price maize	C$		44165	96544	2979856	477.8
Output price maize (O)	C$▲		50000	5000	230000	30.0
Output price maize (M)	C$		137500	10000	295165	30.0
I/O ratio (official)			0.9	19.3	13.1	13.5
I/O ratio (market)			0.3	9.7	10.1	13.5

Notes: ♥ Official Prices of the parastatals ENIA and PROAGRO (Old Córdobas);
♦ Official Prices of the parastatals ENIA and PROAGRO (New Córdobas);
♣ Market Prices (Gold Córdobas), taking the average of different agents;
▲ Official (O) Prices from ENABAS (until 1989/90); Market (M) Prices (Spoor, 1994; 523).
Sources: Data provided by ENIA, BANADES, ESECA, ENABAS; (Spoor, 1994); Own calculations.

Table 2.2: Capital/labour price-ratios (1987–92)

	December 1987	April 1988	July 1988	November 1988	December 1989	October 1992
P(Kc)/P(L)	0.34	2.91	5.33	6.37	5.39	3.57
P(Km)/P(L)	0.96	1.48	3.21	4.67	2.77	1.86
((P(Kc)+P(Km))/P(L)	1.30	4.39	8.54	11.04	8.16	5.43

Note: c = chemical inputs; m = machinery services.
Sources: BND, BANADES, ENIA.

In Table 2.2 the capital/labour (K/L) price ratios are presented for the production of maize at an advanced technological level (i.e. with tractors and sufficient levels of fertilizers and pesticides). As capital was still artificially cheap in 1987, there was a rapidly rising K/L price ratio for maize production after the February 1988 monetary reform, somewhat stabilizing during 1989. Nevertheless, if one takes into account the large share of implicit credit subsidy, these ratios were increasing only gradually over this period, remaining well below the 'real' level of October 1992. By then, after a period of substantial monetary stability and absence of inflation, the overall K/L price ratio was about five times that of December 1987, with chemical inputs increasing tenfold and machinery services doubling in price with respect to labour. This development of relative prices between capital goods and labour is already indicating what is confirmed in the farm surveys. These large price increases induced a radically changed utilization of capital inputs by peasant farmers, commercial farmers and co-operatives, shifting to more labour-intensive production methods, while also reducing the cultivated area of maize.

A comparative farm survey: the north-eastern Segovias

In this section the change in choice of techniques in the production systems of grain-producing peasant farmers and co-operatives is discussed on the basis of data from two comparative farm surveys that were held in what in Nicaragua is known as the north-eastern Segovias, and more in particular in Jalapa, Jicaro and Quilalí. These municipalities share common borders with Honduras and have for long been affected by the *contra*-war.

For three reasons the region of the north-eastern Segovias and the zones involved are of interest in the Nicaraguan context. First, it has all the characteristics of a typical peasant region, producing grains and export crops like coffee and tobacco (often in combination with cattle breeding). Second, the zones of Jalapa and Quilalí are good examples of the mainstream thinking behind the agricultural development strategy of the Sandinista government that combined socio-economic with strategic-military objectives. This broad strategy was based on state-centred accumulation, including a bias towards capital-intensive production and agro-industrial development. From early

1982 onwards, large integrated rural development projects in Jalapa and Quilalí provided access to technological transfer and substantial infrastructural investments. Jicaro, a geographically isolated zone, with a lack of all-season roads, a long tradition of extensive cattle breeding and a correspondingly low level of social organization of the peasantry, did not benefit from this development. Third, the Segovias is one of the most under-researched regions in comparison with the three regions of the Pacific coast. Previous research on peasant production in the north of Nicaragua had concentrated mostly on the arid and semi-arid zones of the western Segovias. For a long time, intensive *contra* activities in the mountains around the valley of Jalapa, in Jicaro and neighbouring Murra, and in the whole of Quilalí, made it difficult to penetrate the mountainous areas, which contain a large number of scattered farms. Therefore, although being priority areas within the development plans of the Sandinistas, little serious research was done on peasant production and rural markets (Spoor, 1994). While geographically situated far from Managua, and even isolated because of the absence of sufficient all-season roads, the north-eastern Segovias are economically important in terms of agricultural production. In particular, the valleys of Jalapa and La Vigía are highly suitable for maize, rice, beans and tobacco production, with coffee or cattle breeding in the highlands.

The 1989 and 1993 farm surveys in Jalapa, Jicaro and Quilalí
The farm survey sample consisted of 43 farms, of which 27 were individual peasant farmers, small and medium, and 16 were small, medium and large CAS-production co-operatives. Within the limitations that continued *contra* activity imposed on rural research, the sample could not be representative. However, stratification was done according to three criteria – degree of specialization, cultivation and mechanization – resulting in three strata of individual farmers and three types of production co-operatives. The individual peasant farmers were categorized as: small farmers, with low or intermediate technology and largely depending on grain production; medium (type 1) farmers, with advanced technology and a mixed (cultivation/cattle raising) production system; and medium (type 2) farmers, with extensive cattle raising as basic production system, and with grains as a marginal activity. The production co-operatives were divided into small work collectives, medium and large CAS (type 1) co-operatives with mixed production systems, and large CAS (type 2) co-operatives with mainly cattle breeding.

Briefly summarized, the results of this first survey were the following. First, the use of subsidized technology transfer had caused the agricultural producers, in particular the capital-intensive medium (type 1) farmers and the medium and large (type 1) CAS co-operatives, to produce maize at excessively high real costs. They were still not sanctioned for such behaviour, as the Sandinista adjustment brought only a gradual indexation of the crucial interest rates for agricultural credit.[10] Second, when asked to indicate a change in choice of techniques for the following season, it was again these strata that were least willing to change, specially as regards the use of chemical inputs such as fertilizers and pesticides. As they were benefiting most from the impact of inflation on rural financial markets and no sanction for their behaviour was imposed, there was no incentive for them to change. However, the post-1990 stabilization and adjustment programmes forced them to adapt. Third, in accordance with the still strong presence of ENABAS in the region, producers sold most of their grain at an early stage, having little option for storage, and no 'market control' by reserving substantial quantities for the non-harvest season.

Of the original sample, only 17 (of the 27) farmers and 10 co-operatives (of the 16) could be revisited in February 1993. The reason for this reduction of the survey sample – as mentioned above – was that those producers and co-operatives that were situated in the municipality of Quilalí could not be visited. When the team arrived in the town to start the survey, fighting broke out between the army and armed rural gangs (*revueltos*), which made the planned visit an impossible undertaking. Apart from this unforeseen factor, one producer was not present in his farm and another had moved outside the region.

Comparison of the surveys: the impact of market reforms

First, from the sample data the marked drop in farm size for the medium (type 2) farmers, and in cultivated area for the medium and large (type 1) CAS co-operatives, is significant, other differences possibly having a more spurious character (Table 2.3). This is in line with the selling of grassland as a form of decapitalization and improving liquidity, and a greater market sensitivity of the co-operatives to the market price development of some crops, in this case beans. Second, taking into account the small sample problem of both surveys, it was observed that the production co-operatives improved yields on the whole, while there is clearly an opposite movement for the private farmers. The seemingly inefficient co-operatives – that during the in-between period were strongly compressed in terms of membership – have not only survived, but also improved their cost structure of grain production.[11] Third, the changes in relative prices during the four years between the first and the second surveys greatly influenced the use of chemical inputs, especially of a variety of (previously very cheap) pesticides.[12]

All strata severely reduced the use of chemical inputs measured in constant (December 1992) prices, with particularly significant reductions in the case of the medium (type 1) co-operatives. For the 1993 sample the overall yields of individual peasant farmers decreased by 29 per cent while chemical input costs per *manzana* dropped by 23 per cent, in comparison with the 1989 survey.

For the CAS co-operatives there was an increase in yields of 20 per cent and a reduction of chemical input costs per *manzana* of 50 per cent. Medium

Table 2.3: Stratification of individual farmers and production co-operatives

	Individual farmers			CAS/CAP co-operatives			
	Number	Farm size	Cult. area		Number	Farm size	Cult. area
Small	10*	(10.7)	(7.9)	Small	(3)	(60.3)	(43.7)
1989		11.3	7.3			60.5	35.5
1993	6	11.3	6.7		2	46.0	31.5
Medium^1	(8)	(79.3)	(23.1)	Med/Large^1	(1)	(739.3)	(206.5)
1989		97.0	33.0			712.9	229.0
1993	3	95.0	31.7		7	693.9	166.4
Medium^2	(9)	(64.9)	(6.4)	Large^2	(2)	(1270.0)	(27.5)
1989		56.8	6.6			1240.0	38.0
1993	8	36.3	6.3		1	700.0	30.0

Note: * On the basis of the full 1989 survey sample.
Medium (1) Farmers = Mixed (crop/cattle) production system.
Medium (2) Farmers = Extensive cattle breeding/low grain production.
^{1} Medium/Large CAS = Mixed (crop/cattle) production system.
^{2} Large CAS = Extensive cattle breeding/low grain production.
Manzana = 0.7 ha.
Source: Sample data from Producers' Surveys Region I, 1989 and 1993.

farmers, who were least willing to change, present an increase of chemical input costs per quintal. This is a surprising result as production co-operatives encountered particular problems with obtaining credit and are confronted with continuing land conflicts. Nevertheless, production co-operatives had the advantage of using their own machinery, where small and medium farmers mostly had no such assets. It produced the result that some co-operatives are now providing machinery services (on a rental basis) to private farms in their areas, something that the state enterprises had previously done.[13] Where in other parts of Nicaragua many co-operatives have parcelized their land and disintegrated, in Jalapa they have integrated themselves in markets in new ways using their economies of scale.

Relative prices and choice of techniques

Taking the 1989 survey data, one can observe no significant correlation between the value of the chemical input package that was used to grow maize and value of output per unit of land (TVP or Total Value Product measured at 1992 constant prices).[14] In fact, the observed correlation coefficient is only 0.06. It is also clear that there is a cluster of co-operatives that can be defined as 'high cost and medium output', indicating a strong overuse of inputs in the production of maize, a phenomenon which was already indicated above. This picture changed radically in the 1993 survey results. The input/output relationship in value terms became a reasonably straightforward one (assuming that equilibrium values of this input/output relationship were

Table 2.4: Costs of chemical inputs (fertilizers, pesticides)

Maize	Individual farmers		Co-operatives	
(Dec1992C$)	Cost C$/Mz	Cost C$/QQ	Cost C$/Mz	Cost C$/QQ
Small			Small	
1989	415.9	10.7	529.6	22.6
1993	235.8	6.1	505.9	10.6
Medium			Med/Large	
1989	606.4	19.0	918.6	23.1
1993	594.2	24.2	397.9	7.4
Medium			Large	
1989	382.8	6.8	196.0	5.2
1993	310.5	9.1	62.1	2.7
Average			Average	
1989	437.2	10.5	768.5	21.2
1993	335.7	10.8	384.5	7.6
Price of maize: 30.0 C$/quintal		Exchange Rate C$/US$: 5.0/1.0		

Source: Sample data from Producers' Surveys Region I, 1989 and 1993.

not reached in our observations, as a consequence of credit restrictions and liquidity problems in the adjustment process). The liberalization of this sub-market indeed caused a substantial shift in producers' behaviour and use of inputs, in particular the group of co-operatives. The correlation coefficient now became 0.78.[15] This result indicates that the previously absent correlation between the value of chemical inputs and the crop output value per unit of land, was re-established during the economic adjustment period under study. Obviously, during the 1988/9 agricultural season the chemical input price was still highly artificial as most had been acquired just before the relative prices were really affected by the Sandinista stabilization measures, or had been held in stock. Therefore, the relative weights of the inputs used did not depend on their real market values at that moment, while this was the case in the 1992/3 season. The erratic use of chemical inputs (fertilizers and pesticides) in the pre-reform situation, as measured in the first farm survey, changed dramatically under the influence of market liberalization and deregulation. In particular, pesticide use dropped from 289.2 C$/unit of land (*manzana*) in 1989 to 110.0 C$ in 1993, while fertilizers diminished from 277.7 C$ to 202.7 C$ (at constant December 1992 prices). Some of the pesticides used (like the herbicides) were substituted by labour and traditional labour-intensive techniques such as weeding with machete have regained a place in the farming systems. However, other reductions in pesticide use have contributed to lower yields, as resistant plagues could not be controlled and integrated pest management is still underdeveloped.

Rational behaviour in 'irrational markets'

The data presented from the Nicaraguan case study indicates that peasant farmers and co-operatives in the 1993 farm survey sample were 'on average' using their inputs efficiently.[16] There are several problems related to this conclusion, such as the assumption that the sample observations are comparable (in spite of existing differences in soil quality), and the linearity of the correlation that was measured. Furthermore, although the north-eastern Segovias is a very important grain producing area, it cannot be taken as representative of all peasant farmers in Nicaragua, in particular not for a large group of very small and marginal producers in the 'agricultural frontier' areas of the country. Nevertheless, returning to the original questions raised at the outset of the chapter, was the behaviour of peasant farmers in the pre-reform situation 'irrational' or 'inefficient'? It can be concluded, on the basis of these arguments and empirical data, that the overuse of chemical inputs measured in the 1989 farm survey particularly reflected their very low relative price. They were held (often for too long) in stock, were sold in bulk and used in barter trade or smuggling practices. Great quantities were also actually used because resistant plagues were developing. Peasant farmers and co-operatives were seemingly inefficient in their production cost structure (at real market prices). However, taking into account the absence of sanctions and the alternative use (hoarding, speculation, barter trade) that was given to cheap inputs, they were behaving rationally within inefficiently (and even 'irrationally') working markets. It is important to note that those private or co-operative farms that received more implicit subsidies, being more capital-intensive, benefited more than the peasant farmers. While appearing inefficient, they were not so from their own perspective.

The change in relative prices (between inputs, and between inputs and outputs) has greatly affected the utilization of these inputs. This process has been gradual during the post-1988 period when for a number of years the credit subsidies softened (or slowed down) this impact. In general, a greater consciousness developed with peasant farmers and co-operatives regarding the purchase and use of inputs and their relation with output levels (or values), which had been practically absent before. This change in the behaviour of peasant farmers and co-operatives was caused mainly by drastically different relative prices (input-input, input-output and output-output price ratios) and their insertion in a reformed set of market relations. These same producers act (at least in the short run) according to their form of integration and the efficiency of the markets themselves, without suddenly having left their supposed inefficiency or having embraced efficiency. A transition from non-transparent, segmented and heterogeneous towards transparent, integrated (interlinked) and homogeneous market transactions will re-establish the standard relationship between the costs of the input package and the value of crop output. However, as was stated in the beginning of this chapter, the change in relative prices is a necessary, but certainly not sufficient, condition for the efficiency of markets. The conclusions from the empirical data therefore cannot be used to suggest that agrarian markets in the post-reform situation in Nicaragua have already developed into integrated and competitive markets, as new tendencies of monopolization are present and there is a severe lack of the new institutional frameworks that are needed for market development (Spoor, 1995b).

Notes

1. An earlier version of this paper appeared as ISS Working Paper, No.165 (January 1994), 'Agrarian Transformation in Nicaragua: Markets, Peasant Rationality and the Peasantry'.
2. See Ellis (1988) for different definitions of peasants and peasant behaviour such as the 'profit maximizing peasant' and the 'risk aversive peasant'.
3. Unfortunately, these zones had again been affected by guerrilla activities, this time from rural gangs formed by *contras* and/or government soldiers. They also absorbed a large part of the disarmed guerrillas who were resettled.
4. This part benefited from comments made by Ashwani Saith.
5. Maureen Mackintosh (1987).
6. Some of the ministries were stripped of their inventories by the outgoing crew. This process is known in Nicaragua as the *piñata*.
7. The term 'facilitative' is taken from Faaland and Parkinson (1991).
8. Field notes of Mario López made during the farm survey of February 1993.
9. One *manzana* = 0.7 Hectare; On average between 250 000 and 300 000 *manzanas* of maize were cultivated during the 1980s in Nicaragua.
10. While these farms were spending only 9.5 per cent and 15.2 per cent of the crop price/unit of output on chemical inputs and machinery services respectively during the 1987/88 season, this had become 79.3 per cent and 118.1 per cent during the 1988/89 agricultural season (Spoor, 1995b: 175).
11. Membership of the ten co-operatives that were revisited in early 1993 was on average 32, while this had been 52 in early 1989. The reduction in membership was caused by outgoing members who returned to their (often deserted) mountain farms or who looked for other rural or urban employment.
12. Note in Table 1 that pesticides like Gramoxone and Atrazine were subject to much greater price increases than fertilizers.
13. Since the 1986/7 season the concept of 'territorial enterprise' had become fashionable, in which the state enterprises would have to articulate better with the private and co-operatives sectors. It was entirely dropped when 'state compression' was introduced during the 1988–90 reforms.
14. This can be done as survey data were also measured in physical units, while prices were collected through other channels.
15. One influential outlier (extreme observation) has been ignored in this calculation (while another was eliminated because of unreliability of the input data), but inclusion of this outlier and the application of a robust regression analysis would adjust the outcome only marginally. The data can also be analysed by a simple, one-factor Cobb-Douglas production function. However, for the sake of the argument the (linear) correlation coefficient is a useful instrument.
16. See Ellis (1988) on the statistical problems connected to analysing the behaviour of the 'average peasant'.

3 Adjustment, agricultural modernization and land markets: the case of Honduras

ANDY THORPE

Introduction: land access and ownership rights

LAND OWNERSHIP AROUSES strong emotions in Latin America. The Mexican Revolution at the turn of the century, with its accompanying images of Pancho Villa and Emiliano Zapata leading peasant armies to reclaim rights to land, encapsulated popular notions regarding the necessity of agrarian programmes. It was generally argued that the profoundly dualistic nature of Latin American agriculture was a severe hindrance to rural, and by implication, national economic growth. On the large *latifundios* or *haciendas*, a combination of low labour and capital utilization coupled with extensive land exploitation resulted in both low output volumes and labour absorption rates. Conversely, *minifundios* were characterized by a high degree of surplus labour and intensive land use (to the point of degrading the soil).

Redistribution was advocated on the grounds that it would (i) increase agricultural productivity, leading to an expansion in output, and (ii) provide a means whereby surplus labour could be redeployed, thereby raising both rural employment levels and incomes. Furthermore, output expansion would either provide the foreign exchange necessary for the import substituting industrialization (ISI) strategies being pursued across the region (in the case of agroexports) or ensure that urban consumers would benefit from lower food prices, thereby reducing industrial costs. Popular demands for land were melded with these theoretical arguments, thereby shaping the actual redistributionist policies adopted. In Mexico (1917), Bolivia (1952), Cuba (1959) and Nicaragua (1979) significant economic and social dislocations dictated that the land reform legislation approved was equally revolutionary. In Chile (1964–70) and the Central American region – Honduras included – a mixture of popular pressure and the exigencies of US Alliance for Progress funds were instrumental in ensuring the adoption of conservative agrarian reform programmes. In the southern cone, however, low levels of rural militancy and/or large expanses of unutilized land ensured that reform never appeared on the agenda (Argentina) or else popular demands were mitigated through colonization programmes (Brazil, Paraguay and Uruguay). The failure of ISI as a development strategy in the region was paralleled by an increased questioning of redistributionist ideas regarding the land resource (See Chapter 1). The new neo-liberal view saw insecurity of land ownership or usufruct rights as the main obstacle to 'long-term investments in the land and in the modernization of agriculture'

(University of Wisconsin/LTC, 1990: 1). Security of tenure became the byword, which was seen as the fundamental agrarian pre-requisite if Pandora's productivity box was to be opened. Land redistribution was now rejected on the grounds that it heightened insecurity. Instead, land titling was ordained to be the most immediate policy need if national land markets were to emerge. Ancillary measures sought to provide greater scope for buying, selling and renting land. An efficiently functioning land market would, by encouraging the cultivation of more profitable crops, it was argued, improve rural investment returns and thereby expedite the 'modernization' of agriculture. In the short to medium term, however, a transition period would be necessary while the market mechanism was created and/or consolidated.

The case of Honduras provides a good insight into the development of Latin American land markets in the era of privatization and market liberalization. Not only has the country recently introduced a structural adjustment programme (SAP), it has also strongly reoriented agrarian policy along neo-liberal lines. Furthermore, both the bifurcated agrarian structure (in the sense of reform/non-reform land) bequeathed by the now rescinded agrarian reform law (ARL) and the current institutional structure of the sector are indicative of the agrarian environment encountered in the rest of the region. In a sense, then, Honduras provides an example through which the consequences of agrarian modernization can be evaluated *vis-à-vis* its impact upon rural land markets. To this end, the chapter:

• analyses how the current priority for land titling (in the neo-liberal sense) originated in the early 1980s, being incorporated into the more robust agrarian policy introduced under the SAP of the early 1990s
• evaluates the impact of neo-liberal policy measures on Honduran agrarian structure using Instituto Nacional Agrario (National Agrarian Institute, or INA) sources and our own base-line surveys (1992–3). In doing so, the fate of the agrarian reform sector, and in particular the agricultural co-operatives will be discussed, as well as the outcome of the land titling programme in relation to the emergence of formal land markets and their functioning.

Land titling and agrarian modernization in Honduras

In September 1981 the Honduran government launched its first formal titling programme, the *Proyecto de Titulación de Tierras* (Land Titling Project or PTT), in seven of the country's 18 departments. This USAID-sponsored programme was initially targeted at coffee producers who were facing potential ruin due to coffee rust (a year later it was extended to all peasant farmers). To the programme designers the crisis in the coffee sector was due to a failure on the part of growers to undertake preventive measures so as to minimize the blight. This in turn was attributed to problems of tenure insecurity that would prevent the producer investing (University of Wisconsin/LTC, 1985: 1). The programme duly promoted land titling among this producer grouping and specifically exempted properties from being expropriated under the ARL of the time. Land titles thus provided security of tenure, and the collateral that such tenure offered could be used to open up access to credit facilities. More importantly, by standardizing titling mechanisms and documentation, the PTT provided the foundation stone for a formal land market to emerge. However, the outcome of the PTT was well below expectations. While the programme had intended to title 3.24 million hectares of land to 70 000 producers over a period of five years, it achieved only 7.5 per cent (of hectarage) and 37.5 per cent (of beneficiaries) of its objectives (Thorpe, 1993: 38).

Agrarian reform land meanwhile remained outside the land market, beneficiaries under the 1974 ARL being prevented from either selling or renting out their properties. This was to change, however, with the assumption of power of the Callejas government in 1990, and the implementation of a SAP in March of the same year. This SAP had a number of important effects upon the agricultural sector. A drastic devaluation (50 per cent) of the national currency substantially improved the domestic currency income of agricultural exporters. Export promotion became the order of the day with the Law to Promote Banana Production – exempting newly planted areas from taxes for the first three years (and a reduced tax rate for a further three years) – of May 1991. Coffee producers also benefited as the government slashed export taxes in half, provided fertilizer subsidies and then, in 1992, reformed the structure of coffee taxation completely. These moves had rather less to do with neo-liberalism and the promotion of exports, however, and rather more to do with the preservation of producers' incomes, as coffee prices plummeted from US$ 134.3 (1989) to US$ 71.6 (1993) per quintal (World Bank, 1994b). Equally, if not more important, was the sectoral SAP, initiated with the Agricultural Modernization and Development Law (LMDSA) of March 1992. This extensive law sought to revise agrarian policy completely, swallowing up the PTT programme, while adding a further number of provisions regarding land, its ownership and use (Table 3.1).

As is evident in Table 3.1, the LMDSA seeks explicitly to promote formal land markets. The illegally occupied national lands ('INOL'), multiple property and minimum size holding provisions increased sharply the area of land that can potentially enter the market by (i) updating the farming requirement, (ii) relaxing regulations found in the previous ARL, which restricted the scope of land titling and (iii) extending the possibility of expropriation to land in the reform sector. A further supply-side boost comes from the establishment of individual ownership rights permitting the piecemeal sale of land in the possession of co-operatives and associative enterprises (EAs), while rental and joint venture provisions provide alternative options to outright land sales. At the same time, the potential demand for property is augmented by the

Table 3.1: Changes in ownership and use rights introduced by the LMDSA

Issue	Position prior to LMDSA	Position after LMDSA's approval (1992)
1. Illegally occupied national lands (IONL)	Individuals who farmed INOL for 10 years prior to 1975 ARL could petition for title (Art.15).	Requirement changed to 3 years prior to LMDSA (Art.50).
2. Multiple properties	Individuals with one or more properties are excluded from receiving further land through the 1975 ARL (Art.15).	Multiple properties now permitted, up to a 200 hectare ceiling (Art.50).
3. Minimum size holding	Intent on eliminating *minifundios* (5 hectares or less) through expropriating, consolidating and then re-adjudicating them (Arts.34,100 and 101).	Re-defines *minifundios* as properties under 1 hectare (Art.50).
4. Large farms and ownership thereof	Ministry of Natural Resources can authorize farm sizes above locally-defined ceilings, though not beyond the 'break-even' point. Large farms must have a 51% local shareholding (Art.39).	Break-even stipulation and local ownership rules are relaxed (Art.50).
5. Rental	ARL beneficiaries are required to farm their own land or have it expropriated (Art.41, 106 and 108).	Renting-out private or ARL lands is permitted (Art.54).
6. Joint Ventures	No provision for joint ventures ('*Co-Inversión*').	Joint ventures permitted (Arts.55, 56, 57 and 65).
7. Individual ownership rights	Land adjudicated to co-operative groupings or *Empresas Asociativas* (EA) is titled to the co-operative/EA. (Arts.104–25) and cannot be sold (Art.106) without INA permission.	The LMDSA permits the granting of individual ownership shares within co-operatives or EAs. These can be sold, as can co-operative lands, subject to certain provisos (Arts.60, 61, 65 and 70).
8. Women's rights	Land adjudication limited to single women and widows with dependants (Art.79).	Both sexes eligible to receive land under LMDSA, subject to certain, gender-neutral, specifications (Art.64).
9. Interim titling	Beneficiaries entitled to a provisional title to land, until full payment for adjudicated land is completed (Art.93).	Provisional title scrapped. Replaced with full title and accompanying mortgage within six months of adjudication (Art.65)
10. Land market promotion	No provision.	State obliged to create the mechanisms necessary to facilitate land market transactions (Art.69).
11. Reform sector land	Exempt from expropriation	Reform sector land, not properly exploited, is also liable to expropriation (Art.52).

possibility to form (or have ownership of) large farms and expanded women's rights established under the Law. The process is further expedited by the commitment both to promote land markets and move to a system of issuing full title deeds promptly. These specific provisions, buttressed by other parts of the LMDSA which intend to modernize agrarian production, such as the liberalization of internal and external agricultural trade, are expected to contribute to the development of an active land market in the country (Thorpe, 1995a). The question is, what happened in practice?

The impact of SAP on rural property rights

The most dramatic change pre-dated the LMDSA when, on 5 May 1990, the co-operative ISLETAS, seen as one of the beacons of the agrarian reform process, sold out to the Standard Fruit Company. This was one of a number of north coast co-operative sales at the start of the 1990s, as the fruit multinationals sought to expand their production area. It was not the first, however, as nine co-operatives in the Atlantic region had sold land between 1985 and 1989 to various cattle ranchers and traders (Ruben and Fúnez, 1993: 47). While such sales were in direct contravention of the then prevailing ARL, attempts to challenge their legitimacy in the courts were unsuccessful. The LMDSA removed the legal barriers that prevented co-operatives selling land. Indeed, a study completed less than six months after the Law's approval, identified 56 co-operatives which had sold a total of 11 770 hectares in the Sula, Aguán and León valleys (*ibid.*). This pattern has been corroborated by both a POSCAE-WISCONSIN study (1994) and unofficial INA figures – and was instrumental in persuading the Liberal government that took office in February 1994 to introduce legislation to prevent further sales. In commenting upon the phenomena of co-operative land sales we need to answer two sets of questions. First, who is selling land and why (how much land, where and for what price)? This is complicated by the fact that land in Honduras is of widely varying productivity. Maize yields from as little as 8.5 quintals per hectare in impoverished municipalities such as 'El Triunfo' in the south, up to 115 quintals on technified production in the Aguán valley.[1] Second, who is purchasing the land – and what are their motives for doing so?

Combined with the data of Table 3.2 it can be seen that of the 2694 peasant bases recognized by INA[2] when the LMDSA was approved, by 1994 a total of 248 or just over 9.2 per cent had already entered the land market as vendors. Furthermore, 30 775 hectares or 6.5 per cent of the 470 572 hectares adjudicated to the reform sector by the ARL in the period 1962–89 had passed out of the hands of the original beneficiaries. However, as there are significant regional variations, the question of who is buying and selling land is best addressed at a more disaggregated level. One can identify four motives for selling land (see POSCAE-Wisconsin, 1994):[3]

Table 3.2: Co-operative land sales by INA region

Region	No. of groups	Original members	Actual (%) members	Adjudicated area (Ha)	Area sold (%)	Principal crops
Atlantic	51	1091	687 (62.9)	5250˙1	3775 (71.9)	Maize, Rice
North♥	25	1420	759 (53.4)	2472˙12	1541 (56.2)*	Maize, Sugar, Bananas
South	50	2358	1142 (48.4)	9478	2741 (28.9)*	Various
Aguan	64	2503	2031 (81.1)	24877˙7	21454 (86.2)*	Maize, Palm, Cattle, Citrus
Morazan	12	321	225 (70.1)	1846˙1	280 (15.2)	Maize, Vegetables
Comayagua	11	330	191 (57.9)	1469˙1	831 (56.5)	Maize, Vegetables
Oriental	11	332	198 (59.9)	896˙7	119 (13.3)	Maize, Sorghum
Olancho	2	64	40 (62.5)	294	43 (14.6)	Maize, Cattle
Total	248	8419	5475 (65.0)	46582	30775 (66.1)	

Source: INA (1994) and personal investigation.

* In these instances not all groups have reported the number of hectares sold. For comparability, therefore, we also exclude hectarage adjudicated to such groups (The number following the asterisk identifies the number of non-reporting groups).

♥ While a further 12 co-operatives were sold in the north, as data (both membership and area) were not made public they have been excluded from the totals.

♦ The EA San Miguel and the Co-operative Dos Caminos sold 39 and 51 hectares respectively more than originally adjudicated.

♣ The Co-operative El Chaguite sold 24.5 hectares more than originally adjudicated.

♠ The EA Miramar sold 36 hectares more than originally adjudicated.

Indebtedness

A number of co-operatives or EAs saw land sales as a means of reducing enterprise indebtedness. This motive was particularly in evidence around El Progreso in the northern region. Here, the co-operative Agua Blanca Sur sold land worth 22.4 million Lempiras (leaving 560 000 Lempiras per member (*socio*) after settling debts) to an MNC (Standard Fruit Company), retaining a further 106 hectares under sugar cane. Another one, Buenos Amigos disposed of 445 hectares to the other fruit giant, the Tela Railroad Company, for 71.4 million Lempiras in July 1991 (60 579 Lempiras per *socio*), retaining an additional 1236 hectares in the Aguán valley (Ruben and Fúnez, 1993: 52/3, Thorpe, 1992: 137). It was also in El Progreso that the companies Grupo Lempira and Azunosa purchased the major part of the co-operative Lourdes (293 Ha) and the *asentamiento* La Libertad de la Sarrosa (322 Ha), leaving the remaining *socios* with so little land per *socio* (1.3 Ha and 2.5 Ha respectively) that it is hard to conclude that these sales were for any reason other than indebtedness. Land sales due to indebtedness have both positive and negative pay-offs. In those instances where indebtedness has reduced access to credit and prevented reform land being fully exploited, the option to sell land to clear debts, recapitalize the enterprise and improve current consumption levels is a positive boon. The downside is in evidence when distress sales occur – the Uchapita co-operative in the Aguán sold all its 77 hectares for a reported price that did not represent even half of its outstanding debt, peasant farmers being squeezed off their land.

Sales to avoid expropriation

The LMDSA also caused co-operatives to offload unused or underutilized land so as to avoid INA exercising its new powers, namely the expropriation of unutilized co-operative lands. This phenomenon is particularly notable around La Masica in the Atlantic region. Here, an average desertion rate of 61.5 per cent (compared to 37.1 per cent for the region as a whole) left high land-to-member ratios in some units.[4] The most extreme case is that of the co-operative La Constancia, where membership had fallen from 12 to 1, the area adjudicated remaining at 84 hectares (In the EAC Ruth Garcia Mayorquin just two of the original 26 *socios* remained in possession of 195 hectares). Thus, of the nine co-operatives that have sold land in La Masica, only two sold up completely, the others simply 'downsizing' to leave themselves with between 2.25 and 12.5 hectares per *socio*. In this sense the impact of the LMDSA has been positive, providing an avenue through which land surplus co-operatives can convert this excess into financial capital.[5] It also, *ipso facto*, sees the transfer of land into more productive hands.

To resolve internal tensions

Co-operatives suffer as much as other organizational forms from internal animosities. These animosities can be resolved in a variety of manners (depending on their severity) including: (i) group arbitration; (ii) outmigration of one or more of the antagonists – although the outgoing member forgoes his patrimony in the enterprise; (iii) increased emphasis on individual, at the expense of collective, cultivation – with a corresponding decline in the internal cohesion of the group. The LMDSA offered two further avenues for resolving the conflict, the creation of individual ownership shares (TPI, *títulos de participación individual*) which can be sold by those *socios* wishing to leave the co-operative, and the sale of co-operative land followed by the distribution of the resulting proceeds. As the TPI still remained on the drawing-board in 1992–3, land sales were seen as the optimal solution[6] in those co-operatives where tensions had arisen between members. In this instance too, the LMDSA appears positive in the sense that it permits the dissolution of unsuccessful 'marriages', distributing the assets that remain between the partners.

Market and non-market pressures

Finally, one must not underestimate the pressures exercised by fruit multinationals, cattlemen, military officers, politicians and in general the rural élite, to 'persuade' peasants to part with their land. This can be market-driven – as in Olanchito in the Aguán region, for example. Here the Standard Fruit Company offered prices of between 1826 and 12 500 Lempiras per *manzana.*[7] As peasants perceived the offer to be a very lucrative one, 16 of the 22 recorded sales in the region, were made to the US fruit multinational. Alternatively, sales can occur as a consequence of threats and other non-market pressures (Ruben and Fúnez, 1993: 92). While threats and the like cannot be condoned, once again the LMDSA appears to offer peasants a 'better deal' on the land front. However, one should ask whose patrimony is it that is being sold, the state – which allocated the land to these groups and thence offered them favourable treatment through an array of tax exemptions and subsidies – or the *socios* (Thorpe, 1992: 137).

Turning our attention to land purchases, there appear to be three main purchasing groups active in the market.

Fruit multinationals

Both Standard Fruit and the Tela Railroad Company (a subsidiary of United Brands) have been active purchasers, as was noted. Their interests in purchasing reform sector land can be linked to two factors, one external, the other internal. Externally, it was expected that access to the highly profitable European market would improve, leading to a commensurate growth in demand for Central American bananas – hence the need to safeguard domestic production.[8] Internally, the Lempiras devaluation (March 1990) and the failure to dollarize export taxes until May of the following year improved domestic profitability. This was augmented by the introduction of the previously mentioned *Ley de Incentivos a la Producción Bananera*, which stimulated banana exports through tax exemptions.

Domestic agro-industrialists

The name that stands out here is that of Miguel Facussé. Through the company (Cultivos de Leán) he acquired four of the nine co-operatives that sold up in Arizona (Atlantic region), for prices of between 8000 and 13 058 Lempiras per hectare.[9] These 229.9 hectares are likely to be placed under African palm, a crop that has an extremely bright future within the Central American Common Market (UE, 1995), as Facussé owns the local vegetable oil-processing plant. He also acquired a further 265 hectares in Esparta (Atlantic region) at a cost of 2.25 million Lempiras and, through another of his companies (Mejores Alimentos, the country's principal tomato paste manufacturer), 638.2 hectares from two co-operatives in the Comayagua region at prices ranging from 1020 to 3571 Lempiras per hectare. A number of other companies have expanded agricultural activities (Pepe Produce, Cultivos Ex Campo, Azunosa, etc.), strengthening their vertical integration, although the shareholders in these companies and their intentions are less clear.

Others

In Esparta (Atlantic region) the principal purchaser is Agropecuaria Comercial, a group of high military and civil functionaries, according to Ruben and Fúnez (1993: 50). More recent data, however, confirm the 'Munguia brothers' as a major purchaser in the region. Paying anywhere between 2000 and 10 000 Lempiras per hectare the 'brothers' accumulated 1086 hectares. In Tocoa (Aguán) Irias Navas, the Congressional leader under the Callejas regime, is named as purchaser in four instances, paying around 2500 Lempiras per hectare for more than 880 hectares. Unnamed military officials and cattlemen are also cited as purchasing land in the region, while military officials were also active in the reform sector land market in Comayagua. The motives for purchase here are not immediately apparent – although it reflects a nationwide trend of growing military activity in the economic field (Arrivillaga, 1993, Martínez, 1994).

To date, there is little evidence, however, that small farmers have benefited from the emergence of a market in reform sector land. While this could be attributed to the continued failure to introduce mechanisms which expedite the acquisition of land by such groups (notwithstanding Article 69 of the LMDSA), a more likely explanation can be gleaned from the pattern of sales that has taken place to date. The present neo-liberal environment has improved the position of tradable agricultural commodities (in particular, bananas) to the detriment of maize, the crop with which smallholders are most familiar. Hence, the major participants in the market to date have been those most closely allied to the export sector.

The private market for land

One problem in trying to identify changes in the non-reform sector is the lack of formal land titles – and hence a formal land market. Cambar Custodio (1990: 1), for example, estimates that just 38 000 properties (1 per cent of the total tenanted properties) had full formal title prior to the initiation of the PTT in 1983. Seven years on, ADAI (1990: 14) suggests 6 per cent of farms are duly titled. When one takes into consideration a 1990 INA land inventory that estimates private lands account for 38.8 per cent (in the case of Santa Bárbara, 53.3 per cent) of national territory, it is apparent just how far the titling process has to go. Nevertheless, a system of 'customary' (Coles, 1988) or 'informal' (Wachter, 1992) rights have become enshrined in local land transfer practices and are often backed up with private witnessed documents. These 'antiquated' practices, however, were seen as hindering the modernization of Honduran agriculture on three grounds: (i) through restricting the development of a market in land they prevented allocative efficiency, (ii) they were inadmissible as collateral within the formal credit system and (iii) technical support was less likely to be provided in instances where there were no formal ownership documents. Hence PTT, and more recently the wider-ranging LMDSA, are seen as promoting tenure security, thereby removing the developmental bottlenecks identified above.

The original PTT baseline study in Santa Bárbara of 1982 was followed by an evaluation of the programme by the University of Wisconsin in 1988. The first study surveyed 569 (Santa Bárbara) and 198 (Ocotepeque, a control region where PTT was not implemented). The follow-up study re-interviewed 491 of these farms in Santa Bárbara, restricting the sample size to those which

Table 3.3: Formal titling programmes and access to credit and technical assistance

1. Percentage of interviewees selling or transferring land in preceding five years

	1982	*1987*	*1992*
Santa Bárbara	n.a.	6.3	16.2
Ocotepeque	n.a.	15.3	19.7

2. Percentage of interviewees receiving credit

	1982	*1987*	*1992*
Santa Bárbara	14.1	22.0	27.4
Ocotepeque	18.0	24.6	50.8

3. Percentage of interviewees receiving technical assistance (visited by agronomists)

	1982	*1987*	*1992*
Santa Bárbara	47.6	31.7	33.5
Ocotepeque	26.8	32.4	55.7

Source: Computed from Larsen (1995).

had since been granted formal title (243 farms). In Ocotepeque, 176 farms were revisited. Fortuitously, Larsen (1995) replicated the study a decade after the original baseline survey, incorporating 191 farms (Santa Bárbara) and 61 farms (Ocotepeque) of the 1988 survey. These studies give us the opportunity to assess whether formal titling procedures are contributing, in the pre-supposed manner, to agrarian modernization. It would appear that rather than promoting land transfers the issue of titles has actually led to their curtailment! While the 'low' 1987 figure in Santa Bárbara could be due to proprietors repressing sales until after formal title had been issued,[10] this should be paralleled by a greater than expected increase in the post-1987 period. However, recorded land sales by farm size (with the exception of those in the 2.6 to 5 hectare bracket) over the 1987–92 period are all greater in the control group. From this evidence Larsen (1995: 118) concludes that: 'it is unlikely that titling has led to an increase in land sales'. One important flaw in this analysis however is her failure to link these changes to differences in the commodity composition of farm output in each region. In Santa Bárbara a larger number of farms (82.3 per cent compared to 62.7 per cent in Ocotepeque) cultivate coffee; furthermore, those farms cultivating coffee in Santa Bárbara devote a substantially higher proportion (excepting the 10.1–20 hectare category) of land to the crop. Given that coffee has a three- to four-year gestation period between planting and the first harvest, and that the record 1986 prices of $243.3 per quintal undoubtably encouraged expansion in cultivated area, it seems probable (despite the subsequent decline in price) that producers would be loath to sell their *cafetales* due to (i) the 'sunk' costs incurred and (ii) imperfections in local land markets. It is perhaps the nature of the crop rather than the nature of the title, then, that has served to stymie land sales in the region.

In terms of improving access to credit, farm size remains more important than legal title when it comes to obtaining credit. Rather more paradoxically, however, Larsen (1995:120) also notes that while there was no statistically significant difference in the likelihood of receiving credit between the two regions in either 1982 or 1987, this was not the case by 1992. The reason, as she goes on to elaborate, 'was due largely to the activities of Non-Government Organisations (NGO) in the department (Ocotepeque)' (*ibid*.: 119). NGOs have proliferated in Ocotepeque in recent years due to the influx of Salvadorean refugees and the region's poor ratings in economic and social development terms. However, their collateral requirements and loan procedures are much more fluid than conventional (formal) credit sources (Thorpe and Restrepo, 1995b: 51). Excluding NGO credits reduces the 1992 Ocotopeque figure to 28.8 per cent, a figure which is not statistically significantly different from that of Santa Bárbara. It transpires, then, that the professed link between legal title and access to credit is perhaps much more tenuous than is often presumed. Finally, although 'visited by agronomists' is a very crude measure of the level of technical support[11] provided to agrarian producers, it does show that titled and non-titled farms received similar levels of support in

1987. While Larsen (1995:123) suggests the 1982 Santa Bárbara figures were probably inflated due to INA titling staff being mistakenly categorized as agronomists by producers, the reversal that is seen a decade later is almost certainly due once again to the efforts of NGOs in the region.

In short, there is little evidence to warrant the assertions that titling may help to improve allocative efficiency (and consequently production levels) through either 'freeing' up a repressed market in private land (Salgado *et al.*, 1994: 47) or increasing the flow of credit and technical assistance to title-holding peasants. Worse, there are two further issues that heighten our pre-occupations over the PTT-titling programme. First, evidence suggests that the majority of subsequent transfers of PTT-titled land are not formally registered. Larsen's (1995: 119) study indicates that just 34.5 per cent of the transfers occurring over the period 1987–92 in Santa Bárbara were witnessed by a notary, and only 20.7 per cent were registered at the local *municipio* offices. The principal reasons appear to relate to either cost or ignorance of the need to register transactions in this way (Coles, 1988, Salgado *et al.*, 1994: 17). Unless registration rates for land transfers improve markedly in the short to medium term then one must be pessimistic over the long-term outcome of PTT policy. Second, the PTT programme has not been introduced in a vacuum. Rather it has been overlaid on existing customary/informal rules of land tenure and transfer. As a consequence: 'PTT became an additional element in local struggles over property rights in land. Instead of abolishing insecurity of property rights over land *PTT has simply modernised the sources from which people draw rules to contest rights over land*' (Jansen and Roquas,1996: 1; our italics). Despite all these misgivings, the ideological baggage of the PTT programme has been absorbed into the LMDSA as given wisdom.

Conclusion

The most explicit manifestation of the new neo-liberal environment governing the way in which agricultural policy is conducted is undoubtably the LMDSA. This law has swept away the distinctions between reform and non-reform land, moved towards standardizing land transfer procedures through its incorporation of the PTT, and dealt a body-blow to cherished notions of the co-operative as the harbinger of social change. While the agrarian reform movement has been decimated in the north, in particular by the scale of co-operative sales, it is unlikely that we shall see sales on this scale again. The LMDSA legitimized co-operative land sales, thereby freeing up a repressed land market. A 'one-off' re-assignment of landholding portfolios occurred, and judgement as to the future of the agrarian reform sector is best made on what happens once the dust has settled. Nevertheless, a number of critical observations can be made.

First, co-operatives such as Buenos Amigos, Isletas and Nombre de Jesus to name but three, were bought up by the fruit multinationals. It is unclear whether these purchases were made in order to obtain fiscal benefits available under the Banana Promotion Law, or whether they represent a fundamental inability of peasant groupings to compete in productivity terms with multinational enterprises employing plantation-style production methods to grow bananas. Second, co-operatives such as El Marañon (Pepe Produce) and El Astillero (Miguel Facussé) were bought up by domestic entrepreneurs, as part of a strategy to expand African palm and citrus fruit production for domestic processing. Although peasant groups have historically played a key role in the production of these crops,[12] domestic processors are now choosing to embrace production risks within a framework of vertical integration and modernization. Third, a number of co-operatives were carrying such high levels of debt[13] that their recuperative ability was low, sale providing a means of freeing up locked-in capital. Fourth, the LMDSA offered the opportunity for co-operatives to 'down-size'. Membership decline had resulted in high land:man ratios in a number of co-operatives, and the LMDSA now offered the option to offload excess landholdings. This decision to sell was induced somewhat by the LMDSA's veiled threat to extend expropriation of unutilized land to the reform sector. It remains unclear, however, if the revenues received were used to reduce indebtedness, to recapitalize, to technify, or were spent on family consumption.

Finally, the attempt to establish a formal market in private land in Honduras appears to be undergoing a traumatic infancy. From the evidence available there appears to be little correlation between access to credit and extension services and formal land title. One can be sceptical over the PTT's claims that it improves security of tenure, and indeed some authors argue that it has merely modernized insecurity. Furthermore, it appears that the development of an effectively functioning land market is crop-driven rather than title-driven, if the Santa Bárbara results are typical. In fact, if shifts in production are taking place (both in the private and reform sectors) as a consequence of relative price changes, it remains to be seen whether the new tenure arrangements facilitate or constrain these shifts.

Notes

1. At prices of 40 Lempiras per quintal, the average price around the time of the LMDSA's approval, annual revenues per hectare from maize production varied between 340 and 4600 Lempiras. Land prices could be expected to show differences of a similar magnitude. Similar differences are also likely in the case of other crops.
2. INA does not recognize peasant units which either (i) lack land or (ii) occupy land without a full or provisional title. Peasant groupings argue that the real number of peasant bases is considerably higher, at 5754 (POSCAE-OXFAM, 1993: 156). As

we use INA data on land sales we shall also use the INA base estimates in this chapter.

3. The sensitivity of the issue at the time meant that the reasons given for land sales were generally couched in vague terms. Hence our identification of motives is based on inferences (following discussions with peasants, other local inhabitants and INA officials, to name but three sources) and should be treated as indicative rather than definitive.

4. High desertion rates are not just a function of out-migration rates. As co-operatives age, they suffer membership decay unless new *socios* are incorporated. If incorporation does not occur (or is lagged), then higher land/labour ratios will result and land underutilization will emerge in the absence of offsetting shifts in either the technology of production or the employment of outside labour.

5. It is important to separate the production decision (do we continue to cultivate land or sell?) from the consumption decision (what happens to the proceeds of land sales?). Newspaper reports at the time were especially critical of the way sale proceeds had been 'wasted' on non-productive activities (gambling, prostitutes, purchase of luxury goods etc.). If there is such a preoccupation about the way the proceeds of land sales are spent, it is not clear why the most appropriate action should necessarily be to prevent such sales in the first place.

6. Needless to say, the decision to sell is not a conflict-free one. A dispute over whether to sell or not left three peasants dead in the Tres Reyes del Diamante Co-operative in Tocoa.

7. In the case of ISLETAS, while all details of the sale were not disclosed, it was estimated that the price paid amounted to 33 500 Lempiras per hectare.

8. We say 'safeguard' as the tendency in the period after the 1954 banana strike had been to contract-out production to independent growers. The arrival of Fyffes and its offer of improved contract terms to independent producers in the early 1990s made 'in-house' production a more attractive proposition to the two fruit multi-nationals already resident in the country.

9. These prices are likely to be underestimates as the LMDSA (Art.70) requires that 20 per cent of the sale proceeds must be paid over to the state in those instances where the purchaser is not eligible to be a beneficiary of the agrarian reform process.

10. This theory is substantiated in part by evidence showing that just 42.9 per cent of the transfers occurring in Santa Bárbara over the 1982–7 period were sales, compared to 70 per cent in Ocotopeque (Larsen, 1995: Table 6.26).

11. The measure has three principal deficiencies; (i) it fails to identify the type, (ii) quantity [in terms of number of visits] or (iii) quality of the support given.

12. INA (1992: 20) calculate that reform sector groupings have produced 60 per cent of the country's African palm production and 50 per cent of its grapefruit production.

13. The only available information on indebtedness is that supplied by Ruben and Fúnez (1993: 68). While, for example, the co-operative San Rafael (debt/annual turnover ratio of 0.6:1) could be considered to fall into this category, the most indebted (Uchapita, ratio of 5.2:1) was not sold.

4 Structural adjustment and agriculture in Africa

PHILIP RAIKES

Introduction

THE IMPACT OF structural adjustment on agriculture in tropical Africa is a very relevant issue, since agriculture is the major source of employment and income, especially for the poorest people, and of exports in most African countries. However, for this very reason, plus several others, it is very difficult to measure. It is not enough to evaluate progress by looking at increases in overall output or exports, given the extent of poverty, inequality and hunger, as food security does not relate in any simple way to levels of production. Most people who go hungry do so because they lack the income or other means of access to it. The level of total output is only one, and not necessarily the most important, factor involved. Therefore the impact of adjustment must be assessed by reference to a multiplicity of aims; increasing output, exports and incomes; improving income distribution; and doing so sustainably and minimizing environmental ill-effects. There is no guarantee that what maximizes one will maximize, or even improve, others.

Nevertheless, even aggregate production data are hard to assemble and are very unreliable. African agricultural sectors are primarily composed of small peasants, producing in part for own consumption, selling much of the rest in local markets, and frequently evading official markets where they exist. All this makes estimation of output levels, or changes in them, both difficult and unreliable – a problem aggravated by the cash-starved situation of African statistical services and of those agencies, such as extension, upon which they depend for information. Relating changes in agriculture to adjustment also poses severe problems of interpretation. How far are the observed effects the result of adjustment, as opposed to other factors like the weather or international price changes? Among the effects of adjustment, how does one assess the relative effects of policy changes induced by it and those of increased aid for which they were the condition? Among policy changes some are clearly more important than others; some seem complementary, others mutually counteracting.

Under the circumstances, composite measures of 'success' conceal more than they reveal and cannot be used for much. This is shown below, after the introductory sections on adjustment and African agriculture, by presenting and discussing some examples. The chapter proceeds with brief sketches of significant processes within the adjustment histories of a few countries. This certainly does not give a full picture, but tells one more than composite measures and it brings to the surface points of relevance and interest which get ignored by such measures – and by a discussion of adjustment dominated by a simplified neo-liberalism, for which the main, if not the only, problem is market distortion due to state interference, with the main solution being to let 'the market' reign.[1]

Precise evaluation of the effects of adjustment is not possible, but its architects have little reason for self-satisfaction. Most African countries are poorer and more heavily indebted than before adjustment started. Poor people, both rural and urban, seem to have taken the brunt of this through increased landlessness, unemployment and reduced real wages. Adjustment has had little success in increasing export-crop production and (with huge declines in terms of trade since the early 1980s) even less in increasing export revenues. So most African countries are more dependent on Western donors than they were before adjustment – both for the aid grants and loans which keep them going and for the subsidized rescheduling of debt service which keeps this manageable – so long as the country respects its commitments to adjustment. Of course, adjustment should not take the blame for all the ills of the past decade or two and certainly not for long-term problems like population pressure on the land. There was plenty wrong with pre-adjustment agricultural policy in Africa (and elsewhere), and world price trends in the 1980s would not have favoured African exporters, with or without adjustment.[2] Some countries (but by no means all) had already started to lower the quality of health, education and rural water supplies before the 1980s, but adjustment seems to have hastened the process.[3] The breakdown of state power and civil order in so many countries during the 1980s and 1990s derives from a wide variety of historical causes, although in some cases it may have been aggravated by intensified competition for resources in the straitened climate of adjustment. It is scarcely coincidental that Somalia's debt was already 26 times its GDP in 1990, the last year for which figures are available.

Adjustment and agriculture

Agriculture is the most important sector in most African countries; that which provides both most of the income and foodstuffs for the majority of the poor, while it is also the major export earner in most countries. Initial arguments for adjustment rested heavily on the poor performance of African export agriculture during the 1970s, which was said to have been caused by urban/industrial bias and excessive state intervention in the economy and to be the most important reason for Africa's external debt and economic crisis.[4] This was the argument of the World Bank's influential (1981) *Accelerated Development in Sub-Saharan Africa: An Agenda for Action* (the Berg Report), which argued that a focus on export production would improve food security since the countries most successful in increasing agricultural exports were also said to have increased food-crop production most. It thus recommended devaluation (to increase export-crop prices and production), reductions in state expenditure on non-productive sectors, control over parastatal marketing to reduce margins and improve prices to producers, and increased investment in agriculture.

It is true that African agricultural exports stagnated during the 1970s. But one could as well blame too much of the wrong sort of policy as lack of concern for agriculture.[5] The asserted link between export and food production is weakly based theoretically, and empirical demonstration depends on picking the 'right' years. The further link to food security is still weaker. It has also proved very difficult to 'invest in' peasant agriculture without increasing spending by the agricultural parastatal monopolies which had been developed for this purpose, but whose power and spending the Berg Report recommended pruning. Indeed, partly as a result of adjustment-induced financial stringency, changed accounting practices and much higher interest rates, the costs and debts of agricultural parastatals often grew faster after adjustment than before, and often with little or no improvement in the level of services.[6] Foreign private investment, said to be crucial for success, has been notable by its absence.

The term *structural adjustment* applies to policies imposed by the IFIs[7] upon African and other Third World countries since the early 1980s. It thus refers in part to the *content* of these policies; a neo-liberal shift away from state intervention in the economy, raising real interest rates, lowering budget deficits and inflation, letting 'the market' allocate resources wherever possible, and providing an 'enabling environment' for the private sector. But it also stands for the mechanisms that have been used since about 1980 to persuade Third World countries, often very reluctantly, to follow neo-liberal policy prescriptions. These have to a very large extent been imposed by making the release of funds by donors conditional on implementation of the required policy changes. Aid conditionality long predated structural adjustment, but its scope, degree and co-ordination increased enormously from about 1980 onwards. Political parties came to power then, in several major OECD countries, concerned to replace Keynesian with neo-liberal policies and unconcerned that imposing this on other countries could be seen as an encroachment on sovereignty. But the ability to increase pressure was closely related to indebtedness and most of this dated from the monetary boom of the mid to late 1970s, which became a crisis, with deflationary policies from 1979 onwards. The deflationary policies of 1979–81 also hit international prices of agricultural commodities exported from Africa and further sharpened the need for short-term funds since, while aid inflows and export revenues were falling, loans were tighter and calls for debt-repayment were increasing. This made it increasingly difficult for African countries to withstand the pressures to adjust, especially as the IFIs put pressure on other donors to cut or delay aid transfers until adjustment agreements had been made.

Adjustment conditionality first focused on specific macro-economic targets for devaluation, reduction in government spending and deficits, controlling the money supply, and raising real interest rates. In agriculture it proposed to invest more, while reducing the margin between producer and export or consumer prices by pressing parastatal marketing agencies to improve their performance. The underlying reasoning was that prices were the main, if not the only, determinant of production. However, even before most adjustment programmes had started, this 'pricist' viewpoint had been criticized by those who found 'structures' also important, pointing out that if roads and transport, processing, storage capacity and finance were not available, increased crop prices at national level might not achieve very much. By 1990 poor export-crops results showed such factors to have been relevant, as was IFI failure to take account of declining international prices and the effect of devaluation on input as well as product prices. In addition, for a variety of reasons including both parastatal inefficiency and the effects of adjustment itself (see note 6) export-crop producer prices often did not rise either in real terms or as a proportion of the export price.

Since the end of the 1980s the emphasis of adjustment has increasingly shifted towards structural factors. The macro-targets remain, but there has been a shift at meso-level, away from resuscitation of state and parastatal economic bodies under financial stringency, towards privatizing or closing them down, and 'providing an enabling environment for the private sector'. Some observers see this as a softening of conditionality, but this seems largely to be a matter of language. The previous focus on reducing state expenditure and disencumbering the 'productive' sectors has been replaced with concern to improve the efficiency of social services, but one which usually turns out to mean reducing state expenditure and introducing cost recovery procedures. Meanwhile, shifting from restricting state activity to enforcing wholesale privatization seems rather an increase in the scope or severity of conditionality. Privatization also tends to imply an increase in foreign ownership of resources, since few locals have the funds to purchase privatized companies of any size or potential value. Ironically, the few local beneficiaries conspicuously include the most successful state-based rent-seekers of the previous period; those who used their positions in the state or parastatal sectors to fill their pockets. Many of these have now re-invented themselves as private entrepreneurs, ready to buy the shells of corporations they have emptied of assets and avail themselves of the many programmes now being run by donors to encourage private enterprise.

No one doubts the disastrous effect of state extravagance during the 1970s, or that painful policy changes would have been needed under any circumstances. But it is worth pointing out how this arose, and stressing that it was not, as widely asserted in IFI circles, the inevitable result of the working out of a state-oriented development path. It is true that as African countries emerged from colonialism they tended (with donor assistance) to increase government expenditure to redress the disastrous lack of education, health facilities and other infrastructure bequeathed to them by colonialism. But this would have been choked off in the early 1970s for lack of funds, but for factors having nothing to do with Africa at all.

The Bretton Woods exchange control system of 1944 came under increasing strain during the 1960s and was buried in 1971 when the USA devalued the dollar. One destabilizing factor was the growth of the Euro-dollar (offshore) market, which both hastened and was accelerated by the demise of Bretton Woods. Two major shocks aggravated the situation. The USA devalued primarily to make its agricultural exports more competitive, and soon thereafter engineered a grain sale to the USSR, so huge as to triple international grain prices. Shortly afterwards, the first OPEC action increased oil prices similarly. This generated both inflation and pressure on Western banks to get the vast amounts of 'petro-dollars' that had been saved with them, out and working, further adding to inflation and reducing real interest rates. The result was a monetary boom, with massive increases in lending at real interest rates that were initially negative and then very low, until 1979. To repeat, this was an international monetary boom caused by a combination of deregulation and speculation. It hit African countries through foreign willingness to spend, not theirs. Its effect on Africa was disastrous. It made financial discipline impossible, encouraged irresponsible spending and led to sclerotic growth of state and parastatal institutions funded by aid money. The World Bank spent this period pouring loans (and so increasing African debt) into building up those institutions which adjustment would tear down. This was the period when Tanzania's disastrous 'crop authorities' were invented (by consultancy firm McKinseys) and vastly expanded with World Bank and other donor funds. In Kenya the World Bank made a bid to take over planning and integration of agricultural development through its 'Integrated Agricultural Development Programme'. All that remained of this by 1980 were the debts. The World Bank had distanced itself from what it now saw as an entirely Kenyan blunder.[8]

The point is not just whose fault it was. In the dogmatic neo-liberal thinking which underlies much the structural adjustment policies, Africa's indebtedness and other ills are often blamed on an inevitable and cancerous growth process within state sectors. But the above suggests that the rapid state and parastatal growth itself arose in large part from international economic cycles rather than from any inevitable tendencies.

The characteristics of African agriculture

In sub-Saharan Africa, agricultural sectors typically comprise two-thirds or more of the total national population, and the poorest part of the population at that. By far the majority are small peasant farmers, so agriculture directly provides much of their income and food security. It also provides cash income through sale, and this affects the incomes of many others as traders, trans-porters, processors, sellers of cooked food and consumers. The very poorest people cannot subsist from their own farm production and must engage in wage labour and petty trading at some times of year, in order to buy food and other necessities.

Large farms and plantations range in importance from negligible to domin-ant in different countries. They are almost always more important in mar-keted or exported production, and significantly *less* important where employment is concerned. Large farm sectors in most African countries employ significantly fewer people now than they did in the mid-1950s as a result of mechanization, and will never absorb more than a fraction of the sur-plus population from peasant agriculture, though they are often still the largest single employing sector. Neither can urban employment accommodate the flood of young people to the towns, driven both by shortage of land and opportunities at home and by the apparently better prospects in the towns. Thus small-scale agriculture will have to continue to provide the bulk of income and food for huge and increasing numbers of poor people.

While much peasant production is aimed directly at household subsistence needs, all households are also involved with markets, selling crops, working for wages, petty trading and engaging in other activities to earn a living and spread risk. This spreading of activities seems characteristic of African accu-mulation and household reproduction strategies at all income levels. Avoiding various sorts of risk, from climate through government policy to civil war, means diversifying and keeping resources mobile, favouring investment in transport and trading over production. It also means mobilizing kin, clan, eth-nic, school or professional influence networks and patronage hierarchies. All of this both reflects and contributes to the political uncertainty affecting so many countries.

The rich man has a job, political appointments and contacts, is involved in transport and trading, has different farms scattered around. He is often a politician or member of committees giving him access to resources and influ-ence and he may be a respected local elder, involved in much of what goes on in local politics. If so, he will have all the requirements for intensifying farm-ing, except the time to get around to it.[9] Lower down the scale, rich peasants diversify into transport and trading, often mixed with political manoeuvring. Still lower down, a poor woman may work on her husband's and her own part of a household plot (or on still less of her own or hired land if she is a widow). Besides this, and looking after children, cooking, fetching water and firewood and other household chores, she may earn money by buying and selling small amounts of crops (including some own produce), be involved in one or more work and/or savings groups with other women, brew beer or liquor for sale, collect forest products for sale, and undertake a variety of other activities, such as pottery and basket-making. Risk-spreading also involves cultivating a network of kinship and other relations, to give improved access to resources and security in time of need. These are often strongly patriarchal, marked by patron-client linkages, and linked into local political structures. Most rural African societies are not particularly egalitarian, and are marked by interpenetration of market and non-market relations even without state intervention (who you are and how closely connected you are to local powers affects a number of prices, including bribes). The combination of multiple activities in personal and household strategies, with the interpenetration at all levels of political, social and economic transactions means that real markets work very differently from the markets of textbooks and adjustment plans.

Men own or control most land and other resources, while women do much of the work especially, but not only, in food-crop production. It is convenient to refer to the household as the basic productive unit, but this can be misleading, since many households function as only partly linked sub-units. In particular, men and women often take on different tasks or concentrate on different products. The decisions of different parties will depend in part on economic calculation, but even that part only as filtered through male-dominated marriage customs, male power and control of property. Farming techniques are in transition over much of tropical Africa. In some cases this is from long-fallowing or shifting cultivation, to permanent cultivation on one fixed farm – under pressure of population increase, the expansion of cash-crop farming and the accumulation of larger land holdings which often accompanies it. In some areas of high rainfall and population pressure, complex methods of soil-regeneration and/or irrigation developed locally – sometimes before the colonial period, at other times during or since. In large- and medium-scale commercial farming, however, the current tendency is to reduce levels of input use as costs rise and subsidies fall. This also seems to be the case for many smallholders who were introduced to 'modern farming' in organized, regimented and subsidized development projects.

Attempts to inculcate 'modern farming' among smallholders have seldom attempted to integrate these with existing cultivation systems, let alone learn from them. Researchers, extension agents and policy-makers have tended to think in terms of replacing 'traditional agriculture' (a term which incorrectly implies lack of change) with a 'modern agriculture' based on use of inputs and machinery, rather than integrating relevant aspects of both. Input-based intensification involves not only knowledge but access to funds or credit to buy inputs, and often extra family labour (or money to pay wages) to carry it out. When colonial regimes started, from the 1950s, to intensify African peasant agriculture they developed a series of processes and institutions having much in common throughout the continent. Outside the areas settled by whites, roads and other infrastructure in rural Africa were and are very bad and the people poor and dispersed. Transport and distribution costs for inputs were high, demand and markets limited, profits uncertain and private businessmen uninterested. Moreover, it was assumed that African peasants being 'traditional' and non-market-oriented would be 'resistant-to-change', an assumption in tune with the 'diffusion-of-innovations' paradigm under-lying extension theory, but out of tune with reality. To overcome this assumed resistance required that innovations (inputs) be made available cheaply and on cheap credit. However, providing credit to small farmers is administrat-ively expensive – and especially since in most of Africa land is not in private property and so not usable as collateral.

There thus emerged a tripartite basis for agricultural modernization. First was research, performed on research stations (not on peasant farms), assess-ing (and often exaggerating) the amounts of fertilizers and other inputs which it is economic to apply, under conditions which few peasants farms can or do emulate for lack of resources (including timely labour). The next is an exten-sion service to translate the research results into recommendations to be spread among the peasants. For this to be effective, it was assumed that the third leg would be needed – an institution which could purchase the crop, sup-ply the inputs and do so on credit 'secured' by a 'crop-mortgage', otherwise known as deduction-at-source. A necessary – but not sufficient – condition for achieving repayment was that the institution should have monopoly control over crop sale, and this also allowed it to be internally self-financing, cross-subsidizing the price of inputs and credit from additions to the marketing margin – that is, deductions from the price received by producers. Thus peas-ant producers had two motives to avoid official markets; to avoid repaying their debts and to get better prices.

From the start there have been problems with this model and its rather rigid focus on increased external input use, its covering up bad advice with subsid-ies, and its failure to connect with advances in local farming methods. How-ever, most IFI observers accept this model uncritically, while heaping the blame on the parastatal corporations which were (as they fail to note) one of its necessary components. Apart from the inconsistency, this just does not fit the facts. Much of the crop development and intensification in Africa has derived from programmes run by parastatal monopolies, though some might well have occurred without them. Neither have they invariably been grossly corrupt and inefficient – nor for that matter has adjustment had much success in improving them. What it does seem to have done is to have removed the basis for policies which it still aims to pursue.

An overview of structural adjustment

Having reviewed the characteristics of the African agricultural sector, we can now turn to presentation and analysis of the claimed results of adjustment, by presenting first some data on adjustment. World economic leaders talking in public forums, express grave concern over the levels of indebtedness of African countries, and discuss how it can be reduced 'responsibly', that is, without letting countries off their payments. One might thus imagine that debt reduction would be a specific aim of adjustment, but that is not the case, except in general statements of intent. As can be see from Table 4.1, African indebtedness as a proportion of GDP has at any rate not fallen since the mid-1980s, and has probably increased considerably. This ambiguity of expression arises from an oddity of the figures presented in the World Debt Tables 1994–5, where the average indebtedness for sub-Saharan Africa did not change between 1986 and 1993, but where the individual country figures show a sharp increase. Table 4.1, section (a) (from Vol.II) contains a frequency distribution of countries in terms of debt as a proportion of GDP, showing a marked upward shift. Section (b) gives average figures, taken from Vol. I, and shows no change since 1986. Even allowing for the omission from average figures of countries whose level of debt and/or political chaos is so high that figures are no longer quoted, it is hard to see how the average could have remained virtually unchanged between 1986 and 1993, while there is such a clear increase in indebtedness for the 44 African countries as a whole.[10]

Few African countries pay the full value of debt-service – few could, given the level of their debts. Most have had their debts rescheduled on favourable terms, but this does not mean that the debt is written off. The favourable terms apply only so long as a country keeps to its adjustment agreement which ties it down still more tightly. If it fails in its implementation not only does it lose large aid inflows, but it also has to repay much larger annual sums in debt-service. How do these figures relate to the 'success' of adjustment? Of the 44 countries included in the World Debt Tables, 32 have been divided (World Bank, 1994a) into three classes regarding their 'agricultural policy' achievements, and achievements regarding three specific agricultural policy targets.[11] The first group of 15 countries, identified as group A, is said to be doing well on 'policy' and at least one (other?) indicator.[12] The next eight countries, forming group B, have 'done well on either policy alone or two indicators',[13] the third group C, with nine countries, is 'doing well on at most one indicator other than policy' (whether this wording means that they are or are not doing well on policy, remains unclear, but they are clearly the third group in

Table 4.1: External debt of forty-four African countries, as share of GDP

a. Percentage of countries having debt/GDP in the given range (percentage of GDP/Year)

	1980	1986	1990	1993
0–<100	26	11	12	11
100–<300	64	39	30	14
300–<500	10	27	30	35
500–<1000	0	14	12	24
>1000	0	6	16	16

b. Average for sub-Saharan Africa (percentage of GDP/Year)

	92	253	230	254

Source: World Bank (1995b); Distribution from Vol II (44 countries), Average from Vol I, p. 216.

terms of assessment).[14] The remaining 12 countries (not included in the 1994 study) can be divided into two separate groups. Group D comprises eight small countries and islands, omitted for reasons not immediately clear.[15] Finally, group E has four countries which have been through such turmoil, in the form of war or internal breakdown, that figures are not available. Interestingly enough, these include Angola, Liberia, Somalia and Zaïre, but not Rwanda (A), Burundi or Mozambique (B), Sierra Leone or Sudan (C). Table 4.2 shows the indebtedness by group.

Given the small sample sizes, not too much attention need be paid to precise figures, but it is interesting that Group A was less successful in reducing debt or preventing its increase than countries assessed as having done worse in policy terms. Most striking is the much better result for group D 'other small countries' which were not assessed for their success in adjustment.[16] There is no evidence at all here for the positive effect of adjustment, but also very little for the opposite conclusion. About all one can learn from these figures is the obvious: that the lower the level of debt beforehand, the easier it is to reduce it.

The same categories are used, in the study cited, for comparison with figures of agricultural growth. It is claimed that Group A did better in terms of agricultural growth both in 1981–87 and 1988–92, with significant improvement between the two periods (Table 4.3). As it stands, this table shows more improvement for group B than for A. However, the weakness of the figures can be shown by replacing the weighted mean (much affected by large countries like Nigeria and Ivory Coast) with the median growth rate (Table 4.4), which shows all growth rates falling between the first and second period, though less so for the 'better' adjusters.

The whole exercise falls still further apart if these figures are compared with those of FAO for the same period, for the 29 countries included in both series. *In about two-thirds of all cases the FAO estimate was over double or under half that of the World Bank.* For a more detailed comparison, one can take five countries which are included in both FAO and World Bank figures, and which were also included as case-studies in a study in which I was recently involved. Table 4.5 compares FAO and WB figures for agricultural

Table 4.2: Overall indebtedness for different groups of African countries (1986–93)

	1993 figures		Change from 1986 to 1993		
	Unweighted mean Debt as percentage of GDP	Median debt	Fell or the same	Increase up to double	Increase over double
A	495	402	25	56	13
B	679	533	50	25	25
C	979	614	44	22	33
D	425	337	88	12	0
E	922	445	0	25	75

Sources: World Bank (1995b), VOl. II; World Bank (1994a).

Table 4.3: Agricultural growth rates for three country groups

Group weighted mean (percentage per annum)

Country group	1981–87	1988–92	Change 81/87–88/92
A	+2.61	+3.20	+0.59
B	-1.74	+0.91	+2.65
C	+0.91	-1.89	-2.80

Source: World Bank (1994a).

Table 4.4: Agricultural growth rates for three country groups

Group median figures (percentage per annum)

Country group	1981–87	1988–92	Change 81/87–88/92
A	+2..5	+2.2	-0.3
B	+2.1	+0.1	-2.0
C	+2.2	-0.5	-2.7

Source: World Bank (1994a).

Table 4.5: Different estimates of agricultural growth

(percentage per annum)

Country/Year	FAO 1979–86	WB 1981–87	FAO 1987–93	WB 1988–92	Change FAO	Change WB
Burkina Faso	6.0	2.6	3.3	0.8	-2.7	-1.9
Ghana	4.0	0.8	4.0	1.6	0.0	+0.8
Tanzania	2.0	4.3	0.0	5.0	-2.0	+0.7
Uganda	2.0	0.2	4.7	3.3	+2.7	+3.1
Zimbabwe	3.5	1.9	0.5	-2.1	-3.0	-4.0

Source: FAO (1995); World Bank (1994a).

growth rates, over similar if not quite the same periods. About the only similarity between the two sets of figures is that in four out of five cases both show changes in the same direction between the earlier and later periods. Nevertheless, actual growth rates bear very little relationship to one another, most especially for Tanzania, where the World Bank has a quite high growth rate increasing in the later period, and the FAO has a small one declining to zero. The point is not that the FAO figures are more reliable than those from the World Bank, but that neither is sufficiently reliable as a basis for conclusions about growth and adjustment policy. Since many studies do try to draw such conclusions, the point is worth underlining. Few African countries have the statistical service or marketing set-up which would allow accurate estimation of total food crop production to within say ± 10–20 per cent. In many cases, official figures reproduce those of the previous years for want of better information. FAO does this still more often, when it does not trust the figures sent in by national governments – and it regularly presents figures rounded to the nearest half million tons. Weather is the major reason for variation in agricultural production over short periods, so further error arises if different years are confused.[17] To produce figures of agricultural growth, these very uncertain production volume figures have to be weighted by the prices prevailing at one (arbitrarily chosen) time during the period being considered, with considerable differences arising from choice of year (or price estimate). In terms of agricultural growth rates this could easily amount to as much as 2 per cent per annum, quite enough to 'demonstrate' success or failure.

The proxies used for policy achievement are not much more useful. That 'policy' in general should be represented *either* by producer-price increase *or* by reduced taxation suggests a limited notion of policy. The fertilizer target is over 3 per cent growth in use per hectare from 1986–91, but is not simply related to adjustment. It is highly likely that fertilizer imports and use did increase in many countries immediately after the signing of adjustment agreements and the associated release of commodity import-support (which not infrequently came in the form of fertilizer). However, the subsequent effect of swingeing devaluation and subsidy removal would have been to increase fertilizer prices and reduce demand – as seems to have happened in several countries. The 'extension' target seems almost entirely subjective – the evaluation by World Bank experts of local extension services. Some two-thirds of 27 countries listed are said to have 'satisfactory' extension services in the early 1990s. These include countries whose extension services are widely regarded, including by themselves, as 'grounded' for lack of transport and resources.[18] The evaluation also seems to hang partly on whether countries have made agreements to introduce the World Bank's own 'training & visit' (T&V) system. This is, unsurprisingly, rated highly by the Bank itself. Many others consider it rigid, non-participatory and expensive. The target for 'infrastructure' seems to be related to rural roads, although whether it measures the extent of rural roads, the rate at which they are being built or whether they are being maintained, is not mentioned. If it is building, this is as likely to reflect a country's success in getting donors to invest as its own priorities. But once again, the point is not so much that these are the wrong criteria and that some superior set would give the 'right' answers. It is rather that almost any set of measures will have large arbitrary elements.

Case studies of African adjustment

In reading the following mini-case-studies, the reader should be aware that they represent a further condensation from a series of studies which were themselves much compressed by being produced as a consultancy report under severe pressures of both space and time. As such, they do no more than present a brief glimpse through the curtains which the composite studies keep closed.

Burkina Faso

The West African country of Burkina Faso is often cited as a good adjuster and is included in the Group A (sometimes refered to as the 'A-Team') above.[19] However, it does not fit into the framework at all. Its first structural adjustment agreement was signed in March 1991 and its first related loan in June of that year could hardly have affected agricultural growth in 1988–92. Moreover, the period of rapid growth in the production of cotton (the main export crop) occurred before the negotiations for adjustment had even started. Several sources speak of declining cereal production during the period, but the figures available do not bear that out, indicating a growth rate in production of about 7.5 per cent per annum between 1983/4 and 1990/1, a sharp increase of about 35 per cent between 1990/1 and 1991/2 and low growth or stagnation (0.5 per cent per annum) since then. Throughout the periods for which figures are available, major crops in Burkina Faso were traded through the sorts of monopoly agency that adjustment has aimed to get rid of.

Cotton production has been organized through state monopoly corporations since first started in the 1920s. This first effort was such a disaster that it led not only to its own dissolution but that of the then Upper Volta. It was started again after 1945, with the French-owned CFDT in control of every aspect of input-supply, credit-supply, extension, price-setting, crop purchase, processing and transport. Production grew slowly from 1950, but much faster after 1961 – when prices were set high enough to attract producers – and production increased by some 20 per cent per annum during the decade. The 1970s saw intervention by a number of other donors, notably the World Bank with a number of projects to increase cotton production, and the replacement of the French CFDT by the local (state-owned) SOFITEX. Assessments at the end of the decade found that a broader-based programme would have been better, given the shortages of cereals, especially during the major drought of 1970–3. Growth in cotton production continued at about 10 per cent per annum until 1986, despite a change in regime and a severe fall in international cotton prices from 1983 onwards. The latter had little effect, since it was covered by SOFITEX's stabilization fund. However, from about the mid-1980s output growth started to slow down. Between 1951 and 1986, 75 per cent of inter-annual changes had been increases. From 1986 to 1994 production rose by only 1.5 per cent per annum and there were more inter-annual reductions than increases. The CFA Franc devaluation in 1994 improved prices, but also increased input prices. Finally, IFI policy in Burkina Faso seems less anti-parastatal than in Eastern Africa, perhaps because of French involvement and interest.

Ghana

Ghana is widely considered to be one of the most successful adjusters among African countries, having started quite early, in 1983 in the aftermath of a decade of chaos culminating in a serious drought (Hutchful, 1996). The government has taken a positive interest in adjustment throughout most of the period since then, and has made serious attempts to comply with its terms. But again, the agricultural figures do not show enormous gains. Ghana's main agricultural export by far is cocoa. Up to the late 1960s, Ghana was the world's leading producer, a position it lost largely because of excessive state exactions on the sector under both Nkrumah and subsequent civilian and military leaders. For some years after adjustment started, the Ghanaian government and the IFIs disagreed over the severity of the means by which the state agency handling cocoa (COCOBOD) should be made more effective, or its functions privatized. By 1995 this had led to a compromise, with various functions contracted out to private firms under licensing control from COCOBOD, whose non-cocoa buying activities had been severely reduced. Nevertheless, all of the growth in cocoa production and exports had already occurred before this, by 1989. Since 1990 there has been stagnation or slight decline. By far the most important reason for this has been the drastic fall in world prices, which in 1992 were less than one-third of their 1985 level. International cocoa users have been finding ways to substitute more cocoa butter with cheaper vegetable oils. Other producers in the world have been replacing their cocoa trees with new varieties having some three times the yield (so has Ghana, but more slowly). And two new producers, Malaysia and Indonesia, now account for about 20 per cent of world production between them. Dependency on cocoa exports turned out to be a high-risk strategy.

The food-crop side of Ghana's agricultural strategy was not much in evidence for the first several years after 1983, with IFI attention fixed on cocoa. From 1983 to 1984, food production did increase very rapidly, largely as a result of recovery from drought and the return of about a million Ghanaians expelled from Nigeria, most without jobs and so forced to expand food-crop production to live. This production increase, in turn, reduced prices and led to reductions in planting in following years. Since then, there seems to have been at best modest growth, although the figures are not very reliable as 40–50 per cent of the estimated total is cassava, much of it for self-provisioning and little, if any, sold through channels subject to statistical assessment. Indeed, 75–80 per cent of the total is composed of plantains and starchy roots, of which the same can be said. Maize, which accounts for over 50 per cent of all research on food crops, and which is the only crop for which a variety of fertilizer and other recommendations exist, caters for 7–10 per cent of domestic food demand. Since the food trade was never effectively state controlled, there has been little change here. As elsewhere, rising fertilizer prices after devaluation have cut into an already low level of use.

Tanzania

The Tanzanian economy was extensively state controlled prior to adjustment. After the Arusha Declaration of 1967, the government nationalized major industrial, financial and trading companies and expanded an already extensive state, parastatal, co-operative monopoly marketing system for crops and live-stock. With accelerating tempo from 1969 to 1975, the rural population was herded into villages and subjected to a barrage of rules and regulations intended to develop and modernize them, but serving rather to disrupt their lives and alienate them. This had already affected agricultural production neg-atively by 1974. Then the mid-1970s monetary boom, and the then World Bank President's enthusiasm for Nyerere's policies, unleashed a burst of donor project investment, which greatly compounded the problems. An investment-induced boom increased consumer demand, while declining export proceeds, and the import needs of the new investments, reduced the availability of foreign exchange. A severe case of Dutch disease* – except that rather than a windfall gain, Tanzania overheated its economy with 'wind-fall' loans (Wuyts, 1994; Raikes, 1986).

Tanzania's assertively socialist policies made it a prime target for IFI pres-sure to adjust. From 1980 to 1986, the country was kept on a very short leash by the IFIs, which approved no new loans and pressured other donors to can-cel or reduce their transfer. After an official adjustment agreement was signed in 1986, came a new burst of donor funds, much as commodity import-sup-port, including fertilizer and materials for marketing rehabilitation. As else-where, the major policy thrust up to 1990 was streamlining and cost-cutting for export-crop marketing parastatals, while reducing or phasing out the activities of domestically-oriented ones. But it took some time to dismantle the grain purchasing monopoly (NMC), and the subsidy programmes that operated through it, since these were part of maize development schemes started by the World Bank and later funded by IFAD. To compound the irony, these schemes were utterly dependent on a system of transport equalization by subsidy (known as 'pan-territorial pricing'), to which the Bank was opposed and which was ended in the early 1990s. This caused the collapse of maize production in south-western Tanzania which the Bank and other donors had spent the previous 15 years building up, and a geographical shift north-wards to the main maize-growing areas – and nothing to compensate those led up a blind alley for so long.

The export-crop targets were not met by the early 1990s. In some cases, the expected improvement in parastatal efficiency had not materialized – rather the reverse. To some extent this was the result of adjustment itself, vastly increasing the interest rates at which already huge debts were held. Moreover, the government 'complied' with IFI pressures by cancelling its subvention for consumer and fertilizer subsidies, without cancelling the subsidies, which thus further swelled the costs and massive debts of the NMC and Tanzania Fertilizer Corporation. The high agricultural growth rate claimed by the World Bank for Tanzania comes solely from crops and products for which there is little accurate measurement, many being 'estimated' either by adding

---

* 'Dutch disease': increased government spending based on the existence of foreign exchange earnings, often relates to existing natural (such as mineral) resources.

a fixed percentage to the previous years' figures or 'finger-in-the-wind' methods. Nor, for that matter, do World Bank figures agree too closely with those produced by the Tanzania Government. There does seem to have been an increase in growth during the 1980s, at least in part as a result of better weather, while price decontrol has, by definition, got rid of shortages, which are now expressed in price increases.

Tanzania's food problems have thus changed, though whether security has improved is another matter, since food security is more closely related to incomes than to physical food production. A study performed by a team from Cornell University claims no serious worsening of income distribution, although figures from a paper citing their results (and taking the same view) by a World Bank economist (Ferreira 1994) implies otherwise. The main finding presented was that the percentage of the population falling below an arbitrary poverty line had fallen from 65 per cent in 1983 (the worst of the pre-adjustment years) to 50 per cent by 1991. In more detail though, the incomes of the bottom 50 per cent had fallen by 20 per cent and those of the bottom 40 per cent had fallen by 30 per cent (thus those of the 'lower-middle' 10 per cent would have risen, pushing them up over the poverty line). That three to four million had moved up out of poverty, while some ten million of much poorer people had got 30 per cent poorer over the same period hardly seems an encouraging result.[20]

Uganda

Uganda started in the aftermath of a disastrous war, with nowhere to go but up. None the less, it does seem that adjustment provided a framework within which the government was (after some time) able to operate. Uganda's first attempt at adjustment was made under President Obote in the period 1981–4 but which, after initial success, failed because of civil war in which Obote was replaced by the National Revolutionary Movement headed by the current President Yoweri Museveni. After an abortive attempt to do without IFI funds, an adjustment agreement was signed in 1987. From then until 1992 the growth rate of GDP increased, but exports did not, nor did most other macro-economic indicators improve. The value of coffee exports in 1993 was only 27 per cent of the 1986 level, a result of falling international prices and failure to improve internal marketing. It is said to have improved since, with internal liberalization and a short-lived increase in coffee prices in 1994–5, the result, as always, of a Brazilian frost. To the limited extent that the marketing of food crops had ever been effectively government controlled, this had collapsed during the Amin and later Obote periods, so there was little to privatize, other than formally. As a result of its geographical position, Uganda has the most secure rainfall and harvest of almost any African country and it can easily feed itself, given peace. There seems little doubt that foreign aid since 1987 has helped to maintain this, though the main credit goes to the NRM regime. It also seems that Uganda has been able to impose a little more of its own agenda on the adjustment process than did Tanzania – albeit this has also involved the regime moving considerably towards IFI policies.

Zimbabwe

Zimbabwe is also part of the composite measurement cited above ('B-team'), despite the fact that it did not embark on adjustment until 1991, so that its results from 1986 to 1992 have nothing to do with adjustment. None the less, growth rates were high by African standards during that period (4 per cent per annum in real terms during the 1980s), the economy was diversified, social services improved dramatically, food security was ensured and debts were repaid without rescheduling; in short, a much better record than most countries which were adjusting (Stoneman, 1993 cited in Gibbon, 1996). Moreover, African maize deliveries to the Grain Marketing Board (GMB) rose from negligible levels before 1981 to almost 60 per cent by mid-decade, although white farmers retained their virtual monopoly of tobacco and other export-crops. IFI sources were far more critical, pointing out that growth fell in the first years after independence. They also found the fiscal deficit high, at about 9 per cent, though macro-economic stability was not a major issue for the IFIs in Zimbabwe – rather, increased growth.[21]

Zimbabwe's adjustment programme started as a local initiative and although taken over by the IFIs, some of the hardest conditions were imposed by the Zimbabwean state. Its main focus was to increase industrial production and exports by stimulating private investment, a programme which up to 1994 had been largely counterproductive, due to an odd choice and sequencing of measures at the behest of the World Bank (Gibbon, 1996). Unlike adjustment in most African countries, agricultural adjustment in Zimbabwe has hardly affected tobacco or other export crops, which are mainly produced by large-scale commercial farmers (LSCFs). Zimbabwean agriculture itself differs from that of most tropical Africa in that LSCFs, mostly white, still control about a third of all agricultural land and some two-thirds of the best land. They employ more labour than the combined industrial sector and still dominate most marketed agricultural production, except for maize and cotton. In the first few years after Independence the Zimbabwe government made some effort to transfer land to Africans under various resettlement schemes, but from about 1983, with high costs and land tied up in passage through a highly bureaucratic planning structure, the steam went out of this programme. Adjustment has concerned itself little with the large-scale sector or its crop marketing and has involved no efforts to increase the participation of peasants.[22]

The major agricultural focus has been on maize marketing and the reduction of parastatal marketing control in general. The GMB had a monopoly of maize sales long before Independence in 1981, prior to which it purchased almost solely from LSCFs. From 1981 it expanded its collection points into the (African peasant) 'communal areas' and, together with the extension service and Agricultural Finance Corporation was largely responsible for increasing African deliveries from a negligible amount to over half of an increased total by the mid-1980s.[23] In the course of this, both parastatals incurred substantial deficits, although there is no evidence of inefficiency or corruption on the scale of Tanzania or Kenya. This lead to reduced producer prices and stagnating production for the rest of the decade. It also led to strong criticism from the World Bank, and pressure to reduce the number of collection points in the communal areas. The World Bank also pressured the GMB to reduce stocks by exporting surpluses. This it did at a considerable loss, compounded by the need to import maize at still greater loss the next year, when Zimbabwe suffered the worst drought of the century. These losses accounted for much of a further massive increase in GMB deficits.

Another component of adjustment was the removal of GMB's monopoly, to encourage the entry of private traders or direct sale to grain millers. In 1994 large-scale commercial farmers, fearing the monopoly power of the millers, lobbied the government to be allowed to deliver solely to GMB. Peasant producers, hit by the closing of collection points, were forced to sell largely to small private traders, occasioning many complaints about poor prices and malpractices. In the following years poor weather and efforts by the GMB to reduce its deficits by cutting producer prices seem to have reduced sales. But with excellent rainfall in 1995/6, maize deliveries for 1996/7 seem likely to be the highest since the mid-1980s, and stocks sufficient to permit exports – this time probably without loss, because of low world stocks and high prices. But while weather is clearly the major factor affecting output, there is little evidence that applying the standard 'state bad, private good' dogma to the quite technically-efficient GMB has benefited either Zimbabwe as a whole or its peasant producers. There is far more to the story of adjustment in Zimbabwe, but little of it is even closely related to the 'composite measures' cited above.

Conclusion

This indeed is the general, if limited, conclusion to this chapter. The sorts of general composite assessment of adjustment performed by and for the World Bank and IMF seem very clearly to have 'bent the stick' in a direction favourable to themselves, possibly provoking an opposite reaction in critics like myself. But far more important than this is that such measures do not even begin to take account of what happens in the different countries – as we have seen, results for Burkina Faso and Zimbabwe are presented although they did not even start on adjustment until the very end of the period measured. So, apart from giving an unrealistically rosy picture of the impact of adjustment, they reinforce simple-minded visions like 'state bad, private good' and make that much more difficult the development of policies relevant to the enormous complexity of even the smallest and poorest country.

Notes

1. Arguments for liberalization depend in large part on eliding the distinction between 'the (ideal) market' and ordinary markets. Private markets in tropical Africa are often as controlled by monopoly and politics as those of the state.
2. But international financial institution (IFI) success with increasing production, elsewhere in the world, of crops exported by Africa, may have contributed to price reduction for products facing inelastic demand schedules.
3. In the mid-1990s, World Bank spokespeople often deny that the Bank ever enjoined African countries to cut expenditures on social services. Whether or not this is strictly true, it certainly is not true in the broader sense that conditionality invariably required cuts in government budgets of sufficient scale to make it unavoidable.
4. The terminology of adjustment is full of words like 'performance', with its implications of assigning grades or marks. But while it is both absurd and obnoxious to see countries as performing animals being forced through hoops by judicious combinations of whip and carrot, this *is*, to no small extent, the way the donors/trainers see it.
5. The Berg Report made much of this supposed ignoring of agriculture in the 1970s. The World Bank's *Tanzania-Agricultural Sector Memorandum of 1994*, shows that in Tanzania (one of the countries criticized), state expenditure on agriculture was higher in real terms during 1975–9 than ever before or since.
6. In Tanzania adjustment released large amounts of 'commodity import support' to re-equip run-down parastatal corporations. Given to Tanzania as grants, these were lent to the recipient corporations at nominal interest rates which rose, under adjustment, from around 5 per cent to around 25 per cent, assuring the rapid growth of parastatal debts. The Tanzania government also cancelled subventions to parastatals to cover costs of policies like fertilizer subsidy or pan-territorial pricing without cancelling the policies, so shifting the financial burden to the parastatal. Many of these institutions were indeed inefficient and corrupt, but the growth of their deficits – trumpeted by the IFIs as evidence of more 'state distortion', was at least partly a result of adjustment itself.
7. 'International Financial Institutions', the World Bank and IMF.
8. Working on a consultancy team in 1976, we were sent in to see the World Bank agricultural task manager, who told us at length about IADP and how our proposed project should be fitted into it. Two years later World Bank personnel seemed unable to remember much about IADP, except that it had been a Kenyan idea, against which they had warned.
9. This is not a trivial point. It is the sort of entrepreneur on whom adjustment focuses, and much extension advice is directed at (male) full-time farmers with sufficient funds or access to finance to intensify farming. But anyone (mostly men) with such control of resources will almost certainly be involved in other activities paying more than agriculture and demanding more of his time and attention.
10. The Column for 1993 in Table 4.1 excludes Somalia (2599 per cent when lasted quoted in 1990), and Sudan (3265 per cent in 1992), as well as Liberia (386 per cent in 1986, but with a civil war since).
11. In this chapter World Bank (1994a) is used, instead of the widely published World Bank (1994f). There are small changes in the compared periods and total number

of countries, but the methodology is nearly the same. Four criteria are used: 'agricultural policy' – seen to have improved if agricultural taxation fell or crop producer prices rose during the 1980s; 'fertilizer' – whether fertilizer use grew at 3 per cent per annum or more over the same period; 'extension' – World Bank assessment of the country's extension service; and 'infrastructure' which refers to construction or maintenance of rural roads.

12. Benin, Botswana, Burkina Faso, Ghana, Guinea, Kenya, Malawi, Mali, Mauritius, Niger, Nigeria, Rwanda, Tanzania, Togo, Uganda.

13. Burundi, CAR, Congo, Côte d'Ivoire, Gabon, Madagascar, Mozambique, Zimbabwe.

14. Cameroon, Chad, Ethiopia, Guinea-Bissau, Mauritania, Senegal, Sierra Leone, Sudan, Zambia.

15. Cape Verde, Comores, Djibouti, Equatorial Guinea, Lesotho, Sao Tomé & Principé, Swaziland, the Gambia.

16. Mean debt of this group would fall to 184 per cent, the median to 138 per cent, with 100 per cent maintaining or reducing, if Sao Tomé & Principé should be considered a 'trouble-spot' rather than a 'forgotten small country'.

17. My own efforts to find one 'best estimate' set of figures for Tanzania unearthed at least fifteen different partial sets of figures for GDP, and made quite clear that among the reasons for difference were factors so simple as that some had transcribed (say) 1990/1 as 1990 and others as 1991.

18. Noted for Uganda and Ghana by Brett (1996) and Hutchful (1996), while noted by the present author in Tanzania.

19. Information largely from Speirs (1996) and Buhl (1996).

20. See further: Raikes and Gibbon (1996), Raikes (1986), and Wuyts (1994).

21. In comparison: 7.4 per cent for Tanzania post adjustment or over 10 per cent before, about 10 per cent without grants for Burkina 1986–93, much lower (about 2 per cent) for Ghana and with figures so sparse for Uganda that it is impossible to tell.

22. Transfer of land was limited by the terms of the agreement ending civil war and granting Independence, which specified that land should be transferred only on market (willing-buyer, willing-seller) terms. But its subsequent pace was further slowed by a World Bank report of the early 1980s, which warned of dire consequences if 'too much' land was transferred, on the basis of misleading evidence about relative yields (Weiner *et al.*, 1985).

23. Another factor was that LSCFs found it more profitable to switch to tobacco and other higher-valued crops.

5 A decade of structural adjustment in Uganda: agricultural tradables, rural poverty and macroeconomic 'success'

DERYKE BELSHAW, PETER LAWRENCE AND
MICHAEL HUBBARD

Introduction

JANUARY 1996 MARKED the tenth anniversary of the Museveni government's accession to power in Uganda after 14 years of intermittent civil war. This chapter examines the country's economic performance over that period, giving attention both to the macro-economic and the sectoral components of the reconstruction programme implemented with the aid of World Bank/IMF structural adjustment packages. The sectoral discussion focuses particularly on the agricultural sector and on the performance of traditional agricultural exports.

Uganda has been hailed as a success story for structural adjustment policies (Sharer, 1994; IMF, 1995; 1996; World Bank, 1994f) and has attracted an increasing quantity of external funds as confidence in its political and economic governance has returned. A major concern of the chapter is the critical role of these aid flows in maintaining Uganda's external balance over this period.[1] Aid has helped to bridge Uganda's increasing trade deficit in the period of adjustment, but has also contributed to real exchange rate appreciation in the latter part of this period, which itself cannot have helped the deteriorating trade balance. As long as adequate quantities of aid, including debt remission, continue to flow into Uganda, this is not a major problem. However, since the adequacy of aid flows cannot be guaranteed, a key question to be raised is the extent to which recent aid flows have been, and are, contributing to increasing Uganda's ability to repay loans. The central argument of this chapter is that, to date, continued aid dependency and widespread poverty suggest the potential stalling of the structural adjustment programme rather than the relatively unqualified success claimed by its supporters. The emphasis on an aid-funded rehabilitation programme based on diversification away from 'traditional' export crops has had little success. By 1994 'non-traditional export crops' accounted for only 12 per cent of export earnings as against 80 per cent from the four 'traditional export crops' – coffee, tea, tobacco and cotton. Effective recovery measures for cotton, in particular, and tea have been seriously neglected for most of the past decade. This neglect has turned Uganda into a virtual monocrop-exporting economy, its capacity to import being highly dependent on the vagaries of international coffee prices and quotas (75 per cent of the 1994/5 export revenue came from coffee).

The next section of this chapter briefly reviews the theoretical framework underlying adjustment programmes and the assessment of their performance to date in sub-Saharan Africa. The third section reviews Uganda's macroeconomic performance over the last decade, looking especially at the degree to which economic reforms have contained positive incentives to increase the output of tradables, including major import substitutes such as sugar. The fourth section discusses the extent to which the reconstruction programme in Uganda has paid sufficient attention to directing aid to projects which assist tradable goods production, especially exportables. The fifth section discusses alternative policies to rehabilitate tradable production and reduce rural poverty. The conclusion draws general lessons for the design of SAPs, as indicated by the Uganda experience.

Structural adjustment: theory and practice

As noted by Mosley *et al.* (1995), there is considerable confusion about what constitutes 'structural adjustment'. The formal separation between the IMF role of supporting internal and external stabilization through demand management, and the World Bank role of funding supply-side reforms and restructuring, has not been as clear cut in practice. The term 'structural adjustment' has become used as a catch-all for demand-side and supply-side policies. World Bank/IMF packages have become best known for policies which 'get prices right'; these have clear demand-side and supply-side effects in theory and practice. Thus, the liberalization of the foreign exchange market is intended to establish an 'equilibrium' exchange rate which achieves external balance. Control over government expenditure, and money supply in general, removal of producer and consumer price controls, increased fiscal effort and the liberalization of interest rates, are all designed to achieve internal balance and, via the real exchange rate, external balance. However, these 'stabilization' policies are also intended to have supply-side effects in encouraging more efficient allocation of resources in response to the liberalized price signals in domestic and external product markets and in the capital market. Institutional reforms, such as reducing the size of the government service, privatizing state enterprises and abolishing statutory marketing bodies, encouraging competition, especially in the financial sector, are more unambiguously concerned with creating the supply-side framework for a more market-oriented economic system.

Assessments of the effects of structural adjustment on the performance of the economies involved have tended to suffer from a lack of clarity as to the objectives of economic reform packages, and from having to consider a relatively short time period. Thus, the World Bank in its own assessments of the effects of structural adjustment has focused on growth rates of GDP as the dependent variable (World Bank, 1989, 1994f), although it is not clear that growth enhancement has been a short-term objective (Mosley *et al.*, 1995). The message of these assessments has been that the more strongly the adjustment package is implemented, the higher the growth rate of GDP per capita. The World Bank assessments have been widely criticized, especially for their methodologies, and other more rigorous analyses have reached either opposite or neutral conclusions (Mosley, 1996; Sepehri, 1994; Mosley *et al.*, 1995). There are several good theoretical reasons why the implementation of adjustment programmes should lead to initial declines in GDP per capita growth and these have been shown to be the case empirically. Increased real interest rates may initially result in investment decline, while reduced government expenditure, increased domestic cost of imports and the removal of domestic price subsidies will all reduce domestic demand. Price incentives through domestic liberalization and depreciating exchange rates are likely to take time to have an effect on total agricultural tradables output, although some short-term switching of tradables from parallel markets may improve the official statistics and taxable income flows. So while the World Bank may be right to look for GDP per capita growth as the dependent variable, the signs on the explanatory variables may be different from those the Bank expected to find.

However, one area of the debate on which there is substantial agreement concerns the negative effect on economic performance of overvalued exchange rates. A recent econometric study for a group of African economies has confirmed the negative effect of real exchange rate misalignment on growth and foreign trade (Ghura and Grennes, 1993). However, once exchange rates have been devalued as a result of structural adjustment packages, less attention has been paid to the effects of elements of the packages, especially increased inflows of aid, on the exchange rate over time. Aid is not only part of the standard adjustment programme, for which economic reform is a *quid pro quo*, but formal adoption of the programme gives countries the seal of approval to apply for aid from other multilateral and bilateral donors. A Computable General Equilibrium (CGE) simulation by Collier and Gunning (1992) suggests that a typical adjustment package involving both aid and exchange rate liberalization will require aid only at the beginning to obviate the likely downward effects on domestically-financed investment (such as there may be) of increased prices of imported capital goods. However, there is much evidence that adjustment periods in sub-Saharan Africa are often longer than expected, and that once a package has been adopted, the first tranche of aid generates further aid (Mosley *et al.* 1995). Based on the 'Dutch disease' framework,* there is a substantial literature pointing to the possible paradoxical effects of aid. Aid in the form of foreign exchange increases the demand for importables and non-tradables (White, 1992; White and Wignaraja, 1992; Lewis and Younger, 1994). Tradable output is reduced either because of increased labour costs, or a shift of domestic terms of trade against tradable producers, or both. The real exchange rate, expressed as the relative price of tradables to non-tradables, therefore appreciates. Thus export promotion, which Collier and Gunning describe as the 'fundamental rationale

* See footnote on page 71

for liberalisation', may well not be the result. Targeted and well-designed interventions are required at the sectoral level to offset this effect.

Uganda's macroeconomic performance

Uganda is widely regarded as one of the success stories of structural adjustment. IMF staff have described this process in the following glowing terms:

> Uganda's achievements during the past six years have been impressive, especially given the substantial deterioration in its terms of trade. Now, with Uganda's terms of trade outlook improving, inflation under control, market-oriented economic policies firmly in place, and the authorities' strong commitment to continued structural adjustment, Uganda has laid a sound basis for many years of solid growth (Sharer *et al.*, 1994).

More recent assessments by IMF staff have re-affirmed this view, and approval was given at the end of 1995 for a second annual Enhanced Structural Adjustment (ESAF) loan:

> With broadly-based real economic growth of 10 per cent and an inflation rate of 3.4 per cent, Uganda had a strong economic performance in 1994/5 and observed all the quantitative and structural benchmarks under the economic programme supported by the first annual ESAF loan (IMF, 1996).

There is considerable justification for the IMF's upbeat view. However, there is also the usual question about whether to choose evaluative criteria relating to observed differences over time or those comparing the actual with an appropriate counterfactual. The IMF has chosen the former. As Collier (1994) has pointed out, however, 'a normal slow-growing African economy would have expanded by around 3.5 per cent p.a.' during the 1970s and 1980s: 'Had the Ugandan economy grown at this rate it would have been double its actual 1986 size'. By 1996, GDP would have been 40 per cent higher than that, implying a recovery growth rate of nearly double that actually achieved over the last 10 years. The degree and speed of approach to a position extrapolated from some *status quo ante* the catastrophe is obviously appropriate to the evaluation of any recovery strategy. The IMF and other donors, however, seem content to compare the rate of recovery from the 1986 nadir with the much lower growth rates which are acceptable in non-recovery situations. As we point out in a later section of this chapter, initial emphasis on the rehabilitation of what previously existed, rather than on new projects, seems likely to have yielded the higher rates of return required to return consumption levels and the poverty gap to either the *status quo ante* or to a reasonable counterfactual extrapolation from it.

Table 5.1 shows the recovery from the negative growth rates in real GDP of the mid-1980s. These rates have averaged 5.7 per cent per annum over the period since 1987. Real agricultural GDP grew at an average 3.8 per cent per annum, while real manufacturing GDP averaged an annual 11 per cent rate of

Table 5.1: Uganda: selected macroeconomic indicators (1979/80–1995/6)

Year (%p.a.)	GDP growth	Budget deficit A	B (% of GDP)	Money growth (%p.a.)	Imports ($US Mln)	Exports ($US Mln)	Trade balance ($US Mln)	Current account ($US Mln)
1979/80	12.3	2.6	2.6	n.a.	318	319	1	−83
1980/81	7.5	3.5	3.6	47.4	278	229	−49	32
1981/82	11.7	3.6	4.3	54.9	338	347	9	−16
1982/83	9.6	2.4	2.5	38.8	428	368	−60	−72
1983/84	−8.5	2.9	3.4	60.8	342	408	66	107
1984/85	−1.9	4.0	4.3	139.3	264	379	115	77
1985/86	−1.5	3.4	4.4	138.6	438	407	−31	52
1986/87	5.7	4.7	5.4	102.6	598	334	−264	−112
1987/88	6.1	1.5	3.3	205.2	658	266	−392	−195
1988/89	6.4	1.7	3.1	123.8	740	278	−462	−260
1989/90	4.0	4.5	6.5	57.5	617	178	−439	−263
1990/91	4.3	4.7	7.4	46.7	545	175	−370	−187
1991/92	4.5	7.4	14.4	70.7	451	172	−362	−132
1992/93	6.3	4.8	11.7	42.7	522	169	−443	−142
1993/94	10.1	5.3	11.3	32.8	672	254	−418	−89
1994/95	8.7	2.8	7.0	27.4	1085	577	−508	−164
1995/96	8.5	2.1	6.7	16.7	1180	555	−625	−114

Note: A Including grants; B Excluding grants.
Source: Republic of Uganda, *Background to the Budget* (various issues).

growth (Republic of Uganda, 1995). These relatively good performances by usual, non-recovery, standards compare with growth rates for agriculture and manufacturing of 4 per cent and 8 per cent respectively for the 1960s and early 1970s. Getting inflation down to single digits has been another vaunted achievement of the liberalization policy. The data show that inflation rates fell from annual averages of over 100 per cent to 8.4 per cent by the end of 1995. Two factors are associated with bringing inflation under control. First, the budget deficit, which appeared to be getting out of control in 1991/2, has been sharply reduced, both by tight expenditure controls and improved tax collection, assisted by substantial external grant aid. Second, there has been more strict control over money supply growth. Further, negative real interest rates have now become highly positive as nominal rates fell slowly, at the same time as inflation has dropped sharply.

On the external front, the current account deficit was almost eliminated in 1994/5 and there have been considerable increases in the level of foreign exchange reserves. Table 5.1 also shows the balance of trade and payments through the 1980s: strong negative balances on trade and payments, the smaller negative payments balance accounted for by official and private transfers (official and non-governmental grants and remittances). Although it looked as though performance in 1991 was showing the effects of earlier real exchange rate depreciation, with exports rising slightly and imports falling sharply, these trends have been reversed from 1993. Central to the reforms has been the deregulation of the foreign exchange system. In 1991, a free market in foreign exchange was introduced alongside an official one, with a policy of continually depreciating official rates towards free market rates. Since November 1993 a unified rate has been determined through an inter-bank market. Far from this process resulting in an even greater depreciation of the Ugandan shilling, there has been some stabilization and even appreciation of nominal exchange rates and evidence of real exchange rate appreciation, recognized both by the IMF (1996) and by the Ugandan government (Republic of Uganda, 1995). The stabilization of the exchange rate, combined with positive real interest rates, has led to agents holding assets in shillings rather than dollars, thus reinforcing tendencies for the nominal exchange rate to appreciate.

An appreciation of the real exchange rate is quite consistent, of course, with an improvement in the current account balance of payments. In Uganda, one contributory factor to real exchange rate appreciation has been the 1994–5 coffee price boom. However, the main cause, which pre-dates and post-dates the coffee boom, would seem to be that the considerable increase in the inflows of hard currency in the form of official and private transfers (itself a product of Uganda's World Bank/IMF-induced reform policy) has outstripped the demand for dollar-mediated imports. Data on aid (including private remittances) and the real exchange rate for the last decade show first a high positive correlation between these two variables as the massive depreciation of early 1987 is preceded and followed by sharp increases in aid. After that, there appears to be a negative relationship between these two variables, especially between 1989 and 1991, when inflows fell and the real exchange rate depreciated, and 1993–6, when these inflows, especially private remittances, increased sharply and the real exchange rate appreciated equally sharply (IMF, 1996; Republic of Uganda, 1996). If a lack of effective demand for hard currency-mediated consumption goods plays a significant part in the explanation of exchange rate appreciation, then questions about the heavy skewedness of income distribution and the persistence of rural poverty in northern and eastern Uganda are critical factors to be taken into account.

Although Uganda's current account balance of payments has improved substantially over the period, this has not been the case for Uganda's *trade* balance (see Table 5.1), something which might have been expected to occur as a consequence of the original massive currency depreciations after 1987, and which is still awaited. For despite the increase in export income from both coffee and non-coffee exports, there has been a much bigger increase in imports consequent upon freely available foreign exchange and import liberalization. Increasing aid flows have lead to increasing indebtedness and debt service burdens. In 1985, Uganda's debt stock stood at US$ 920 million, while in 1995 it stood at US$ 3384 million, or US$ 1860 in present value terms. Uganda's ratio of debt service payments to exports in 1994/5 was approximately 26 per cent. Although this compares well with the previous year's figure of 66 per cent, almost all the improvement is the result of the coffee boom (Republic of Uganda, 1992 and 1996; World Bank, 1996).

How far the real exchange rate appreciation has led to the persistence of a large trade deficit is a pertinent question. Certainly it could be argued that imports are higher than they would have been, but it is difficult to argue that such appreciation, in isolation, has made much difference to export perform- ance. From the Amin period in the 1970s onwards, Uganda has become an export monoculture based on coffee. This accounted for 75 per cent of total export revenue in 1994/5 (Republic of Uganda, 1995: A16). The collapse of world coffee prices after 1989 severely affected Uganda's export revenue. However, because of increases in producer shares of the export parity price, following the liberalization of Uganda's coffee marketing arrangements from 1990 onwards, the fall in world price and the real exchange rate appreciation were offset to a significant extent by reduced marketing costs. Consistent with this, there was no evidence of reduced coffee procurement, but neither was there any significant new coffee planting or replacement of old trees. The ever-present possibility that the world price of coffee would once again increase sharply as the result of another Brazilian frost, became reality from mid-1994. Uganda's export revenue has gained by at least as much as it would have if investment in new planting had occurred during the price trough of 1989–94, when replacement costs (mainly the loss of three to four years of coffee produced by over-aged trees) were at their lowest.

Table 5.2 traces the performance of traditional export crops from 1980 to 1995. Tea and tobacco recover slowly after 1989, but from a low base.

Table 5.2: Exports of principal agricultural crops (1980–95)

(× 1,000 Tns) Year	Coffee	Tea	Cotton	Tobacco
1980	110	1.0	2.0	0.0
1981	128	1.0	1.0	0.0
1982	175	1.2	1.8	0.0
1983	144	1.3	7.0	0.7
1984	133	2.5	6.7	0.7
1985	151	1.2	9.5	0.3
1986	141	2.8	4.9	0.0
1987	148	2.1	3.4	0.0
1988	144	3.1	2.1	0.0
1989	176	3.2	2.3	0.5
1990	141	4.8	3.8	2.3
1991	125	7.0	7.8	2.5
1992	119	8.0	7.5	2.3
1993	114	10.0	2.5	4.1
1994	194	11.0	3.8	4.1
1995	169	11.0	5.6	3.5

Source: Republic of Uganda, *Background to the Budget* (various issues).

Cotton's attempts to get off the floor suffered two sharp setbacks because of adverse farmer experience at the hands of unreformed institutions. As for coffee, it is arguable whether the exchange rate appreciation has slowed export crop recovery in general, but it is certainly the case for coffee that low producer prices consistent with low shares of the export parity price have had a more significant effect. Table 5.3 shows that the producer price share of the export price at official parity rarely exceeded 30 per cent until 1994 and was, of course, lower at parallel (open market) exchange rate parity. The export price at official parity failed to hold its improvement after exchange rate depreciation from 1987, because of low world prices prevalent between 1989 and 1994.

Although producer prices started to rise after 1987, the major increases took place after 1990, and particularly with the boom in world prices in 1994. Clearly the ability, before the coffee boom, to raise domestic prices despite stagnating world prices does suggest that it would have been worth placing more emphasis on rehabilitating coffee production to build up coffee exports. However, coffee procurement and export volumes remained steady through this period with producers appearing not to respond to the increased export parity prices until the 1994/5 boom, when procurement rose by over one-third.

Table 5.4 presents volume and value data for the five major crops at the late 1960s/early 1970s peak baseline (i.e. the four traditional exports and sugar as the single most important import-substituting tradable commodity). These five

Table 5.3: Producer share of export parity price (1980–95)

Year	Producer Price (Ushs/tonne)	Producer share of PXR (%)	Export Parity Price OXR (%)
1980	0.2	8.5	64.5
1981	0.5	12.6	52.6
1982	0.8	15.0	44.4
1983	1.3	17.1	36.1
1984	2.7	23.3	27.8
1985	4.7	20.3	30.5
1986	8.5	6.6	21.7
1987	24.0	9.7	26.6
1988	60.0	7.1	31.4
1989	60.0	6.7	17.9
1990	120.0	17.5	28.0
1991	210.0	21.6	29.8
1992	240.0	24.2	26.1
1993	330.0	28.4	28.8
1994	750.0	44.2	
1995	900.0	39.0	

Note: PXR = parallel exchange rate; OXR = official exchange rate.
Source: Republic of Uganda, *Background to the Budget* (various issues).

Table 5.4: Output of principal cash crops (1986–94)

	Year of peak production	Peak volume (x 1000 Tns)	Peak vol. Exports (x 1000 Tns)	1986 output (x 1000 Tns)	1986 value of exports (US$ m)	1995 output (x 1000 Tns)	1995 Value exports (US$ m)
Tobacco (Cured)	1967	52	3	1	0	6	7
Coffee (Green – all types)	1972	200	224	160	394	181	384
Tea (Made)	1973	21	23	3	3	13	9
Sugar (Milled)	1968	152	47	15	0	59[2]	0
Cotton (Lint)	1970	91	78	5	5	6[1]	10

Notes:　[1] Export Voume; [2] 1994.
Sources:　Government of Uganda, *Background to the Budget*; FAO, *Production Yearbooks; Trade Yearbooks* (various issues).

crops dominated both the agricultural sector and, for reasons already stated, the national economy as a whole. The basic data are compiled on different assumptions, but the resulting variations are relatively small and do not invalidate the pattern observed over the long time periods involved. By 1994, tobacco had exceeded the absolute pre-catastrophe peak production and coffee, in a peak price year, was approaching it (with a little help, no doubt, from coffee smuggled into a competitively efficient Ugandan market from Rwanda and Tanzania's Kagera Region, as well as the reported harvesting of semi-ripe berries (Republic of Uganda, 1995:9)). Tea and sugar in 1994 were still under 60 per cent of the peak volumes, and cotton had even slipped below the level of the 1986 trough.

Table 5.5 applies three criteria to this record: the 1995 volume and value figures compared with the same for 1986; the relative position of 1986 and 1995 performance compared with the historical peak export volume for each crop; and third a modified 'counterfactual gap': the relationship of the 1995 value data with the value of a quantity based on peak volume plus average year-on-year growth of Collier's counterfactual growth rate of 3.5 per cent. The verdicts are increasingly less favourable as one moves from left to right across Table 5.5.

Disincentives to tradables?

In contrast to the stagnation in export crop production, the last decade has seen the output of food crops grow on average by 7.5 per cent per year. Table 5.6 shows how each category of food production has performed. These large increases in food output can be explained by expanding urban markets, with corresponding upward pressure on food prices, allied to poor prices for traditional crops. These growth rates compare well with 'counterfactual'

Table 5.5: Output of principal cash crops (1986–94); alternative evaluation

	1995 Output/ 1996 Output	1995 Value of exp./ 1986 Value of exp.	1986 Volume/ peak volume	1995 Volume/ peak volume	1995 Value of exports/ 'counterfactual estimate'[1]
Tobacco (Cured)	650	inf.	1	141	57
Coffee (Green – All Types)	113	97	80	81	32
Tea (Made)	380	289	13	56	24
Sugar (Milled)	393	0	10	39	0
Cotton (Lint)	n.a.	100	5	4	3

Note: [1] The hypothetical figure assuming export volume growth from peak volume at 3.5 per cent p.a. to 1994, times the mean 1995 export value (Uganda is a price-taker in all export markets under consideration).

Sources: See Table 5.4.

growth rates of food output of 3–4 per cent prior to the early 1970s. Although possible negative interactions between aid inflows, real exchange rate appreciation and the failure to improve Uganda's trade balance have been identified, the question remains why the various structural adjustment packages have had so tardy an effect on the recovery of the main tradables – the agricultural cash crops. Even with the loss of competitiveness implied by exchange rate appreciation, there is some evidence that competitiveness as measured by domestic resource cost (DRC) actually improved over a key part of the period under examination. In late 1992, at an exchange rate of Ushs/$US of 1211, (the nominal exchange rate had appreciated to Ushs 968 per US dollar in 1995) the DRC ratio in financial prices for robusta coffee was 1.01 and 1.25 for cotton, indicating that actual costs of production and marketing to the border exceeded their value at the border. The equivalent figures for late 1989 were 1.61 and 0.89 respectively, suggesting that over the three years 1989–92 coffee market reforms increased its competitiveness despite a low world price, while cotton became less competitive (data courtesy of the Bank of Uganda). Long-term comparative advantage cannot be deduced from these ratios, since the cost figures reflect the well-recognized inefficiencies in processing and marketing which should and can be reduced by internal competition.

The key to the explanation of the tardy response of the tradable producing enterprises in the agricultural sector lies in the relatively slow process of institutional change. The previous section noted how long it took for producer price shares to be raised in relation to border parity prices. The former monopoly of the parastatal Coffee Marketing Board was abolished only in 1990; by 1992 vigorous competition between co-operatives and private buyers had reduced the marketing margin considerably. This partially offset at the farm gate the decline of world prices to the historical lows, in real terms, of the 1930s depression years. However, the length of time taken to change institutional arrangements for coffee reflected donor, political and intellectual attitudes which were strongly 'anti-coffee' in the 1990–4 period, stressing crop diversification instead. Low world prices and a high level of dependence on coffee for export revenue suggested a policy of crop diversification would be more appropriate. Nevertheless, widespread frost in Brazil in mid-1994 showed that prices could move up as well as down and led to a minor coffee boom, with prices staying above or around long-run average levels in 1995/6. The failure to recover lost coffee potential during the years of low prices meant that the opportunity to replace ageing trees with new hybrid varieties at least investment cost (lowest levels of coffee income forgone over the three-year gestation period) was almost completely missed.

An even longer delay in implementing institutional reforms in the cotton sector is largely responsible for the poor performance of this crop since 1986. Cotton generated around 40 per cent of Uganda's export revenue in the 1960s. As world production is less volatile than with frost-sensitive coffee, it provided a partial counterbalance to the effects of coffee price fluctuations on the

Table 5.6: Selected food crop production indices (1985–95)

(1987 = 100)					
Year	Cereals	Roots	Pulses	Oilseeds	Bananas
1985	96	91	90	82	97
1986	87	98	93	100	98
1987	100	100	100	100	100
1988	115	104	115	113	104
1989	134	110	130	126	106
1990	130	108	133	158	111
1991	129	106	130	162	115
1992	143	102	136	167	111
1993	154	109	144	181	117
1994	159	92	132	176	121
1995	166	97	136	179	128

Source: Republic of Uganda (1996).

international market. The crop is entirely produced by smallholders who were organized under marketing co-operative societies and unions which in turn came under the Lint Marketing Board (LMB), a statutory monopsony. By the mid-1980s the co-operative movement and the four domestic textile plants had become heavily indebted, and farmers were continual victims of both underpayment and delayed payment for their output. Mainly for this reason, the 1986 Canadian Mission[2] (IDRC, 1987) had recommended the abolition of the twin layer monopoly provided by the co-operatives and the LMB and its replacement by a vertically-integrated system. This would allow farmers to contract with either domestic textile companies or international export firms that would provide seed, extension advice and other inputs as well as owning or financing ginnery services. In the event, the Lint Marketing Board was not abolished until 1994 and an independent cotton promoting agency – the Cotton Development Organisation – began operations only in late 1995. The largest textile plant was not privatized and resuscitated until 1996. The reasons why the rearguard action brought by the cotton co-operatives and marketing board was more successful than their counterparts dealing with coffee, are not clear (a recent paper on export marketing [Katorobo, 1995], despite its general title, examines the coffee institutions only). A possible answer lies with the support and advice given by a few key donors to the Uganda Cooperative Alliance. The virtual total failure of the cotton recovery programme to date has had a particularly severe impact on regional income distribution. Large parts of the east and north of Uganda are registering poverty levels last experienced in the 1920s[3]. The diversification into maize and legume production has been unable to compensate for the loss of the cash-earning opportunity which cotton provided.

In the case of tea, delayed institutional reforms and low international prices coupled with the Uganda shilling revaluation on the domestic currency market in 1992–5 explain the unexpectedly sluggish recovery of a perennial crop (abandoned tea bushes growing to 8–10 metres in height can be brought back into production in six months or so). With sugar, levels of investment and the rate of recovery of output have been far below expectations. Most of this crop is produced on large private estates owned and managed by two 'Southern' transnational corporations. The alternatives of giving a greater role to smallholder producers through outgrower or resettlement schemes, as recommended in the Canadian Mission report, have been ignored by government and donors alike. Tobacco, on the other hand, is a relative success story, produced by smallholders operating under contract in a vertically-integrated production-processing-retail monopoly for the domestic market. This was established and is operated by a 'Northern' transnational corporation. Historical processing capacity had become a constraint by 1992 but was being expanded in the mid-1990s.

The poor recovery performance of the main cash export crops has ironically assisted the tendency towards appreciation of the real exchange rate. Hard currency aid and remittance inflows have exceeded the rate of generation of enhanced employment and incomes which would increase the demand for hard currency-mediated consumer goods imports, that is, there is a poverty-constrained demand for hard currency. Although there are problems associated with the measurement of poverty, it is clear that the heavily skewed income distribution is a factor in distorting economic incentives. Efforts to reduce levels of poverty are hampered by debt-driven resource constraints. Uganda's debt service over the next decade will average between US$ 210 million and US$ 240 million per year (close to half the value of total exports in 1994–5). The Uganda government sees renegotiation of this largely multilateral debt as a way of reducing this burden and diverting resources to 'human development expenditures in order to reduce poverty' (Republic of Uganda, 1995: 42). However, it is argued in the next section that rehabilitation policies are more likely to ensure reduced aid dependence and a declining debt burden than will a negotiated debt write-off, dependent as it is on donor goodwill.

Policies to accelerate recovery

In this section, two different sets of policies are considered: first, policies concerned with managing the exchange rate; second, policies which concern the rehabilitation of tradables production. The management of the exchange rate is necessary to prevent renewed real appreciation generating disincentive effects on the output of tradables, while rehabilitation policies are designed to rebuild and renew production-supporting institutions, such as agricultural research and financial institutions. Achieving the latter is likely to help exchange rate management in two ways: increasing incomes and employment and therefore demand for imports; and generating hard currency inflows which can be used to repay debt in order to reduce the required level of net inflows of hard currency.

Managing the exchange rate

Even if price incentives increase production for export, exchange rate management under current conditions may not be feasible (Lewis and Younger, 1994). First, the Bank of Uganda has to offload aid dollars and import support even if this means real appreciation. Second, dollars cannot be bought without creating too much domestic bank credit; the government can mop up shillings only by issuing treasury bills, but this is politically difficult to do on a continuing basis because of the reaction of aid donors. Nevertheless, there has been market intervention by the government to buy up dollars in order to stabilize the exchange rate, but this has meant the expenditure of scarce government funds which may have a high opportunity cost in terms of expenditure on poverty reduction.

Government funds could be used in a different way to increase effective demand for imports. In particular, counterpart funds to import support could be used to fund an across-the-board employment subsidy to correct capital-labour price ratios and increase employment. Targeted cash-for-work on specific labour-intensive public works would have a similar effect. Counterpart funds could also be used to support the prices of exportables in order that a longer-term view involving investment in realistic diversification and in renewal of traditional activities (for example, replacing old coffee trees with new varieties). Strategies for increasing export revenues will on their own lead to exchange rate appreciation, but through their effects on effective demand they will also increase import demand, and slow or even reverse any tendencies to appreciation. However, as noted earlier, any increased net export revenues could be used to repay debt and so increase demand for dollars. Once again, the question is how far the major donors would accept anything other than their view of what will work (see Helleiner, 1992). In any case, such policies as outlined above attempt to influence different price variables in such a way as to generate market-based solutions. It is the burden of our argument here that more than simply making markets work is necessary to produce sustained economic recovery. The next section looks for policies for recovery which lie beyond the market.

Rehabilitation and institutional reform

A successful economic recovery programme also requires the design of effective activities at sectoral and project level, including the choice of appropriate institutions and procedures. A few of the most relevant principles are summarized below (Faber, 1993):

(1) In the circumstances of economic decline, it usually makes better sense to invest in the rehabilitation of existing projects (activities) than in the construction of new ones.
(2) Given the right policy framework, these rehabilitation projects are capable of showing high rates of return.

(3) Such policy framework embraces macroeconomic policies (exchange rate, control of inflation, containment of government deficit, etc.) as well as appropriate sector policies (pricing policies, controls, lease and licensing regimes, labour policies, etc.)

(4) Even when longer-term capital and foreign exchange for imports have been obtained, short-term local credit can be a problem; a strong partner eases its availability.

(5) The abolition of restrictive rules and regulations may be the cheapest and most cost-effective way of achieving the rehabilitation of many projects.

(6) Rehabilitation projects can act as 'bright spots'. Each successful one makes the next easier to establish. When a sufficient number of them exist, the whole economy will be on the way to recovery.

In the Uganda case there is no evidence for the systematic application of these principles. In fact, both donors and the Ugandan intelligentsia have applied considerable resources and ingenuity in the pursuit of agricultural diversification rather than to the recovery of lost market shares and the use of already installed capacities and skills in the production, processing and transport of major traditional export and import-substitute crops.

Any assessment of this strategy has to analyse how much aid actually goes into projects likely to increase tradable production and how much into projects which increase demand for non-tradables. Data on aid and rehabilitation expenditures show that industry, mining, and social infrastructure take the bulk of resources, while low proportions of expenditure go to agriculture and agricultural tradables, especially to infrastructure rehabilitation (see e.g. Republic of Uganda, 1992). This is despite the fact that agricultural GDP still comprises nearly half of overall GDP and that traditional exportables, all agricultural tradables, provided 75 per cent of export earnings in 1994/5. There could be a sustainability problem as an increasing proportion of recurrent expenditure is taken by wages and salaries and interest repayments. As has been shown, recovery in the agricultural tradable sector has been poor. Co-operative and state industry insolvency has resulted in delayed payments to producers, and inputs financed by aid have been diverted from intended recipients by co-operative unions, banks and public sector institutions.

The policy corollary of this brief analysis of aid expenditures is that aid targeted to tradable production-inducing projects which rehabilitate 'traditional' sectors is likely to yield high rates of return and enable the ensuing debt to be repaid in the longer run. Aid for the improvement of infrastructure, especially that supporting a liberalized marketing system, aid to improve management of capital projects and marketing, and aid to increase farm productivity by replacing old varieties and tree stock, has the virtue of building on existing knowledge and activity with well-established markets. Such clearly targeted aid could also be linked to structural reform; for example, transferring the production components from estates and large schemes to smallholder or outgrower systems. This combined approach of rehabilitation and structural reform links well with the attack on poverty which is a central part of government policy, but which so far has yielded little result.

Conclusion: contradictions of economic liberalization

This chapter has argued that market-based macroeconomic reforms are insufficient to effect the kind of economic recovery that would allow Uganda to reach the level of economic activity which would have prevailed in the absence of the political turmoil of the Amin and Obote II years. The failure to engage in the institutional reform of agriculture simultaneously or shortly following liberalization has led to a recovery far less rapid than was needed to alleviate widespread poverty and achieve sustainable economic recovery. The policy of eschewing the systematic rehabilitation of the traditional cash-crop sectors in favour of diversification into both tradable and non-tradable agricultural commodities has resulted in missed opportunities to improve the balance of trade, increase import demand, alleviate rural poverty, and through these measures manage the real exchange rate. The sustainability of the present aid-dependent economy is in serious doubt.

Such concerns make it very important that project aid is implemented effectively. However, at the macro-balance level, there is a possibility that as long as the aid keeps flowing, policy adjustments to increase export income and increase imports can be viewed as unnecessary. In other words, no agency has an immediate interest in changing the *status quo*. The international institutions have a vested interest in pointing to Uganda as one of the SAP success stories. The Ugandan beneficiaries from the aid inflows – largely in the public and formal sectors – have little or no incentive to adopt policies which may divert resources to smallholder agriculture. The typical view that investment in traditional cash crops is mistaken because of poor world prices and identification with a previous era may be right, but this is not the way the World Bank model is supposed to work.

Notes

1. An earlier version of this chapter was presented at the Annual Conference of the Development Studies Association (DSA), University of Reading, September 1996.
2. This was, in effect, the one and only structural adjustment mission.
3. For an excellent survey of poverty in Uganda, and especially the importance of rehabilitating cash crops in the poor areas of the country, see: Appleton and Mackinnon (1995).

PART II

AGRARIAN TRANSITION IN FORMER SOCIALIST ECONOMIES

6 Agrarian transition in the former Soviet Union: the case of Central Asia

MAX SPOOR

Introduction

THIS CHAPTER CHALLENGES the mainstream position which claims that between the pace and extent of privatization and market liberalization in transitional economies, and their speed of recovery, exists a simple positive causal relationship, as is put forward quite forcefully in the recent World Development Report entitled *From Plan to Market* (World Bank, 1996). In order to do so, the current agrarian transition in the five Central Asian States (CAS) of the former Soviet Union (FSU) is analysed, i.e. in Kazakhstan, Kyrgyzstan, Tajikistan, Turkmenistan and Uzbekistan. Although the supposed positive correlation, that is the foundation-stone of the World Bank's conclusion, can already be questioned on statistical grounds, as is shown by Kekic (1996), our argument against this one-to-one relationship will be of a more analytical and qualitative nature. It will be shown – by using a comparative method – that agrarian transitions embrace extremely complex and often contradictory processes, in which a crucial role is played by various factors, such as: (i) initial conditions; (ii) intersectoral relationships and dependencies; and (iii) the dynamic interplay between macro-economic adjustment policies and sectoral development.

A brief analysis is then presented of the macroeconomic crisis that affected the CAS, emphasizing the influence of resource endowments, initial conditions and the differential impact of macroeconomic contraction at a sectoral level. The next section focuses on two aspects of the agrarian transition: the land privatization process, and the break-up of the state-dominated agricultural marketing and distribution systems under the influence of market liberalization and deregulation. The agricultural sector reforms are reviewed, with special reference to Kazakhstan, Kyrgyzstan and Uzbekistan, showing that in spite of slow privatization and the formation of only an incipient private family farm sector, a wide variety of farm types and production arrangements is appearing, which points to a dynamic and diverse development, even if a country scores low on the World Bank's 'Reform Progress Index', such as Uzbekistan.[1] In the final part some conclusions are drawn which underline the basic argument in this analysis: in these transitional processes there are no simple recipes nor ideal outcomes, but mainly complex dynamics and unexpected, or sometimes unintended results of adjustment policies.

The Central Asian economies in crisis (1990–5)

All FSU republics have suffered from severe economic contraction in recent years. The Central Asia States are no exception to this rule, as sustained negative growth can be observed in all of them since 1991 (Table 6.1), sometimes even starting earlier (Spoor, 1996a). Kazakhstan and Kyrgyzstan saw their GDP, by the end of 1995, being reduced to around 46 per cent of the 1990 level; Tajikistan's GDP, suffering from the impact of civil war, even declined to 36 per cent. For Turkmenistan (in spite of the rich oil and gas reserves) the 1995 level stood at 64 per cent; while finally in Uzbekistan, the largest economy in terms of population, GDP had decreased to 82 per cent, being relatively the 'best' performing economy.[2]

In comparison with the average GDP for all the CIS countries, which was 58 per cent of the 1990 level, the Russian Federation being at 62 per cent, the CAS performance was fluctuating widely around the average (StatKom SNG, 1996:11). Furthermore, taking into account the substantial out-migration of skilled labour from Kazakhstan and Kyrgyzstan, the drought that hit the region in 1991, and the civil war that raged in Tajikistan, the economic situation is without any doubt precarious. Nevertheless, according to the latest reports the trough seems to have been reached in Kazakhstan and Kyrgyzstan, and a further contraction in the Uzbekistan economy, in which industry grew in 1995, has been contained.

During the Soviet era the CAS benefited structurally from the all-Union budget transfers that provided investment resources for agricultural, industrial

Table 6.1: GDP development in central Asian FSU states (1990–1995)

% Change (p/a)	1990	1991	1992	1993	1994	1995
Kazakhstan	−0.8	−11.8	−13.0	−12.9	−25.0	−8.9
Kyrgyzstan	3.2	−4.2	−16.4	−16.4	−26.0	−6.2
Tajikistan	−1.6[a]	−8.7[a]	−31.0	−17.3[b]	−21.3[b]	−12.4
Turkmenistan	1.8[a]	−4.7[a]	−11.0	−6.0	−15.0[c]	−6.0*
Uzbekistan	1.6	−0.5	−11.1	−2.4	4.0[d]	−1.0[c]

Notes: *   January–May 1995 estimate; Other 1995 data come from StatKom (1996) that was published in January 1996, most likely to be taken as estimates as well, but for the whole of 1995.
    [a]   As estimates for GDP are lacking, NMP (Net Material Product) growth is used.
    [b]   EIU (1995) estimated NMP growth at −27.6 and −20.0 per cent for 1993 and 1994 (suggesting a somewhat greater drop in GDP). World Bank EIU (1996) gives −15.0 per cent for 1994. The data in the table are taken from StatKom SNG (1995).
    [c]   EIU (1995) estimated NMP growth in 1994 to be positive (!) at 1.7 per cent. The different GDP figure of the CIS Statistical Committee is used here. Differences cannot be explained but the EIU suggests that the original IMF estimate cannot be justified.
    [d]   EIU (1995) gives −2.6 per cent for 1994. StatKom SNG (1995): −3.5 per cent.
    [e]   World Bank (1996: 173) gives −2.0 per cent for 1995.

Sources: EIU (1995); Zhukov (1995); World Bank (1994d); Spoor (1995a); StatKom SNG (1995); StatKom SNG (1996); Author's Calculations.

and mining infrastructure or social sector institutions. Nevertheless, the development model of the CAS within the Soviet Union reflected the increasingly one-sided inter-republican division of labour, in which countries such as Uzbekistan, Turkmenistan and Tajikistan specialized in cotton, known as 'white gold'; Kyrgyzstan emerged as one of the Soviet Union's main wool producers, and a supplier of uranium, gold and mercury; Kazakhstan became a bulk grain producer, with expanded areas of cultivated land as a result of the virgin lands campaign of Khrushchev in the 1950s, while simultaneously developing oil and gas production, just like Turkmenistan. This inter-republican division of labour also created dependency on mono-cultures, while the consequences of ruthless exploitation of natural resources with a general disregard of the environment remains a major long-term problem for public health and socio-economic sustainability.[3] Furthermore, most of the CAS (with the exception of Kazakhstan) imported more and more food, while agricultural and industrial inputs also came from elsewhere. On the one hand, many of the raw materials or primary agricultural products were 'exported' to other republics of the USSR without any form of processing, while relatively little processing capacity was built locally.[4] On the other hand, industry was established with a total disregard of comparative advantage by simply subsidizing transport costs between the centre and the periphery.

Because of the structural dependency that grew between the 'centre' and the 'peripheral' economies of the CAS, the disintegration of the Soviet Union had a dramatic impact on them. Previous inter-republican trade had more the character of planned transfers at the level of a central ministry or a *kombinat* (industrial complex), and markets (if one can speak of markets in this context) were purely captive ones. After 1991, the CAS were forced to pay much more (sometimes at world market price levels) for their imports, while on the other hand traditional export markets for cotton, wool, gas, oil and meat could not immediately be replaced by hard currency market outlets. Hard currency payments within the CIS for exports from the CAS are often delayed or even refused. The external shock caused by the disintegration of the FSU particularly affected those CAS with sectors largely dependent on forward and backward linkages within the former Soviet economy, such as Kazakhstan and Kyrgyzstan, with their industry, while those economies with substantial primary sectors (agriculture and mining) were able to provide a cushion from the shock.

Agricultural sector reform

A large part of the population in the CAS is rural, as in Uzbekistan and Kyrgyzstan where the share is around 63 per cent. Agricultural production represents an important share of GDP, with sub-sectors such as cotton (Uzbekistan, Turkmenistan and Tajikistan), wheat (Kazakhstan) and mutton and wool (Kyrgyzstan). For example, in the two most industrialized CAS, Kazakhstan and Uzbekistan, agriculture contributed 31.4 per cent to NMP

(1993) in the former, while this was 33.6 per cent in the latter (1994). Nevertheless, the share of industry in GDP is still slightly larger, mainly because of the extraction (and in some cases processing) of mineral resources, such as gas (Uzbekistan), oil (Kazakhstan), coal (Kyrgyzstan), aluminium (Tajikistan), tungsten, gold, and the production of thermal energy. A comparison of NMP data in the last year before the collapse of the Soviet Union shows that Kazakhstan had the strongest industrial sector of Central Asia, followed by Uzbekistan, with the other republics depending largely on agriculture and mineral resource exploitation.[5] In particular because of the inter-republican dependency relations of industry, and its inability to compete in foreign (non-CIS) markets, the contraction in this sector was dramatic (Spoor, 1996a). In contrast, the agricultural sector was less affected during the first half of the 1990s, although grain production in Kazakhstan showed a very negative trend, with spectacular declines in production in 1991 and 1995 (see Table 6.2).

Why was there such a differential impact of the economic crisis during the transition? First, agricultural production such as cotton, grain, meat and wool formed a nationally integrated production process, depending only on some external (extra-republican) inputs. Therefore the disintegration of the former USSR in 1991 had a smaller direct impact on the agricultural sector of the CAS. Second, it seems that although the terms of trade generally did not improve, as the costs of inputs (fertilizers and pesticides) increased much faster than output prices, the importance of newly demanded high value agricultural products (such as vegetables) grew, stabilizing agricultural incomes, at least somewhat. Third, agricultural commodities, in particular food staples, remained 'marketable' with relatively little competition from imports. Fourth, specifically for the important cotton sector, the revenues earned with hard currency exports (such as in Uzbekistan and Turkmenistan), provided finance for the import of spare parts, fertilizers and pesticides, which previously were transferred, or bought at administrative prices. These factors have contributed to the fact that agriculture became a cushion for the shock of economic contraction in the CAS.

Furthermore, initial conditions of the major economic sectors at the outset of the transition were quite different for the five CAS, whether it be industry, agriculture or the important sector of mineral resources. They have played an important role as to the impact of the reforms, and overall in the outcome of the transition process so far. As we focus here on the agrarian transition in the CAS for agricultural production this diversity can be shown by looking at some major agricultural crops (Table 6.2).

The data presented on grain, cotton and potatoes output during the 1990–5 period, reveal some interesting features. Firstly, Kazakhstan's crisis with respect to grain production is obvious, although there were also visible violent fluctuations in output, caused mainly by weather conditions. Also in Kyrgyzstan this sector contracted, a phenomenon that was in both cases related to the severe crisis in the livestock sector. Grain output was greatly affected by

Table 6.2: Output main crops Central Asian FSU states (1990–5)

(x 1,000 t.)	1990	1991	1992	1993	1994	1995
Grain (cleanweight)						
Kazakhstan	28 488	11 992	29 772	21 631	16 454	9514
Kyrgyzstan	1503	1374	1516	1508	1063[a]	991
Tajikistan	313	286	257	253	250	240
Turkmenistan	449	517	737	974	1130[b]	1011
Uzbekistan	1899	1908	2257	2142	2467[c]	3200
Cotton						
Kazakhstan	324	291	252	200	206	180
Kyrgyzstan	81	63	52	42	54	72
Tajikistan	842	814	442	542	529	417
Turkmenistan	1457	1433	1300	1341	1283	1304
Uzbekistan	5058	4646	4128	4234	3938	4200
Potatoes						
Kazakhstan	2324	2143	2570	2296	1953	1720
Kyrgyzstan	365	325	362	308	310	431
Tajikistan	207	181	167	147	140	110
Turkmenistan	35	30	39	32	30	11
Uzbekistan	336	351	365	473	562	500

Notes: [a] In 1994 the grain situation (food and feed grains) had become so precarious that the Kyrgyz government had to make and urgent plea for EEC food aid.
  [b] Although official sources give the figure of 1.1 million tons, in a recent interview by the author with a high Turkmen official (December 1995, Ashgabad) this was scaled down to 0.8 million tons.
  [c] Although the precise output figure is missing here, the grain acreage increased from 347 000 ha in 1993 to 643 000 ha in 1994 (with a plan to reach 972 000 ha in 1995!).

Sources: EIU (1995); World Bank (1994d); Spoor (1995a); StatKom SNG (1995, 1996).

the dramatic decrease in demand for feed grains (Liefert, 1995: 4), as there was a shift towards less meat consumption, and areas reserved for fodder production shrank dramatically (Table 6.3). Nevertheless, other factors, such as the strong decrease in fertilizer application, also contributed to the decline. For example, in Kazakhstan the use of fertilizers dropped from 26.8 kg/ha (during 1986–90) to only 5.4 kg/ha in 1994 (USDA, 1995: 10). Second, Turkmenistan and Uzbekistan began stimulating their grain production, mostly by converting irrigated cotton lands to grain cultivation.

This change in crop-mix shows the determination of these countries to reach a situation of food self-sufficiency, even at high cost, as imported grain from Kazakhstan (if available) in some cases would be relatively cheaper for both countries. For Uzbekistan and Kyrgyzstan, this strategy is also visible in the expanded potato sector. Third, the cotton sector was affected negatively, although cotton output dropped less than might have been expected because of the access to foreign exchange revenues that guaranteed the purchase the necessary inputs, such as fertilizers, pesticides and machinery.

Table 6.3: Changes in land use in FSU Central Asian states (1990–94)

| | Sown Area | Grain | Sub Total | Industrial Crops | | | Potatoes | Vegetables | Fodder |
				Cotton	Sugar	Sun Flower			
Kazakhstan									
1990	35 182	23 356	440	120	44	137	206	71	11 065
1994	31 672	20 706	604	111	56	281	218	75	10 054
Kyrgyzstan									
1990	1294	538	62	30	0	—	25	21	641
1994	1248	586	87	26	10	—	34	22	516
Tajikistan									
1990	824	230	315	304	—	—	15	23	229
1993	793	279	289	275	—	—	12	23	180
Turkmenistan									
1990	1232	187	625	623	—	—	4	35	338
1993	1324	435	580	579	—	—	4	21	266
Uzbekistan									
1990	4194	1008	1876	1830	—	—	42	140	1040
1994	4236	1522	1579	1538	—	—	53	157	877

Source: StatKom SNG (1995).

Agrarian sector reforms

Rapid privatization of state and collective farms in the FSU is generally seen as crucial in restructuring the farm sector. However, until now it has proven to be very difficult to execute. Even in the Russian Federation, where most of the attention of foreign donors is focused, the process has been very slow and complex (Czaki and Lerman, 1996). According to one World Bank study, by early 1993 only 8 per cent of the farm sector was really privatized (Brooks and Lerman, 1994: 42). Furthermore, many changes – such as the formation of joint-stock companies, farmer's co-operatives and forms of *tovarishchestvo* (limited liability partnership) – represent formal rather than real changes (Brooks and Lerman, 1994: 42; Czaki and Lerman, 1996). This development reveals the existence of political and social forces that represent vested interests, but in some cases it also points to a certain hesitation among the farming population to embark upon private farming in view of often non-existent or malfunctioning rural input, output and credit markets.

In the CAS similar phenomena can be observed with respect to land reform, albeit with substantial country-specific factors involved. Why is there still relatively little land really privatized (although the governments of the CAS consider some of the above mentioned – mostly quite superficial – ownership transformations as 'privatization')? There are a number of reasons. First, there are insufficient incentives to break away from the remaining collective structures. New markets for inputs and outlets for agricultural production are emerging in a very slow and fragmented manner, while credit for private farmers is often not available.[6] Furthermore, the social infrastructure of education and public health is still related to the old parastatal or collective structures. Second, the rural *nomenklatura* clings to power, or even hopes to increase it. Keeping the previous structures intact (albeit under another name) gives the *nomenklatura* better options to remain in social and political control of the rural areas (Spoor, 1995a). However, when privatization of land is taking place it is also the former party élite that seems to get control of most of the best land. Furthermore, newly established enterprises (joint stock companies, farmer's co-operatives etc.) are still closely tied to the remaining large-scale state trading and processing companies (as in Uzbekistan and Kazakhstan), forcing them to keep their structure and previous forms of operation intact. Third, the governments of the CAS genuinely fear that a land privatization process will lead to conflicts along ethnic lines, as were witnessed in 1990 in Osh, where access to land was a major issue in the violent and bloody riots between Kyrgyz and Uzbeks (CPSS, 1996). Equally, there are future tensions to be expected in Kazakhstan, in particular between the Russian farming population in the northern plains and the Kazakhs. Therefore, although leasing of land (often with rights of heritage, and long periods of leasehold) has been the most advanced step on the road to privatization, most land is still owned by the state. Distribution of usufruct rights to farm on small plots of state-owned land by households is widespread, while subcontracting of collective land to households has recently emerged in response to popular demand for land. However, there is no visible sustained movement for an economically viable private farm sector (Table 6.4 – page 105).[7]

The agrarian reform – in terms of the formation of private family farms – has actually seen limited progress in Kazakhstan, Kyrgyzstan and Uzbekistan, and even a little in Tajikistan and Turkmenistan. However, there is a widespread belief that privatization in the agricultural sector has already been more or less completed in the CAS that are considered as the 'reformers' of the CAS (Kyrgyzstan and to a lesser extent Kazakhstan) and absent in the 'non-reformers' (Uzbekistan, and even less Tajikistan and Turkmenistan).[8] Actually, most of formal land reform has taken the shape of paper exchanges, where state farms are transformed into joint-stock companies or co-operatives, and collectives into limited liability companies (*tovarishchestva*) or into leasehold companies. Often the change meant nothing more than taking away the old name plate above the main gate and hanging a new one there.[9] Nevertheless, land in the CAS has been 'privatized' in different ways, which makes it difficult to assess what share of agricultural land is currently in private usufruct or *de jure* ownership. As in the Soviet era, more land is in private use than is noted in official statistics. Previously, members of collective farms or workers on state farms had a small family plot, which produced a substantial part of the household cash income. In the post-1991 period additional land has been privatized in this manner. Therefore, what is not shown in Table 6.4 is a strong increase in the private household plots and *dacha*-gardens or orchards (that already existed in the Soviet era), but more importantly, in the use of contracting schemes within the currently remaining collectives (Khan, 1996: 77).

An example of the deliberate expansion of household plot production is Uzbekistan, where the government distributed, in the form of leasehold, 500 000 hectares (around 12 per cent of total arable land) until 1992, in order to satisfy the increasing private demand for land.[10] Most of this land was fractionated into tiny pieces (EIU, 1993). During 1993 nearly all *sovkhozi* (state farms) were transformed into joint-stock companies, while some were divided up into a number of collectives (Khan, 1996). However, the formation of a new private farm sector remains incipient. In some cases land issues led to ethnic tensions, concentrated mainly in the densely populated Ferghana Valley (that borders Kyrgyzstan). Since February 1994, supported by a number of presidential decrees on private property and entrepreneurship, land was distributed (actually leased for long periods) to peasant farmers, based on a minimum area per head of cattle owned – varying between 0.3 and 2.0 hectares per head – in order to promote the emergence of viable peasant farms (Republic of Uzbekistan, 1994: 77, 90). For this purpose another 100 000 ha were reserved for distribution in 1994. Interestingly enough, in one of these decrees the government of Uzbekistan showed itself to be extremely self-critical about the economic reforms in rural areas which were seen as

'extremely slow and superficial' (*ibid*: 83). In November 1994 a field visit to
an area north of Tashkent confirmed that these decrees had indeed started to
be put into practice, with farmers obtaining between 10 and 20 hectares of
land. However, with the system of allotting land through the powerful
khokims or mayors, vested private interests in the public sector promote privatization of land to the benefit of the rural *nomenklatura*. Even with the most
recent government decisions on land distribution, land ownership is still a
monopoly of the state, while peasant farmers can obtain leasing (or usufruct)
rights.[11] The latter are partly exempted from taxes but are still obliged to sell
a substantial part of their output (cotton, grain, meat and milk) to the state at
'negotiated' (below market) prices.

In Kyrgyzstan land reform, although having progressed somewhat further,
is also not without contradictions. With a recent history of violent conflicts
between Kyrgyz and Uzbek people in the *oblast* of Osh,[12] land privatization
contributed to further inter-ethnic tension in 1992. However, with an increasingly depressed economy and the collapse of marketing, the privatization programme was suspended until the beginning of the 1993 agricultural season.
In that year land reform again showed modest progress, in particular the
(mostly formal) transformation of state farms into joint-stock companies.
Nevertheless, during this period the government gave special support to state
and collective farms with an emergency programme (World Bank,
1993a:126), a move that provided a strong disincentive to start private farming. In early 1994, at the same time as in Kazakhstan and Uzbekistan, the
Kyrgyz government gave a new impulse to the reform process, reducing the
quota that private farms had to sell to the state. While land is still state owned,
private farms got usufruct rights for 49 years, although after the parliament-
ary elections of February 1995 legislative changes were announced in order
to make private land titling possible. The land distribution and privatization
programme is now exclusively in the hands of the Ministry of Agriculture,
including the National Land Fund, which aims to reserve at least 25 per cent
of arable land for ethnic Kyrgyz farmers.[13]

The land reform programme has developed with substantial inconsistencies, but most recently also with increasing dynamics. This can be shown by
two quite contradictory observations. On the one hand, on a recent trip in
Kyrgyzstan (June 1996) I paid a visit to a former collective farm about 70
kilometres north-east of the capital Bishkek, which combined dairy farming
and crop production. Although the farm was recently reconstituted as a
'farmer's association', in the interview with the farm manager it became clear
that the land titling process had not induced the formation of viable family
farms. Each adult member of the farm and even some children had received
usufruct rights for a standard acreage of 0.85 hectare (!). On the question of
whether anybody had left the association, taking with her or him the allotted
land, the answer was understandably negative, as there would be no way to
survive with such a tiny plot. Overstaffing still remained a problem, but the

continued employment was seen as providing a safety network for the agricultural workers (rather than 'farmers') and no reference was made to efficiency. On the other hand, it seems that during 1995 a strong boost occurred in family farm production. According to the Statistical Committee of the Kyrgyz Republic the total acreage of family farms in 1995 as compared to the previous year, increased from 10.1 to 23.1 per cent of agricultural land (somewhat more than is reflected in Table 6.4), while the proportion of these farms engaged in the production of grain increased from 10.4 to 26.7 per cent. Household plots and private family farms together represented 91.0 and 80.4 per cent of potatoes and vegetables output respectively (StatKom KR, 1996: 147–49).

In Kazakhstan, agrarian reform advanced with many ups and downs. Previously agricultural production had been dominated by more than 2000 *sovkhozi* with an exceptional average size of 80 000 hectares and around 430 *kolkhozi* of about 10 000 hectares. Although initiated in the early 1990s, the privatization process has only progressed gradually, with renewed reform impetus given to it during 1994–5. Initially most 'privatization' meant the establishment of joint stock companies with only internal stock-holders (managers and workers), although in Kazakhstan the amount of land available for private use by households within these enterprises increased substantially. It is interesting to see that similar contradictions and dynamics occurred as in Uzbekistan and Kyrgyzstan, although government policies have been quite diverse. In a sector study undertaken in 1994, the World Bank remarked that the 'large inefficient' *sovkhozi* were simply transformed into 'large inefficient' collective or co-operative farms (World Bank, 1994c: 39). Some of these enterprises still functioned under the same operative regime as before, albeit having changed their name. This could be observed on a field visit in June 1996 to the Chengyldy farm, about 130 km north-east of Almaty, where an irrigation rehabilitation project of the World Bank was planned. It seemed that some sub-contracting activities had been allowed, but basically the old structures of management of the collective (including the brigades) had been retained. Nevertheless, privatization of land in family farms has led to medium sized farms that can be economically viable (Table 6.4), while there are recent reports that in the north of Kazakhstan even entire collectives and former state farms have been acquired by private (mainly Kazakh) investors. These have retained their giant size, and thus may still conserve the previous problems of scale-inefficiency, in spite of changing forms of ownership.

Altogether, it is apparent that the demonopolization and privatization of at least some of the important state companies of agricultural services (procurement and inputs) have contributed to the current dynamic in the formation of private farms in Kazakhstan. Land reform has gone somewhat further in Kyrgyzstan and Kazakhstan than in Uzbekistan, while being largely absent in Tajikistan and Turkmenistan. Nevertheless, a viable private farming sector is

Table 6.4: Private farms in Central Asian FSU states (1991–5)

	1991	1992	1993	1994	1995
Kazakhstan					
Number	3 300	9 300	16 300	22 500	27 900
Average Size	238	533	406	348	376
Farm Area	800 000	4 900 000	6 500 000	7 800 000	10 500 000
Total Agricultural Land	271 646 000	. . .	. . .	. . .	. . .
Total Arable land	35 497 000	. . .	. . .	. . .	. . .
Kyrgyzstan					
Number	4 100	8 600	12 800	17 300	19 600
Average Size	25	44	67	43	63
Farm Area	103 100	374 800	868 200	744 000	1 236 800
Total Agricultural Land	10 549 000	. . .	. . .	. . .	. . .
Total Arable land	1 345 000	. . .	. . .	. . .	. . .
Tajikistan					
Number	4	4	100	200	. . .
Average Size	16	25	14	131	. . .
Farm Area	65	100	1 400	19 800	. . .
Total Agricultural Land	4 490 000	. . .	. . .	. . .	. . .
Total Arable land	968 000	. . .	. . .	. . .	. . .
Turkmenistan					
Number	100	100	300	1 000	. . .
Average Size	10	10	8	8	. . .
Farm Area	1 100	1 100	2 800	5 900	. . .
Total Agricultural Land	42 500 000	. . .	. . .	. . .	. . .
Total Arable land	1 351 000	. . .	. . .	. . .	. . .
Uzbekistan					
Number	1 900	5 900	7 500	14 200	17 700
Average Size	7	8	9	14	15
Farm Area	13 700	45 100	70 600	193 100	257 300
Total Agricultural Land	27 900 000	. . .	. . .	. . .	. . .
Total Arable land	4 775 000	. . .	. . .	. . .	. . .

Note: For comparative reasons it is useful to note that in Russia (1/1/1994) only 1.7 per cent of agricultural land (or 5.4 per cent of ploughed land) was in the private farm sector (not counting family plots and *dacha*-gardens). For the five CAS the share of agricultural land is within 0–10 per cent, except for Kyrgyzstan, while shares of arable land (although the composition is unknown) would be substantially higher in the cases of Kazakhstan and Kyrgyzstan.

Sources: USDA (1993b, 1995); StatKom SNG (1995, 1996).

still far from firmly established. As is the case in Russia, only a relatively small percentage of agricultural land is owned or controlled by family farms. Where peasant farmers started to produce, they were often confronted with severe problems. This was because of the near total collapse of support services in the case of Kyrgyzstan, or because existing services are still geared exclusively to state and collective farms, as in Uzbekistan. From this observation it follows that a push to rapid privatization and parcelization, within an environment of inefficient and sometimes non-existent markets, will jeopardize the viability of these peasant farms. Accompanying institutional change in agrarian markets would provide a real incentive to the formation of private farms. Nevertheless, one can already observe the emergence of a great variety of farm production arrangements, from farmer's associations to sub-contracted family production. However, in all CAS, the outcome of land and service sector privatization depends particularly on rural (and related urban) power relations, in which the vested interests of the former party élite play a decisive role. Related to this, the land reform that is currently being undertaken has a strong ethnic connotation, which partly explains the cautious approach of CAS governments to this issue. Finally, control over water as well as land resources is an important issue. Water resources and their management are crucial for Uzbekistan's whole agricultural sector, and for Kyrgyzstan – particularly in the populated Chui and Osh *oblasts*. The complexity of privatization of water rights and the introduction of water charges (on a cost recovery basis) – that some Central Asian governments are currently promoting – are nevertheless being underestimated in the economic reforms. A structural water reform, improving water management and emphasizing the scarcity of the resource, needs to be put high on the agenda. As 'land without water is no land' in the CAS, water reform should certainly not become a residue of land privatization. In particular, in those countries where large-scale systems of irrigation exist, such as Uzbekistan and Turkmenistan (the main water users of the region), water reform is a highly complex and sensitive problem area in the process of agrarian transition.

Reform of the state order system
In the Soviet era all support services for agricultural production, such as input distribution, agro-processing and trade, were closely linked to the 'state order system'.[14] In Uzbekistan this is still largely intact, although in recent years its scope has diminished to a small number of agricultural products (albeit dominant in the agricultural sector) such as cotton, grain, meat and milk. The procurement quota, or share of the harvest that has to be sold by collective or other farmers to the state, has also gradually diminished since 1991. In 1993 this share was still 75 per cent for cotton. By 1995 this was reduced to 50 per cent, and further reductions are planned (Khan, 1996). The state order system provides the farming sector with subsidies, including negative interest rates for bank credit due to high inflation. However, a breakdown of trade relations and higher international prices for fertilizers and pesticides have substantially reduced their availability and use. On the other hand, the prices paid by state companies for agricultural products are only a fraction of border prices.[15] Even 'free market' prices for non-quota production are lower than international prices, mainly because export of cotton is still a state quasi-monopoly. With an exchange rate still lower than purchasing power parity this is not surprising, but even with low input prices for agricultural producers there is a substantial net outflow of resources from agriculture, estimated in 1993 for Uzbekistan to be 0.9 billion dollars.[16] However, during 1994–5 procurement prices were raised substantially and a tendering system was introduced for

above-quota sales. The cotton trade still remains largely under state control, but the grain trade became partly deregulated in 1995. Although such reforms were announced in early 1994, and the complicated licensing system (which is open to corruption) has come under attack since then; in practice it is still rather difficult for a private company to enter into export activities, in which state companies often remain dominant actors. Vested interests are likely to feel threatened by any form of trade liberalization. However, Uzbekistan is struggling to (re)establish trade relations with FSU countries as well as elsewhere in the world market, and is doing so quite successfully, nearly doubling its non-CIS exports in 1995 in comparison with the previous year (Stat Kom SNG, 1996: 250). From an initial reaction of heavy protectionism common to all Central Asian States, licensing and import quotas are gradually being changed into a more rational tariff system, while export tariffs were recently reduced (Republic of Uzbekistan, 1994), and the Common Economic Space, formed in 1994 by Kazakhstan, Kyrgyzstan and Uzbekistan is starting to function in practice.

In Kyrgyzstan, during 1992 and 1993, output marketing was still state controlled. For commodities such as cotton, wool, wheat and tobacco, the state order system remained in force, paying to domestic producers prices far below international market levels. In early 1994, after the emergency programme was abandoned and a new wave of market reforms initiated, obligatory state procurement was abandoned and replaced by 'domestic supply agreements'. Prices were not yet freed, as several state monopolies, such as the Bread Products Enterprise and the huge Tamak-Ash agro-processing company, still remained and prices were being negotiated. Most minimum shares to be sold to the state were established at a level of 20–30 per cent of producer's output (except for tobacco for which the share was substantially higher). Similarly to Uzbekistan, there is sometimes a lack of real understanding by the leadership of how markets should work, particularly when a private farming sector has been formed (Duncan, 1994: 86). The state order system was geared to serve the state and collective farm system, and has difficulties in adjusting to the needs of the emerging private small farm sector. On the other hand, privatization of the huge parastatals is a complex matter, as most of them are formally bankrupt. The absence of outlets offering competitive prices, both for domestically traded food crops or for exportables, still leads to net transfers out of agriculture. Obviously this has negative consequences for agricultural production, particularly in the dairy sector. An example was the drastic reduction in milk production in 1993–94. As farmers saw the price of silage rising, they slaughtered their milk cows to concentrate on meat production. The disarticulation of the marketing system and reduced production was subsequently felt by the agro-processing sector. A milk factory 30 km from Bishkek (visited in early December 1994) with a daily capacity of 50 tons of raw milk, received only 5 tons. Lacking credit and transport facilities, it could not compete with the emerging street market in fresh milk in the outskirts of the capital.[17] Finally, in terms of external trade, Kyrgyzstan has liberalized much more than its neighbour Uzbekistan. Trade with Kazakhstan is lively, and many consumer products enter the country, although the cheap Kazak and Chinese imports that enter as a consequence of external trade liberalization choke to death local Kyrgyz industries that produce with outdated technology at high costs.

Finally, in Kazakhstan the government had initially taken a rather gradualist approach towards the privatization and deregulation of the marketing and agro-industrial processing sectors (1991–3). This meant, for example, that the state order system for grain remained relatively untouched until 1994, when the state still bought under obligatory procurement arrangements around 4.1 million tons of grain (Liefert, 1995: 14). Nevertheless, since then procurement arrangements have been somewhat relaxed (and eliminated for non-grain crops), while in 1995 a system of state procurement was introduced based on a competitive tender system. During 1994–5 in Kazakhstan the reform in this sector received a new push, as many state enterprises were transformed into joint-stock companies or privatized (in part through auctions). The government has also introduced extensive legislation to break up the monopsony powers of many of these companies, in order to improve competition at the farm gate and promote a reduction of marketing costs for the main agricultural commodities. Nevertheless, agricultural markets are still fragmented, inefficient, and in some cases state monopolies have simply been transformed into private monopolies.[18] In summary, the state order system is still largely in force in Uzbekistan, has been practically broken down in Kyrgyzstan, and is currently in a process of rapid transformation in Kazakhstan. In all cases the newly emerging small private farmers face considerable obstacles as they operate in monopolistic, sometimes segmented, and often non-existent markets. Where transfers through the pricing system provided disincentives to producers (whether private or collective), the absence of proper marketing channels and manufactured products that can be bought with income is also felt. The emergence of new support services (and the relevant institutions) for farmers is still slow, although there are private initiatives and government-supported programmes that are trying to fill the gap left by the withdrawal of the state (or the disarticulation of 'old' institutions).

Conclusions

In focusing on the process of privatization and market liberalization in the five Central Asian States during the last half decade, the picture emerges that the impact of reforms – taking into account the differences in initial conditions and the political-economic context of the CAS – is not at all straightforward. The inter-republican division of labour of the former USSR defined strong links of dependency for the industrial sectors of the CAS, and the particularities of regional agricultural production patterns, such as the concentration on cotton in Uzbekistan, Turkmenistan and Tajikistan, on grain and extensive cattle raising in Kazakhstan, and on dairy production, mutton and wool in Kyrgyzstan. Although the dependency on a mono-crop such as cotton in the current context of the world market, and its negative impact on the environment, creates substantial problems, it also supports the role of agriculture as a cushion for the overall contraction of the CAS economies. The shift in agricultural production towards more food staples and vegetable crops, in particular stimulated by changing demand patterns (apart from meat consumption), concerted government decisions, as well as increased small-scale household plot and *dacha*-garden production, seem to strengthen this development. It is not altogether clear whether the current emphasis on food self-sufficiency is coherent with the gradual opening up of these economies, because it seems to happen in situations that differ substantially in terms of 'reform performance', to use the World Development Report (1996) terminology. Nevertheless, from a national perspective – at least in the short term – it looks a rather consistent change of strategy.

In the analysis of the process of agrarian transition it was shown that land privatization – as is the case in Russia – has not progressed very far, at least in terms of the establishment of a substantial and viable private (family-run) farm sector. This is one of the reasons why the CAS do not score very high on the World Bank's 'Reform Progress Index'. Even in countries such as Kyrgyzstan and Kazakhstan, normally seen as the main reformers of the Central Asian region, there is still a predominant role for the heirs of the former *sovkhozi* and *kolkhozi*, having recently been transformed into joint-stock companies (often in the absence of a relevant stock market), farmer's associations, or reconstituted production co-operatives. However, the progress of land privatization cannot be judged only by focusing on the number of private farms and the share of agricultural or arable land that they own or control in usufruct. There are many other production arrangements, including family contract farm systems, which function within collectives or production co-operatives, or other forms of legal and illegal land tenure arrangements, that have emerged in various countries, including Uzbekistan where, formally speaking, land reform has not progressed very far. Therefore, the real changes that are taking place, in particular in Kazakhstan, Kyrgyzstan and Uzbekistan (and to a lesser extent in the other two CAS) represent dynamic changes, are quite complex in nature and are often highly differentiated according to region, district or village community. Finally, and in line with the above conclusion, it is argued that the impact of privatization and market liberalization on the agricultural sectors of these economies cannot be linked in a linear manner to growth performance. If one analyses agrarian reform in relation to economic recovery (and the initial degree of contraction), the pace and extent of privatization and market liberalization can hardly be positively correlated, particularly when one compares the two 'extremes' on the 'Reform Progress Index': Uzbekistan and Kyrgyzstan. The complex relationship between the initial conditions and country-specific idiosyncrasies, the structural dependencies and the macro-development may provoke different (and often unintended) results. Institutional changes that take into account the observed grassroots developments in the agricultural sector are most likely crucial to the transition process, although emphasis seems to remain on the degree and pace of privatization and market liberalization.

Notes

1. The WB index is a weighted average of performance in economic liberalization (domestic market liberalization, external market opening, and entry of new firms). Although the authors of the World Development Report (see World Bank, 1996) admit that such an index is 'judgmental and necessarily approximate', it is used all the way through the report, and divides the 28 transition countries, including Vietnam and China, into four groups. Not surprisingly, of the five CAS, only Kyrgyzstan is in group 3, while the other four are in the tail group 4 of the 'reform tip-parade'.

2. Interestingly enough, Uzbekistan would score high on the list of those transitional economies that have contained their contraction to a minimum. However, its reform profile does not coincide with the conclusion that 'stronger, more sustained liberalization spells a smaller output decline – and a stronger recovery' (World Bank, 1996: 28). In this case it seems that the country has been conveniently eliminated from the graph that relates the 'rate of liberalization' with output contraction (*ibid*: 26).

3. Rumer (1989) and Martin (1994).

4. In the early 1990s only 12 per cent of Uzbekistan cotton and 60 per cent of silk cocoons were processed in the country (EIU, 1993, p.101).

5. Valuation of current output at world market prices gives an obvious advantage to those who produce high-valued raw materials and energy resources, which before had administrative (and mostly extremely low) prices. Previous StatKom SNG and World Bank data seem to indicate that in 1991 the agricultural sector contribution was much higher than currently (which probably represents the dominantly rural side of Central Asia). The variations in sectoral shares in GDP and NMP in recent years relate particularly to inconsistencies in methodology, abrupt changes in exchange rates, and severe problems of valuation, which unfortunately are left undiscussed in most CIS or Western sources.

6. In some cases it might also be the absence of private property rights that forms an obstacle for providing credit, as no collateral can be given.

7. In Uzbekistan the government has signed an agreement with the World Bank to undertake a comprehensive 'Farm Restructuring Study' that might be the first step towards de-collectivization and the formation of private farms.

8. World Bank (1996). Nevertheless, the current reform movement (including some political democratization as well) in Uzbekistan is slowly being seen as more coherent and acceptable to the IFIs.

9. This aspect was raised by several participants from the CARs, during a World Bank/EDI Seminar in Washington, January 1996, dedicated to Rural Project and Investment Analysis. The particular session was led by Roy Southworth, team leader of a number of CAS-agricultural sector reviews produced by the World Bank.

10. Parts of this section draw on a previous publication, Spoor (1995a), in *The Journal of Peasant Studies*.
11. Interview with the Chairman of the Agricultural Economics Institute, (now the Institute of Market Reforms), Tashkent, October 1993.
12. In June 1990 ethnic tensions erupted in the city of Osh, with hundreds of people killed in only a couple of weeks. Only sending in a Russian regiment somewhat defused the tension (Field notes, Osh, October 1993). The Osh *oblast* in the southwest of Kyrgyzstan forms part of the Fergana Valley and is inhabited by many ethnic Uzbeks.
13. Until mid-1994 land privatization was jointly governed by the State Property Fund and the Ministry of Agriculture.
14. 'The State order system regulated economic relations between collectives and state farms and the government. The government determines the output (*planned* output) of farms and the proportion of output (*quota* output) that they must sell to government enterprises'. (World Bank, 1993c: 118).
15. It is somewhat difficult in this case to equalize 'border prices' with world market prices. First, the quality of Uzbekistan cotton is relatively low. Second, most is still sold in the captive markets of the FSU, often under barter agreements.
16. The subsidies for agriculture are estimated at 0.7 billion dollars, the implicit taxation of agriculture at 1.6 billion dollars (World Bank, 1994b: 50). This calculation was made by valuing input and output at border prices.
17. Field notes from a visit to a milk factory in Chui valley, December 1994. It was striking that the factory was well equipped, with experienced staff and producing a good quality cheese. As it was still part of the collective farm structure, no independent decisions could be made and no working capital or means of transport were available. The grim prospect for this factory seemed to be closure, with serious capital destruction. Strikingly enough, cheese is now being imported from some EEC countries (partly because of the export restitution payments under the Common Agricultural Policy), although the population prefers local cheeses.
18. Remark made by Roy Southworth of the World Bank in the above mentioned World Bank/EDI Seminar in Washington, January 1996.

7 Transition, land reform and adjustment in Bulgaria

DIANA KOPEVA

Introduction

THE TRANSITION TO market economy is a complex process. In this chapter this is shown by focusing on agrarian reform in Bulgaria, in particular on the following aspects of it: the restitution of land property rights; the dismantling of the former collectives (TKZS); the privatization of non-land assets (buildings, machinery, equipment, animals); the elimination of monopolistic structures that existed downstream and upstream in the agricultural sector; and the development of a private sector in agriculture. Hence, in our discussion of agrarian reform in Bulgaria attention will be given to two major processes carried out in parallel: land reform and structural economic reform or adjustment. As a result of the land reform programme in Bulgaria the previous bi-modal agrarian structure, with large collective enterprises and small household plots, has been disarticulated. It is being replaced by a new agrarian structure, in which new farm types emerge. However, this is still influenced by the past, and the pre-reform socialist agrarian structure should therefore not be ignored. The main objective of this chapter is to identify the main factors that have influenced the transition period, and to analyse the outcome of land reform and farm restructuring. The second section of the chapter briefly presents the macroeconomic framework and analyses the factors that influence agriculture during the transition process. The third section discusses the land reform and the outcome of the land restitution process, followed by an overview of the structural changes in Bulgarian agriculture during the transition, and their legal foundation. The next section presents the progress of privatization and the emergence of private farms in the first half of the 1990s, while the last section contains a summary of the major findings and some preliminary conclusions.

Bulgarian agriculture and transition period

The process of successfully transforming Bulgarian agriculture from a centrally planned to a market oriented economy demands economic adjustments in the following directions: (i) macroeconomic stabilization aimed at creating a favourable environment for long-term investments; (ii) structural reform which stimulates the emergence and development of economic agents characteristic of market economies; (iii) the implementation of food and agricultural policies to underpin the process of adjustment and to minimize the social costs of transformation.

Land restitution and the dismantling of collective farms have been the key elements of structural reform in Bulgaria. They have focused on: (a) the restoration of property rights over land to former owners; (b) dismantling collective farms and the distribution of their assets; (c) the creation of conditions favourable to the spontaneous development of new farm types, such as owner-occupied farms and new forms of co-operatives, each at scales of operation which reflect the prevailing technological and economic conditions. In this regard, an indispensable component is the establishment and creation of conditions for an efficient functioning of a land market.

Nearly half a decade after the start of agrarian reform Bulgarian agriculture is still at the crossroads. In the context of the transition from a state owned and centrally planned agriculture to a privately owned market system the strategic aims should be focused on the degree of private ownership of land and capital and the level of liberalization or openness of the agriculture sector to international markets. However, the current status of Bulgarian agriculture does not meet the desired level of marketization and privatization. Agriculture still generated 12 per cent of GDP in 1995, and if the food industry is included its share of GDP adds up to 20 per cent. It emphasizes its importance, knowing also that 22 per cent of Bulgarian exports comes from these two sectors, while they employ 25 per cent of EAP. However, current data for 1990–4 on agriculture and the food industry show a severe crisis. Total agricultural production decreased by 32.5 per cent, with the most serious drop in the livestock sector, where the contraction in heads of different animal categories vary from 57 per cent (cattle) to 38 per cent (poultry). In the same period cereal production decreased by 28 per cent, beans by 39 per cent and industrial crops by 44 per cent. The irrigation systems are almost in ruins and an estimated three-quarters of all agricultural machinery is fully depreciated, and in need of urgent replacement. The food industry is also in a critical financial and technical situation, and confronted with inefficient or lack of markets.

While some recovery was noticeable in 1995, most of the reforms such as land restitution and privatization, macroeconomic structural adjustment, and development of agricultural credit, price and trade policies for the agricultural sector, showed signs of stagnation. This section will identify various factors that play a role in this phenomenon. Markets in Bulgaria are not well integrated, and economic performance of productive units often depends on the available infrastructure. Production co-operatives and the newly emerging farm sectors such as part-time farmers, private entrepreneurs and family farms have difficulty in surviving in a highly hostile market environment. A land market hardly exists, while only rental markets for land have emerged. Market information is poor, fragmentary and incomplete, while rural communities remain rather isolated. Variable production inputs are erratically available, their quality varies, and supply is mostly through informal market channels. In most cases agricultural labour has low levels of education and technology. Machines and equipment operate at low levels of efficiency, lacking spare parts and replacement investment. Finally, there is a slow process of privatization of the food industry.

In thinking about whether a speedy transition to a market economy is possible, it is necessary to analyse which are the major impediments to such a process. This is also important in the process of comparing the economic adjustment in various CEE countries and finding out whether there are substantial differences in the achievement of the transformation process between individual countries. The factors that have such a negative influence can be classified as general and specific, the former referring to the unique process of transformation of the entire economic and social system, the latter to reform policies. The socialist economy in Bulgaria was characterized by state ownership, state decision-making and central resource allocation. Self-sufficiency in agricultural production and the generation of agricultural surpluses were achieved by centrally determined prices, indicative planning targets, physical production quotas and collective management. Replacing the centrally planned with a market system, diametrically opposed, is difficult and time consuming. The market economy needs an entirely different legal framework, role of the state and other public institutions; democracy as a 'social construction'; market infrastructure, etc. The Bulgarian experience shows that half a decade is an insufficient period for creating all the prerequisites for the installation of a market economy. Furthermore, another general impediment to a speedy transformation of agriculture is rooted in the fact that overall transition began when the centrally planned economic system was in deep crisis. During the 1980s economic growth in Bulgaria had slowed down markedly. Structural imbalances appeared in the Bulgarian economy and the pace of technological change and productivity declined. The emerging macroeconomic disequilibrium at the end of the socialist period needed urgent structural measures. Initial stabilization was pursued by introducing a restrictive monetary policy supported by high nominal interest rates, and complemented by a market-based exchange rate and fiscal restraints that, however, created an unfavourable climate for agricultural development.

Dismantling the state collectives and the emergence of new farming units meant different decision-making processes and changes in crop mixes and production frontiers. However, to ensure that the process is efficient, it needs the availability of credit and the functioning of other resource markets.[1] The restrictive macroeconomic policy created severe rationing of capital (while finance for activities such as trade and industry still prevailed). This created a shortage of capital for agricultural production and difficulties for the emerging newly established (or already existing) private production units. Insufficient access to credit creates sub-optimal economic decisions at the microeconomic level and hampers the creation of economically viable farming units. The macroeconomic policies, aimed at creating a long-term efficient allocation of resources, limited current economic activity in agriculture.

The specific impediments to the development of agricultural production refer to the programme of land restitution, structural adjustment at sectoral level, foreign investments, the extent of market liberalization and finally, price, finance and trade policy. While some of these elements will be discussed later in this chapter, they can be partly dealt with here. With regards to price and trade policy, a number of issues are quite interesting to note. First, there was taxation on farmers during the whole period 1990–4,[2] but although the level of taxation declined during the period it was still significant (Ivanova, 1993). Based on preliminary data, taxation of cereal producers in 1995 increased. It has to be mentioned that this increase in taxation was mainly due to the increase in the world price of wheat, which made the price gap between domestic and world prices wider, and was not so much due to changes in agricultural policy. Implicit taxation through the price system continues, as government intervention and price distortions cause income transfers from producers to intermediate and final consumers. Processors of agricultural products[3] were taxed relatively less than farmers. Second, there was income transfer to traders during the whole period, in particular towards the end. Although there was some taxation on traders dealing with milk and milk products, it is estimated that income redistribution influenced by agricultural and food prices was in favour of final consumers during the first three years of the period, and in favour of traders in the last two years. This indicates that price and trade policies had a substantially negative impact on producers and insufficient positive impact on final consumers (as price differentials were often absorbed by informal trading channels).

Apart from the incomes of agents in the agro-food chain, agricultural policy has an impact on the efficiency of agricultural production, budgetary revenues and foreign exchange earnings. Analysis of the effects of agricultural policy, while focusing on some major agricultural products (like cereals and meat), shows that dead-weight losses in production and consumption were substantial at the beginning of the period but declined during the first half of the 1990s (Ivanova, 1995). The only exception to this tendency was wheat, for which there was some increase in net economic losses in 1994 and 1995 (Mishev, 1995). This is not surprising, taking into account the social importance of the price of bread. If farmers' income losses are about three times higher than consumers' income support the question arises whether the implemented policy is the most appropriate one. As may be expected, the impact of the policy on the budget was relatively positive, but during the last two years of the period it was less obvious. The main reasons for this were: the ban on the export of cereals and substantially higher export taxes on live cattle which prevented their export, thus diminishing budget revenue. Furthermore, the negative impact of the policy on foreign exchange earnings was also substantial.

Substantial problems also exist with financing agricultural activities. There is an absolute shortage of finance, as during the economic crisis, with macro-economic imbalances, scarce capital resources are concentrated in those sectors with a speedy turnover. Furthermore, the banking system lacks the tradition, experience, managerial capacity and infrastructure that exist in market economies. In the agricultural sector, these difficulties are reinforced by some additional factors: (i) uncertainties regarding property rights and serious difficulties in land registration and issuing titles, which means that collateral effectively cannot be used for agricultural credit, while the absence of land markets makes the banks reluctant to consider land as collateral; (ii) the structure of the banking sector and its slow rate of change makes the financial system inadequate to deal with thousands of emerging small farms. Due to these factors farmers find it difficult to finance not only investment but also working capital. Nevertheless, improvements in technical efficiency and product quality do require new investment, and are consequently difficult to finance in this fragile market situation. Furthermore, the bad debts of the agro-industry were more than 17 billion Leva (260 million US$), in May, 1995 with the result that processing enterprises delay payments to farmers. A shortage of working capital does not allow them to buy agricultural products when they are cheaper (after harvest), creating an environment for the emergence of many middlemen who buy cheaply from farmers and sell at high prices to the food processing industries. Finally, foreign investments since the beginning of reform have been very limited, as of the total inflow of foreign capital in Bulgaria, in terms of direct investments up to the end of 1994 – which amounted to 470 Million US$ – only 71 000 US$ were for agriculture. Foreign investment would mean new technology and the penetration of new markets. Deferring these investments delays the transformation to a market economy in the agricultural sector. In summary, all these factors, and the ones related to privatization and land reform which will be discussed in the following sections, have a strong impact, both indirect and direct, on the future development of Bulgarian agriculture. They also influence the choice of future and current private farmers to participate in one or another structure, to join the new co-operatives or farmers' associations, or to develop commercial farms (with privately owned or leased land).

Land reform: the Bulgarian case

The legal and institutional framework for land reform
The legal basis for the current process of land reform is the Law of Ownership and Use of Agricultural Land (LOUAL) of 1991 (amended in 1992, 1994 and 1995) and Regulations concerning the Law's application. The institutions primarily responsible for initiating the process of land restitution throughout

Bulgaria are the 301 Municipal Land Commissions (MLCs). These are responsible for over 4800 so-called Territories Belonging to Settlements (TBSs) occupying nearly 5.6 million hectares of land. The main objective of the reform was to restore private property rights to owners or their heirs, of land in their possession before the creation of the collectives and in accordance with the land area determined by the Law of Land Ownership of 1946 (Kopeva *et al.*, 1994). Under the new land legislation, land can be restored in two ways:

(a) By restoration within existing or restorable old boundaries.[4]   Old boundaries which have been preserved on the terrain are defined with respect to topographic features including roads, fences, areas of trees or shrubs, rivers or reservoirs, ravines, and dry river beds, if their location had been unchanged after inclusion in the collective farm. Also, restorable boundaries of former estates are those which can be determined from the cadastral maps of settlements, and the reallocation or surveyor plans elaborated prior to the establishment of the collective farm. The size and category of the estate, its location, borders, neighbours, and any reductions in the area of the property must be specified.

(b) Through land reallocation plans.[5]   Where it is impossible to provide evidence of boundaries but it can be established that former owners or their families are entitled to have land restituted, this is to be achieved by land reallocation. Importantly, owners should receive consolidated land to avoid problems of farm fragmentation, and if possible, allotted land of equivalent quality and quantity in areas where most of the original estate was located. Moreover, restituted land holdings needs to be suitable for cultivation and have access to transportation. Small estates should preferably be located close to settlements.

It is important to note that land restitution under reallocation schemes is implemented in two stages. First, ownership rights are restored in abstract terms. In other words, the right to own land of a specified area and category is formally recognized before any specific location is designated. Second, following a plan of land reallocation, actual restitution takes place. However, when people want to cultivate their land immediately, land can be allocated for temporary use while they are waiting for all the procedures to be completed.[6] Procedures for the reinstatement of property rights are lengthy, and the stages involved which incorporate the aforementioned provisions are as follows:

1) Former landowners or their heirs present a petition to the relevant MLC for restitution of their property.

2) Within one month of receipt of the petition, the MLC has to issue a decision on the reinstatement of ownership rights. This is either:

  a) land can be restituted in real boundaries and so the issued decision is final. Owners recover their actual land property which they can farm immediately, or

  b) land cannot be restituted in real boundaries, but a right to ownership is acknowledged. Owners must await the final decision regarding the specific area of land which is allocated to them until after the plan of land re-allocation is enacted. If they want to use land temporarily, they must submit a separate petition.[7]

 3) A sketch of each plot must be prepared by the MLC with reference to existing or new cadastral maps. The act of receiving the sketch from the MLC means that owners are considered to be 'granted possession'.

 4) A notary issues a legal deed of ownership based on the MLC's final decision and a sketch of the plot.

According to the law, therefore, a distinction is drawn between economic (1 and 2 above) and juridical (3 and 4 above) restoration of property rights. The deadline for the submission of claims was set at 4 August 1992. Applicants had to provide both a description of the estate concerned and evidence of ownership. Proof of ownership could be given by act of notary, notarial deed, deeds of partition, TKZS protocols, land registers, applications for TKZS membership, rent ledgers, or any other written evidence. If written evidence was not available, the applicant could attach to his petition a signed statement, certified by a public notary, which declared the applicant's ownership. In cases of misinformation, the signatory was liable for prosecution under the Criminal Code.

The current status of land reform

Some 1.7 million applications were made, almost all from individuals resident in Bulgaria, with only about 0.4 per cent from so-called legal entities, such as churches, monasteries, agricultural schools, municipalities, and the state. Of nearly 5.7 million hectares available for restitution, 91 per cent was claimed by individuals, 1.4 per cent by the state, 5.1 per cent by municipalities which held communal land before collectivization, and 2.4 per cent by other legal entities. By April 1996 2.4 million decisions had been issued. The land area subject to restitution in real boundaries [Article 18g(1)] accounted for only 17 per cent of the total area of all claimed land. In all, 758 428 final decisions for restitution of land ownership within real boundaries were issued, accounting for some 0.97 million hectares. By contrast, nearly 1.6 million decisions were enacted for restitution under land reallocation, accounting for 79 per cent of all claimed land. These include nearly 0.7 million decisions under Article 18i, for temporary use, which covered almost 1.95 million hectares, or 34 per cent of all land subject to reallocation. In addition, some 551 000 decisions were issued under Article 27 whereby plans for land reallocation were completed and their provisions implemented, covering 1.8

million hectares. An estimated 49 per cent of all claimed land had been returned to recognized owners or their heirs by April 1996. Of the total, it is known that at least half was being farmed. It must be remembered, however, that restitution is formally complete only when the final legal title to land is issued. A mere 70 000 notarial deeds had been issued relating to only 224 000 hectares.[8] Without deeds, there is no legal foundation for trade in land. Nevertheless, the current signs are that land reform in Bulgaria will be a protracted process, for the following reasons.

Fundamental problems in the land reform
The new land legislation and its implementation by the MLCs was a highly complex matter. However, the LOUAL and its Regulations were insufficiently complemented by the necessary private property and pension legislation. This created difficulties for its implementation and uncertainty for land owners. Furthermore, the complex administrative procedures for reinstatement of property rights gave ample opportunity for many disputes to be solved by court verdicts. Finally, 0.32 million more hectares of land were claimed than physically existed. These problems are closely linked to the legal and financial aspects of the reform. The low wages of the MLC staff cannot be neglected, since they result in a lack of qualified staff at the executive level, which slows down the restitution process. Finally, the amount and quality of the equipment are both insufficient and need up-grading. The land reform administration is financed by a non-budget fund, which has been relatively constant for the four-year period 1992–5, not taking into account inflation. While the budget went down slightly from 819.2 million Leva in 1992 to 725.0 million Leva in 1995, in real terms the annual budget in 1995 had shrunk to a value of only 22 per cent of the 1992 figure, insufficient even to cover the cost of the reform. There are problems with contractors who carry out the land reallocation. As the contract price is not indexed to inflation, the companies cannot cover their expenses, leading to work disruptions in some places. The co-ordination between the MLCs and the contractors is very often unsatisfactory. Another reason for delaying the reform is that some of the contracting survey companies have won too many tenders for their capacities. Being unable to reinstate the owners of several TBSs simultaneously, they do it piecemeal.

Psychology plays an important role in property identification. People want their land exactly where it has been and of the size they can prove. The law and the implementation rules allow for land consolidation. However, owners often do not agree with proposed land consolidation, specially in the mountainous and semi-mountainous regions, where land categories and fertility vary significantly. Furthermore, fear and indifference coexist with the desire of the owners to receive their land back. All these problems, combined with a liberal heritage law in Bulgaria, lead to the expectation that after the completion of land reform there would be over 5 million land owners with an average landholding of 0.8–0.9 hectares. The prognoses are that over 20 million parcels of 0.2–0.25 hectares on average will be established. The result will be diseconomies of scale and difficulties in the development of new structures in agriculture. There is therefore an urgent need to include in the current legislation the following elements that can speed up the land reform: to put on an equal footing land owners and persons who have become land owners after buying land, exchange of land, or in possession of land under the restitution law; to provide compensation to land owners who were allocated or restituted land polluted with heavy metals and chemicals and eroded soils; the obligation of MLCs to pay compensation and to provide land to landless farmers from municipality and state domains should be determined and put on the juridical basis; finally, and not the least important, making work conditions more attractive for those with high qualification and skills.

Towards a new agrarian structure

Since the beginning of the reform it was assumed that the pre-reform bi-modal agrarian structure, comprising a small number of large state farms or collectives, and many small household plots, would fundamentally change. It is being replaced by a pattern of multiple structures. A key part of transition in agriculture is that the farms and agri-businesses must switch from being state-managed enterprises to privately-managed businesses, in which all land and other assets are privately owned, a complex process which has political as well as economic elements. The agrarian transition in Bulgaria has already been going on for four years and will doubtless take many more. To assess the progress in structural transformation, a critical step is accurately to characterize and describe the farm structures that exist at any point in time.[9] This can be done, following Buckwell (1994), by taking into account the legal basis of the business, land ownership, economies of scale, labour supply and management structure. Applying these characteristics, five broad groups can be defined: (i) state farms; (ii) organizations under liquidation; (iii) new co-operatives; (iv) partnerships and farming companies; and (v) individual farms and household plots. Assessing the data of July 1995 (Table 7.1) it can be observed that the former bi-modal structure has indeed changed fundamentally, and become more complex. State farms still accounted for an estimated 7 per cent of total land (0.32 million hectares), but the biggest single category, with nearly 2.4 million hectares, i.e. 52 per cent of total arable land, was operated by private farms, coming primarily from the land restitution programme ('organizations under liquidation', in particular the TKZS). Hence, part of this land is still recorded as unrestored ownership. Also shown as unrestored property is part of the land occupied by the new co-operatives. This amounts to 1.9 million hectares (41 per cent of the total). The most significant observation is that land indeed moved from public to private ownership (or at least management). However, the process has not yet gone very far.

Table 7.1: Farm-types in Bulgaria, 1993–5

	Number			Arable land (Hectares)			Share of Arable Land (%)		
	1993	1994	1995	1993	1994	1995	1993	1994	1995
State Farms	1196	1009	980	34 564	328 085	304 651	7	7	6
Org. Under Liquid.	114	142	122	1 980 000	849 057	0	43	17	0
Farm Enterprises	1166	500	0	54 461	39 946	34 590	1	1	1
Co-operatives	1524	1873	2344	1 072 211	1 411 299	1 910 972	23	30	41
Private Farms	1 897 454	2 010 961	1 777 122	1 234 622	2 058 545	2 462 250	26	45	52
Total				4 375 858	4 686 932	4 712 463	100	100	100

Source: National Statistical Institute (1996).

Development of private farms

Private organizations are gradually becoming dominant in Bulgarian agriculture. According to data from the National Statistical Institute there were nearly 1.8 million private farms that cultivated 52 per cent of arable land in 1995 (Table 7.1). Some of them used land given for personal use or leased from collectives that are not yet liquidated. The overall average size of private farms was in 1995 around 1.39 ha, following an increasing trend. However, this overall average hid the strong tendency of land concentration that we can observe (Table 7.2). While during the four-year period 1992–5 the number of private farms decreased by 9 per cent, the amount of privately farmed land increased twofold. There was a decrease in the number of small farms (of up to 5 hectares) and on the other hand a dramatic expansion of land farmed in units larger than 10ha, with an average landholding rising from 35.5 ha in 1993 to 252.7 ha in 1995 (see Table 7.2)! In order to classify the private farm sector a number of factors have to be taken into account: their market orientation (producing for self-sufficiency, for the market or for both); the share of agricultural income in the total household income; and the relative share of household owner and external factors of production and inputs. Such a classification ranges from self-sufficiency peasant farms to fully commercial farms.

1) Most significant is the large share of farms less than 0.5 ha (72 per cent), as the average size of their land (between 0 and 1 hectare in Table 7.2) is not more than 0.22 hectare. Because of the advanced age of many of their owners and continued rural-urban migration, their significance and number can be expected to fall gradually. However, the expectation is that there will not be a significant change in the short run in the number and average size of these farms.

2) In total 27 per cent of private farms (from 0.5 to 5 ha) farmed 46 per cent of private land. Most likely, after the completion of the land reform these farms will be widespread, as they guarantee part-time employment and additional income for the land owners. Adaptation to market conditions will take place gradually with specialization and production for the market.

3) Less than 1 per cent of the newly established farms are in the group of 5-10 ha, but they occupy 12% of the privately farmed land.

4) As a sign of rapid land concentration, 41 per cent of private land is farmed by 0.2 per cent of the farms which are over 10 hectares, but with a much higher overall average. They predominantly function on leased land or land that is allocated for temporary use and which is to be consolidated, specializing in grain or industrial crop production.

In general, the activities of the second group concentrate on the production of labour-intensive crops and animal husbandry, although the latter has low productivity and is largely non-competitive. Illustrating this thesis are data for the average number of livestock per private farm. Of an estimated 221 100

Table 7.2: The development of the private farm sector (1992–5)

Farms by landholding	Arable land (hectares)				Number of farms				Average size (hectares)			
(Ha)	1992	1993	1994	1995	1992	1993	1994	1995	1992	1993	1994	1995
0 to 1	NA	400 003	652 147	631 139	1 783 808	1 537 462	1 555 090	1 535 111	NA	0.22	0.42	0.41
1 to 2	NA	328 934	371 567	312 184	128 874	248 772	342 340	156 092	NA	1.32	1.08	2.00
2 to 5	NA	264 097	407 180	342 145	42 520	91 980	93 568	68 429	NA	2.87	4.35	5.00
5 to 10	NA	98 007	160 361	168 421	8 608	15 195	15 762	13 483	NA	6.44	10.17	12.49
over 10	NA	143 581	467 290	1 008 362	580	4 045	4 201	4 007	NA	35.50	111.20	252.70
Total	1 438 000	1 234 622	2 058 545	2 462 251	1 964 390	1 897 454	2 010 961	1 777 122	0.73	0.65	1.02	1.39

Source: National Statistical Institute (1996).

farms that breed cows, 80.9 per cent have only one cow, and 14.8 per cent of the farms have two. Similarly in pig breeding, 64 per cent of farms breed only one pig; 22.3 per cent two, and 9 per cent from three to five pigs. In sheep breeding, on 40 per cent of the farms there are no more than three to five sheep, with six to ten sheep on 27 per cent of the farms. One of the main problems for farmers, in particular small and medium ones, is the inefficiency (or absence) of marketing, servicing and credit institutions such as co-operatives. The new farmers used the services of newly established production co-operatives, while part of agricultural production is purchased by existing regional consumer co-operatives (RPK). But in both cases the relations are not put on an equal footing and are not very stable.

The reasons for this situation are: first, these co-operatives are often local monopolies, and second, private farmers can use the services of the co-operatives only if there is machinery and equipment available. As they tend to consider their land area and family labour as natural restrictions on their activities, these farmers will mainly be members of emerging co-operatives that are active in input purchasing, including credit, machinery use and output marketing. In spite of the desire and capacities of farmers to organize viable and competitive farms, the economic crisis, an undeveloped land market, high interest rates, and the monopolies of some processing and purchasing companies, impede the fulfilment of such plans. Land restitution leads to non-utilization of some parcels (especially in mountainous and semi-mountainous regions), and also to land fragmentation. Even with areas of arable land that allow the full use of machinery, it is often necessary to move it several times a day from one parcel to another. Finally, only 13 per cent of land owners intend to lease their land out, and those who are inclined to sell cover scarcely 1 to 2 per cent. The lack of government policies to put an end to land fragmentation is practically stifling the development of the relatively larger, and economically more viable, farms. The current practice of leasing land every year discourages the right rotation of crops and causes improper land use. On the other hand, the lack of proper legislation regarding the relation between lessors and tenants is one of the reasons for the problems of default in lease payments.

Private farms will 'play the first violin' in the near future. However, it is very difficult to make any prognosis for the future of Bulgarian agriculture under such uncertainty and when the processes of land restitution and structural changes are still going on. Nevertheless, it is to be expected that after the land reform is complete the most significant share of farms will be that of the *minifundia* (up to 1 hectare). This group includes the traditional household plots, whose number remains relatively constant. The farmers in this group produce for self-sufficiency and supply part-time labour. However, they will not play an important role in the production of surpluses for market.

A second group includes farms from 1 to 5 hectares. These are marginal farms, in the sense that part will move to the first group after decreasing their size. The rest will switch to the next group by increasing in size through buying and/or leasing of land. These farms cannot guarantee full-time employment for the members of the household and during the first years of their existence they will use the services of local production co-operatives. Gradually they will be able to establish associations.

More important for commercial production will be farms from the group of above 10 hectares. It is estimated that the group between 10 and 50 hectares will number between 10 000 and 12 000, producing mainly intensive crops (vegetables, forage) and breeding livestock. The commercial farms of 50 to 100 hectares are estimated to reach a number of between 5000 and 10 000 farms. They will cultivate family-owned land and/or enter into informal associations of farmers (three to five maximum) for farming land. In the near future they will become the main founding members of marketing, servicing or credit co-operatives. The final group of commercial farms includes those roughly between 100 and 1000 hectares. In this group there are co-operatives as well as private landowners and big tenant farmers. These farms, together with the former group will form the core of Bulgarian commercial farming.

Conclusions

The programme of land restitution implemented in Bulgaria is complex and protracted, but its outcome will cause a structural adjustment of Bulgarian agriculture. A variety of farm types have emerged, operating on the basis of different types of land ownership. The real situation on the ground is dynamic and changes are continuous, which makes it impossible to quantify them in any reliable manner. Amendments to the Land Law (more than 12) also affected the land reform and structural changes of the agricultural sector. While there are laws which define the farm types and the ownership of land, there is a gap between the letter of the law and its application in practice. There is a great deal of informal activity which crosses the legally defined boundaries, both in organizational forms and in land ownership and land transactions. It is interesting to note that in comparison with other Central and East-European countries (CEECs) Bulgaria differs significantly, in the level of private land ownership and in market structures. In recent years it has become conventional wisdom of many observers that in the former socialist CEECs agricultural sectors will evolve that are dominated by family farms following the model of Western Europe. Whether such expectations are realistic, or whether other systems of tenure will predominate remains to be seen, but there are important reasons for attempting to assess the possible outcomes now. The practice shows that the main structures in most CEECs are co-operatives (new type) and reregistered co-operatives into limited liability companies. Such has been the extent of disruption to agricultural production in Bulgaria since economic transformation began, that it is vital that misguided or misinformed farm policies are not allowed to worsen an already serious situation. Undoubtedly, the chances of avoiding mistakes can be increased by careful consideration of the key variables that are expected to influence the direction of agricultural adjustment.

Notes

1. The process of redistribution and restitution of fixed assets, machines and animals to the members of collectives was accomplished with large losses: some of the machinery, equipment and buildings were sold through auctions to people outside the agricultural sector; assets like barns and other infrastructure could not be sub-divided. Because many machines and equipment are fully depreciated, it means that unless there are investments amounting to 125 billion leva (at June 1995 prices) before the end of the century we should expect a collapse of machine and tractor fleets and a severe crisis in agricultural production.
2. The calculations of PSEs have been made on the basis of OECD producer subsidy equivalent (PSE) methodology, as some specific peculiarities in Bulgaria are taken into account (there were no input subsidies during the period analysed but the difference between domestic and parity prices of inputs is considered as input sub-sidies). PSEs were calculated for wheat, barley, maize, sunflower, tobacco, veal, pork, chicken and milk.
3. Processed products analysed are: flour, bread, veal, pork, chicken, milk, yoghurt, white and yellow cheese.
4. Article 18g (1) of the Regulations of LOUAL.
5. Article 18g (2) of the Regulations of LOUAL.
6. Article 18i of the Regulations of LOUAL.
7. Article 18i of the Regulations of LOUAL.
8. National Statistical Institute, reference on the pace of land reform, 26 March, 1996.
9. The process of defining farm structures was not based on an examination of data on the nature of each individual farm, as such data do not exist. The analysis was informal and was based on available published, mostly national, aggregate data, which at best are good estimates (particularly as far as numbers are concerned). Under the conditions of rapid change and lack of resources for comprehensive farm surveys it is unlikely that these data are completely accurate.

8 Romanian agriculture in transition

MIHAIL DUMITRU

Introduction

SINCE THE 1990s Romania has embarked on the path toward a market-oriented economy. While during 45 years of post-World War II socialism the large state and collective farms have proved their inefficiency, a new agrarian reform is being undertaken, continuing as well as juxtaposing the chain of land reforms that occurred before and during the communist period in Romania. However, the more the current agrarian reform advances, the less evident becomes the new agricultural model that is pursued, due to an important number of constraints still blocking the development of the agricultural sector. One of these obstacles is the absence of an efficient land market in Romania. Agrarian reform has aimed primarily to restore private ownership rather than to improve the performance of the sector. As a direct result of this privatization effort, land ownership shifted from agricultural operators to non-agricultural owners (43 per cent of the new landowners are city dwellers), providing new complexities in the search for an agrarian development model in this transition to a market-oriented economy. This chapter will analyse Romanian agrarian reform and show that although the privatization effort has fundamentally changed the agrarian structure, this was not complemented by other reforms such as in agrarian institutions, financial markets, land markets and input and output marketing, which has made the position of the newly established – mostly very small and highly fragmented – family farms extremely difficult.

In search of a new agricultural model in Romania

Due to the collapse of the planned economies in Eastern Europe at the end of the 1980s, the search for a new agricultural model has been on the agenda of transition already for a number of years. With the return to a market-oriented economy in this part of the continent not only did a debate emerge on the characteristics of this new model but also the path to follow in order to get there. In this debate the historical evolution of the 'agrarian pattern' in Central Europe should be taken into account (Sivignon, 1992). According to this author, by agricultural pattern (or model) is meant the organizational system which is based on a specific agrarian structure together with its labour force, capital and technology, that carries out the agricultural production process within a given economic system. Thus, the current de-collectivization movement that can be observed in all Central European countries should be seen in the historical context of the transition between two agrarian structures, dominated by large estates and by smallholders. In the eastern part of Europe, after World War I and again immediately after World War II, the dominance of large estates was questioned, and small peasant farms became more important. However, where an almost balanced situation of land ownership has been reached by the recurrent agrarian reforms, this trend was interrupted through the advent of forced collectivization during the early socialist period. This induced a new form of large agricultural farms based upon state and collective ownership of land and agricultural machinery, and the collective organization of wage labour. Peasant farmers lost their personal relationship with the land that they cultivated, becoming wage workers in the chain of agricultural activities.

In Western Europe the agrarian structure which is now operating proceeds from two agricultural patterns, the Anglo-Saxon one and the Danish one (Sivignon, 1992). The latter, unlike the former, has spread widely over all of North-Western Europe. Today the Danish pattern is the foundation of rapid agricultural development, stimulated by the common agricultural policy of the European Union, with the pivotal role of the modernizing family farm, while the Anglo-Saxon pattern is still based on the large owner-operated or rented farms. Most of the Central and Eastern European (CEE) countries are still searching for the agrarian model and path they wish to follow in an agrarian transition, while having to take into account the requirements of compatibility with Western European agrarian structures and policies, as they desire to join the European Union. The key problem is obviously not only agricultural but primarily rural. It is well known that most of the CEE countries have a high ratio of rural dwellers in their population; in Romania this is more than 45 per cent. Constructing the most productive and efficient pattern would mean ensuring an increase of agricultural labour productivity by the transfer of labour from agriculture to other rural sectors that are more productive, so that a general gain in productivity in the whole economy would occur, albeit without moving this population from the rural area. Thus, the agricultural restructuring must be closely accompanied by the expansion of non-farm rural employment.

The choice of the agricultural pattern must also be in accordance with its economic efficiency. This results from the most efficient size and forms of enterprises, related to the optimal combination of factor use. According to the theory of the firm, the first economic ground for the increase in farm size is to a large extent the economies of scale argument. Factor allocation and average cost structure will change with the size of enterprises. The farm enterprises strive to combine production factors such as as land, labour and capital in such proportions that they will yield the best output at minimal cost. Economies of scale in agriculture have important implications for the number of farm units and the degree of concentration of production, but overestimation of its role can provide a shift towards the other extreme, such as happened during the communist era. In Romania, as in all CEE countries that followed the Soviet pattern, large farms have had at their base the assumption of increasing returns to scale. They considered that the more the size increases, the more the average cost of production decreases. However, many of the socialist large farms were in the curve's part of decreasing return to scale, well beyond the point of lowest-cost production. In some cases, the size of the farm had reached a point where the transport cost of inputs and outputs increased total costs enormously. However, the possible technical advantages of large size and specialization should not be the only consideration.

First, there is ample proof of an unresolved incentive problem for farm workers, who preferred to spend more time on their private household plot than on collective or state land. The existence of the 'free rider' as an outcome of the rather egalitarian wage-system was one of the endemic causes of low productivity on the state and collective farms in Romania (as well as elsewhere in the socialist countries). Second, one vital factor remained fixed, i.e. the overall management capacity of the farm. Even if the supervision of different activities within the farm was well regulated, technical and managerial inefficiencies were liable to rise. Reasons commonly advanced for increasing inefficiency are managerial limitations, and not least, bureaucratic red tape and political interference. As farm size increases, the manager encounters increasing difficulty in maintaining control over his organization; communication and co-ordination become more difficult and mistakes are both more frequent and more costly; as a result the total cost rises. Obviously, it can be questioned whether the collectivization decision in the CEE countries was actually based on the economies of scale argument, as motivations were complex, being influenced both by the assumed superiority of large-scale farms as well as by political and social objectives.

The restoration of private land ownership in Romania is opening up the debate on problems of articulation between land ownership and land operation, between capital and labour, and the structural problems that have occurred in the field of stimuli and productivity (Maurel, 1993). The choice of a new agricultural model will therefore reveal a complex of economic, social and political motivations. In Romania, the family farms, as in all European rural societies, have strong social significance. The high value placed on personal freedom can be associated with the desires of peasants to be in control of their own destiny. Ownership of farmland satisfies farmers' beliefs favouring freedom and independence. The family farm has been considered the best way of keeping the economic rent of the land inside the farm, as well as providing the best articulation between the labour and capital. According to Coulomb (1991), the performance of the family farm should be considered in accordance with the capital accumulation process. However, in the present day reality of Romania, in spite of the strong social and economic advantages of the family farm, most are in a deplorable state. In most cases, the present agrarian reform has

induced the passage from the large collective farms to very small and even fragmented peasant holdings. The fragmentation of land among a large number of
peasants (and urban dwellers as well), constitutes a crucial problem for the
agricultural sector. Because of their small size they hinder the formation of capital as well as the increase in productivity, and maintain the low level of technology in the rural sector. In this situation the co-operative movement is
considered to be a fair alternative (taking into account the history of agricultural development in Western Europe). However, due to the bad memories of
the collectives during the *ancien régime*, today the Romanian peasant farmer
has great suspicion and generally rejects the co-operative movement. On the
government side, despite the declarations encouraging the development of a
modern co-operative movement, the present legislation (Law no. 36/1991) still
restricts the commercial activities of co-operatives.

Agriculture in the national economy and foreign trade

The share of agriculture of the Gross Domestic Product (GDP) increased
from 14.2 per cent in 1989 to 21.1 per cent in 1993, followed by a slight fall
in 1994 to 19.6 per cent (Table 8.1). In the early 1990s agricultural output
decreased in real terms, suggesting that the increase of the agricultural share
in GDP was primarily due to a sharp fall in the contribution of other sectors,
such as industry. The agricultural sector provides employment to more than
three million people, and it is interesting to note that the share of agriculture
in the total labour force (EAP) increased from 27.5 per cent in 1989 to 35.0
per cent in 1994. Romanian agriculture has served as a 'short-term shelter' in
the present economic crisis.

Among the CEE countries the evolution of Romanian agriculture has followed a particular path. During the 1980s the sector was under very tight control by the state. Some signs of decline in Romanian agriculture had already
appeared, particularly since 1985 when a crisis became evident. Yield and
productivity decreased for most products in both crop and animal production
before the reforms, and not only afterwards, as was the case in most of the
CEE countries. The crisis induced by the reforms has therefore added to the
recession that started in the early 1980s. The financial situation of farming
enterprises was already very precarious by the end of the decade and, as a
result, internal supplies of many agricultural products contracted. This bad
situation dominated Romanian agriculture on the eve of the reforms that followed the collapse of communism. Annual average food consumption per
capita in 1993 was about 91 per cent of the 1989 level for meat and meat
products, 86 per cent for milk and dairy products, and 86 per cent of cereals.
However, since 1993 a recovery can be noted (see Table 8.1), both in terms of
the real value of agricultural output and of exports. Until 1989 the agricultural
sector was an important source of foreign currency, reaching a peak in 1980
with a 12.8 per cent share of total exports (Table 8.1). After 1989 the agricul-

Table 8.1: Macro-indicators of the agricultural sector

	1980	*1989*	*1990*	*1991*	*1992*	*1993*	*1994*
Share of agriculture in total GDP (%)	12.6	14.2	18.1	18.9	19.0	21.1	19.6
Share of agriculture in total employment (%)	29.4	27.5	28.2	28.7	32.1	33.0	35.0
Volume of agricultural exports (millions US$)	1448	554	171	249	291	330	399
Volume of agricultural imports (millions US$)	1184	543	1372	770	988	966	664
Agricultural trade balance (millions US$)	264	11	(1201)	(521)	(697)	(636)	(265)
Share of agricultural exports in total (%)	12.8	5.0	3.7	5.8	6.7	6.8	6.5
Share of agricultural imports in total (%)	9.0	3.2	20.0	13.3	15.8	14.8	9.3
Indices of agricultural output (1980 = 100)	100	92	78	79	68	77	—

Source: ComStat (1994).

tural trade balance became negative, having been positive for a long period. In 1993 the 'coverage rate' of imports by exports was only 25 per cent. This was caused particularly by a fall in cereal output between 1990 and 1993 for which Romania had to import substantial quantities of grain.

With an agricultural sector that provides employment to more than a third of the economically active population, the agricultural reforms and the length of the transition will be strongly affected by the direction and pace of adjustment in the rest of the economy and vice versa. A new agricultural model should take into consideration the very large part of the population that must find non-farm employment. At present, the poor macroeconomic environment is the most binding constraint on agricultural development.

Present restructuring of Romanian agriculture

From the beginning of reform in Romania the main elements in the transition towards a market-oriented competitive commercial agricultural sector were: (a) the restoration of private land ownership, and (b) enterprise reform and privatization; input and output price liberalization; legalization of a land lease market; the breaking of state monopoly upon agricultural trade; relative liberalization of agricultural external trade; establishment of a new agricultural tax system; and promoting agricultural support services.

The restoration of private land ownership

The development of the private sector is an essential pillar of Romania's economic reforms. A major step toward a free market economy in agriculture has therefore been the restoration of private land ownership over the land previously belonging to collective farms. The new land reform was backed by the Land Fund Law (LFL, Law no. 18/1991), which stipulated that restitution of private ownership over land held by co-operatives must be done according to the following principles: (i) private land ownership was given to: former co-operative members or their heirs who brought land into the co-operative; any other person whose land was taken over by the co-operative during the communist regime; and co-operative members who did not bring land into the co-operative, but who participated in the work in the co-operative during the last three years prior to the reform; (ii) the restoration of private land holdings relates to the land situation of co-operatives as of 1 January 1990 recorded in the land cadastre; (iii) private ownership can be restored to a maximum of 10 hectares per family, but not less than 0.5 hectares per capita; (iv) it is prohibited for foreign nationals and entities to own and use land in Romania; (v) the maximum limit of agricultural land that can be owned by a family household is fixed at not more than 100 hectares in equivalent arable land; (vi) in semi-mountainous areas reinstatement of private land ownership is done within previously existing land boundaries where they have remained intact, while in the plains this is done within the boundaries established by the newly established Land Boards.

The institutions empowered to carry out the land reforms are the Land Commission chaired by the mayor of each locality and set up by the prefecture's decision as well as by the Liquidation Commission of Assets. The Land Commission is responsible for: (i) determining the right of ownership; (ii) the effective allocation of land to the owners within the boundaries established according to the law; (iii) issuing property titles. The land remaining after the restitution of land to the registered claimants is available to the Land Boards to be managed by the Agency for Rural Development and Planning (ARDP), which has still to be set up. The Liquidation Commission evaluates and establishes co-operative assets and liabilities. The Land Fund Law stipulates in Article 28 that the fixed assets of former co-operatives will be transferred into the ownership of the Agricultural Associations for joint cultivation of land if they are so constituted. For the land of state-owned farms the former proprietors or their heirs can become shareholders of the newly created commercial companies. The number of shares that they can obtain will be proportional to the land taken over by the state, but not more than the equivalent of 10 hectares of arable land per family. The sales of land in the emerging land market are to be supervised by the ARDP which, furthermore, is responsible for: (a) insurance of the pre-emption rights; (b) land consolidation of farms; (c) administration of the land ownership of state-owned farms; (d) allocating credit to farmers who want to buy state-owned land. The enforcement of the Land Fund Law in effect began by mid-1991 when the agrarian structure was as shown in Table 8.2. The LFL, according to official statistics, affected 9 162 711 hectares in total and an estimated 4 995 190 persons, although meeting enormous difficulties in its application.

Under the implementation of LFL, it was reported that by December 1994 4258 agricultural production co-operatives had been dissolved and private holdings accounted for 70 per cent of agricultural land, if agricultural associations are included. It can be seen in Table 8.3 that by the end of 1994 – three and a half years after LFL came into force, only 34 per cent of proprietors received their ownership titles and 89 per cent of them had been affected by the reform. After three years of LFL enforcement three main forms of agricultural enterprise appeared: the family farms and associations, agricultural associations and commercial companies (Table 8.4). These forms of enterprise are highly differentiated in term of land holdings, with the average size of farm ranging from 2.6 ha in the case of private family farms to 2372 ha in the state-owned commercial companies.

Table 8.2: Pre-reform agrarian structure in Romania

Type of units	Area (ha)	%	Number of units	Average size of unit (ha)
State farms	2 055 500	14	411	5 001
Collective farms*	9 162 711	61	4258	2 105
Private farms	1 420 100	10	340 900[1]	4.17
Other state land users	2 354 400	15		
Total	14 992 711	100		

Note: [1] according to livestock census 1984; * including personal plots.
Source: ComStat (1990).

Table 8.3: Advance of agrarian reform (December 1994)

	Total area concerned	(%)
Area to be restored under private ownership	9 162 711 ha	100
Area already transferred	8 603 780 ha	94
Companies and agricultural associations	3 402 572 ha	40
Total persons involved	4 995 190	100
Persons already affected:	4 456 597	89
Companies/agricultural associations	1 538 171	35
Certificates issued[1]	4 325 416	99
Land titles issued	1 557 858	34
Shareholder certificates		
Commercial companies	195 525	32

Note: [1] This is a temporary deed establishing the ownership without any information about location of land, neighbours, number of parcels, whereas the property title contains all information and is registered at the Land Cadastre.
Source: Data provided by the Ministry of Agriculture and Food.

Apart from these main categories of enterprises that owned land as a main factor of agricultural production, the agrarian structure was complemented by 573 Machine and Tractor Stations (MTS), 106 Hydro-amelioration Enterprises (HE) and 365 Food Industry Enterprises (FIE).

The family farm

Among the new agricultural enterprises the most important in terms of numbers and overall area occupied is the family farm. With the process of land restitution, 41 per cent of land now belongs to family farms, but this new subsector is highly fragmented. As a consequence of the agrarian reform, farm land has been split and scattered more than it was 50 years ago, before collectivization. The average land holding is around 2.6 hectares per household, often held in a large number of separate parcels. The total number of parcels resulting from the implementation of the LFL is even estimated to be 23.5 million. Moreover, the ageing of the heads of farming households is the most evident feature of the new social structure in this sector. Thus, 56.7 per cent of them are over 60 years old, 22.7 per cent between 50 and 59 years and only 20.6 per cent are younger than 50 years. Another important consequence of land reform is the shift of land ownership from peasants to urban dwellers: 43.1 per cent of the new land owners reside in towns and cities; 39.1 per cent are wage earners and rural pensioners, while only 17.8 per cent are peasants of working age. As a result, among five new landowners only one is effectively a peasant farmer. It can be seen that as a sub-sector the peasant family farm, even if it becomes the predominant kind of agricultural enterprise in terms of area held, is relatively less important in terms of turnover and marketed surplus. Most of the recently established family farms are not economically viable for a range of crops, and a majority produce basically for home consumption, selling only a small surplus. For this reason a process of land reconsolidation is absolutely essential for the development of an efficient agricultural sector. However, if we take into account similar processes that occurred in Western European countries, the consolidation process will be slow and technologies and operational systems, such as part-time farming

Table 8.4: Agrarian structure of Romanian agriculture (December 1994)

Enterprise Type	% of total agric. land	Number	Average size (ha)
Private family farms	41	2 321 000	2.6
Family associations	14	18 176	114.0
Agricultural associations	15	4 009	447.0
Commercial Companies	13	799	2372.0
Communal land	17	2 668	93.5

Source: Institute of Agricultural Economics, Sofia.

already present, could be expected to evolve in a similar way to the situation in Western European countries.

Family associations

Among the new kinds of agricultural organizations that emerged after the recent agrarian reform, the most unstable is perhaps the family association. It is an informal sort of farm enterprise without any formal judicial status. Despite the above mentioned rejection by peasant farmers of associative initiatives (especially when named 'co-operative'), it is possible that in the near future these will play an important role in the Romanian farming sector. A number of reasons leading to this can be enumerated. These are: 1) the preference of current politics for associative farm organizations; 2) the extremely fragmented land ownership which does not allow land owners to form viable private farms, nor to achieve an acceptable agricultural income; 3) the private interests of agricultural managers who are handling the affairs of the village, in maintaining their social position and their own employment; 4) the inability of landowners to create private farms due to such reasons as advanced age, lack of initial capital and other unfavourable economic conditions, lack of entrepreneurship, and lack of interest on the part of the new generation towards the agricultural sector; 5) the absence of an efficient land market – an important economic factor for the development of family farms as well as a mortgage-based credit market; 6) the many inheritors of land who presently reside in town, and who to a large extent are not interested in cultivating land but only in collecting rent; 7) the lack of agricultural machinery, while association with other producers provides access to AGROMEC (state-owned companies supplying mechanization services); 8) priority for newly constituted associations to obtain the fixed assets of former APCs following the liquidation of their inventory, a preferential treatment that is established in the LFL.

In the absence of conclusive data concerning the family associations' movement in order to point out the magnitude of the problem, we know only that between April 1992 and December of 1994 the number of associations increased from 11 057 to 18 176. Currently, this form of agricultural enterprise is in third place in terms of land area held among the newly constituted property forms. With proper structural policies a new co-operative movement, based on modern co-operative principles, could be a potential source of competition and vitality in supplying input and marketing agricultural products. The restrictions on the commercial activities of the associations (laid down in Law no.36) should therefore be eliminated and a new co-operative legislation should facilitate their reorientation from production to services. The co-operative movement in the agricultural service sector could then achieve real acceptance by the peasant farmers. Nevertheless, the associative form of family farms raised suspicions, being perceived as a new attempt at collectivization. For this reason the modern co-operative movement is still resisted by a large number of peasants.

Agricultural associations

These are new forms of agricultural enterprises which are engaged only in agricultural production, as a consequence of the attempt somehow to maintain and benefit from the existing assets of former Agricultural Production Co-operatives (APCs), as stipulated in the LFL. This form of agricultural enterprise tends to be more of a corporate form than a co-operative one. The agricultural associations differ from the former APCs not only in terms of income allocation – related to land, labour and capital shares – but also because these societies are an alliance of individuals with definite property rights. The shareholders of the associations have the right to make bargains with their shares and to abandon the society when it does not serve their interests. If we compare the number of dismantled co-operatives with the number of newly constituted farming societies, we can note an apparent continuum. From 4 258 dismantled co-operatives, 4 009 agricultural associations or farming societies have resulted. However, they have only a quarter of the total area held by the former co-operatives. According to the available data, the average size of these agricultural associations is 447 hectares, which ensures relative large-scale production. Three main factors have contributed to their constitution: 1) stipulations in the law encouraging this form of agricultural enterprise; 2) the private interest of agricultural managers who constitute the main actors of LFL application, and an important political lobby; 3) the large number of new landowners who presently live in town and are not interested in farming the land. It is questionable whether these agricultural associations really represent associative groupings of private land owners, as their name suggests. A new legislative framework needs to be created in order to ensure the development of service co-operatives in Western style, in which also the agricultural associations can be transformed.

Commercial companies (state owned farms)

As the former co-operatives have been dissolved by the LFL, the former state farms were also – at least marginally – affected by the agrarian reform. Nevertheless, enterprise privatization is a declared objective of Romanian economic reform. By the end of 1991 essential elements of the regulatory framework for privatization and private sector development were in place, particularly the Law on Restructuring of State Economic Units. Under this Law the former state farms were converted into commercial companies. These are operating about 1.9 millions hectares (slightly less than before 1989) of the most fertile and best located land in Romania and continue to supply a substantial share of marketable agricultural production. However, taking into account the economies of scale argument, they are oversized. Furthermore, apart from the former state farms, the enterprise reform is also affecting the parastatals engaged in agricultural trading and services. The former MTS were converted into just over 500 AGROMECs – commercial companies for supplying mechanization services; the former 365 parastatal food industries were transformed into about 430 commercial companies.

By the middle of 1991, the formal incorporation of these enterprises in the reform process had largely been completed. However, the current commercial companies cannot really be described as 'commercial' because of continued heavy state interference in company affairs. From the previous parastatal agrifood system, two main agricultural state enterprises remain important policy instruments for the government: AGROMEC and ROMCEREAL. The latter is a quasi-autonomous parastatal under the Ministry of Agriculture and Food (MOAF), maintaining the country's strategic grain reserve. It is the executing agency for importing foodstuffs and farm inputs for the government, playing an important role in internal market regulation. Also, ROMCEREAL is, in effect, the largest enterprise in the agro-industrial complex, by far the largest user of Agricultural Bank credit and therefore a main recipient of state agricultural subsidies. Finally, it is also a major wholesale channel for fertilizers, seeds and pesticides, and a major financier of mechanization services for private farmers. AGROMEC is the successor of the MTS, with its branches supplying mechanization services to the farmers, mainly as subcontractors to ROMCEREAL. Its workshops, distributed throughout Romania, own more than one-third of the tractors in the country and a similar proportion of other equipment. They still exert important state control over the villages' agricultural activity.

Other agricultural sector reforms
Apart from the privatization programmes, the agricultural sector has been affected by a large number of (sometimes) partial reforms, ranging from price liberalization to the introduction of a new tax system. Many of these reforms (such as the change in ownership relations) are still in a state of flux, and certainly not in any way complete. They will now be discussed briefly.

Input and output price liberalization   Overall price liberalization in the Romanian economy, even if necessary, affected the agricultural sector greatly during the first years after liberalization. The agricultural sector is at a disadvantage compared to other economic sectors. The two-and-half million agricultural operators cause the demand for agricultural inputs, as well as the supply of agricultural output, to be highly fragmented, while the suppliers of agricultural inputs and the food industries still have a monopoly position. In both cases agriculture appears as a price taker rather than price setter. Indeed, during the last four years of the economic reform, the terms of trade, although slowly improving, have not yet recovered from the initial 'cost push' of input price increases in 1990–1 (Table 8.5).

However, in individual cases the terms of trade have varied substantially each year. This can be observed in the case of wheat, where in 1991 it was necessary to sell 50 tons of wheat in order to buy one 65 hp tractor; in 1993

Table 8.5: Terms of trade for the agricultural sector (1990 = 100)

	1991	*1992*	*1993*	*1994*
Price indices of agricultural output (P_o)	642	1401	4418	9402
Price indices of agricultural inputs (P_i)	1702	2758	6591	12844
Terms of trade (P_o/P_i)	37.7	50.8	67.0	73.2

Source: Economistul 38/1994.

this was 60 tons of wheat, while in 1994 it had decreased to 34 tons. Fluctuations both in input and output prices are the cause of this.

Legalization of land lease market   This is one of the most recent steps undertaken in the direction of the constitution of a land market. While the landlords can now lease their land and receive land rent, the market for selling land still remains blocked by the LFL, which stipulates ARDP's role. The latter is to facilitate land reconsolidation by enforcing the pre-emption rights of co-owners and neighbours and to issue permits for agricultural land development. Its absence hinders the concentration of land into larger owned or operated farms and is thus affecting the consolidation of a viable modern family farm structure. The Land Lease Law, however, also makes two reservations that might have significance for future agricultural evolution: the prohibition for state-owned agricultural units to let land, and for the AGROMECs to rent it.

Breaking the state monopoly over agricultural trade   The state monopoly in agricultural trade was dismantled in the first stages of the reform and different kinds of farms now compete in Romanian agricultural markets. Despite this development, two kinds of markets still exist in Romania, the free market and the state procurement system. On the one hand, state procurement prices are well below free market prices, on the other hand the official prices of food products are equal, or near, to private operators' prices. This is because the state used to buy agricultural products from state-owned farms, whereas the food industry started to compete in the market with the private operators. Important inequalities still exist in market functions between private and state traders. The latter still benefit from former channels of distribution and other government facilities, as well as from old mentalities and behaviour of state agencies.

Relative liberalization of external trade   From the beginning of the reform, important steps were undertaken toward external trade liberalization. These steps mainly concern the removal of control on companies wishing to engage in exports and imports, allowing private trading companies to engage in external trade in agricultural products and inputs. This policy was combined with a limited convertibility of national currency and a gradual liberalization of the foreign exchange regime. Moreover, Romania's imports are affected by import tariffs, but with an upper limit of 25 per cent. In turn, the export of several agricultural products are subject to volume restrictions (bans and unilateral quotas). Nevertheless, an important step towards external trade liberalization is evidenced by the Association Agreement between Romania and the European Union signed on 1 February 1993. Despite the main economic goal of the agreement – to further the establishment of a Central European free trade area – full trade liberalization was still considered impossible, and special arrangements were created for agricultural products.

Establishment of a new agricultural tax system　The main tax reform was the introduction on 1 July 1993 of value added tax (VAT) under which agricultural products are taxed at 18 per cent. Certain basic items like bread, butter and sugar, were exempted from the VAT, and starting on 1 January 1995 a reduction in the rate of VAT was introduced for some other food products. By the middle of 1994 an income tax system was established on the basis of the average net revenue per hectare. Nevertheless, this is more a land tax system than an agricultural revenue tax because only the revenue gained from crop output is taxed and not the revenue from animal production. If we take the low prices of agricultural products into account, and the high levies per hectare, the new agricultural tax system hinders the capacity for capitalization of small peasant farms – and even medium size farms. If we consider that the average yield on wheat is 3 tons/ha and the state procurement price was 220 lei/kg (in 1994), the tax for arable land accounted for 15–20 per cent of gross returns per hectare, which is very high indeed. The remaining state subsidies do not represent an equitable redistribution of revenue, because the main beneficiaries are state-owned farms and some agricultural associations, while excluding the family farms and family associations.

Changing agrarian structure and factor mix

The shift from the large collective farms to small private farms or farm associations have induced several deep transformations in the Romanian model of agriculture. The most evident result of the present restructuring is the passage towards a more capital-extensive and labour-intensive kind of agriculture and the transfer of the production's destination from state marketing company to home-consumption or farm store. The sudden shift in land structure as a result of the changes in the economic and political system resulted in some major imbalances in the agricultural production process. This arose especially from the incompatibility of the size and nature of existing production factors. Hence, the new land structure that represents the framework for a new production pattern requires a lapse of time in order to adjust the other production factors to it. In Romania the reformers of the agricultural sector did not take this into account, as the reform of the agricultural sector was not

Table 8.6: Tractors and agricultural machinery (December 1994)

| Equipment | Total | State | | Private | |
		Commercial companies	AGROMEC	Family farms	Agricultural associations
Tractors	160 499	37 978	62 104	50 580	9 837
Ploughs for tractors	99 209	20 634	39 454	33 139	5 932
Fertilizer sprayers	10 565	3 962	5 680	407	516
Harrow disks	49 872	11 395	19 005	15 875	3 597
Sowing machines	45 373	5 690	22 315	10 201	3 167
Grain combines	35 115	7 142	25 399	1 565	1 009
Corn combines	2 610	1 231	1 283	60	36

Source: Ministry of Agriculture and Food, *Information Bulletin* No. 9, 1994.

accompanied by the structural adjustment of input industries. All agricultural equipment produced or imported under the socialist regime, as well as the industry producing this, were developed (blueprinted) to serve large-scale farms. For example, by the end of 1994, 78 per cent of agricultural tractors in Romania were over 65 hp (Table 8.6). To adjust the agricultural equipment to the current land structure and to the needs of small peasant farms, requires an adjustment of the whole industry producing these, as well as abandoning important fixed assets represented by inadequate agricultural equipment.

Another important problem arises from the separation between the ownership of land and other fixed assets, especially agricultural equipment. In late 1994 the state still kept within the commercial companies and, especially AGROMEC, 62.4 per cent of tractors, 60 per cent of ploughs, 62 per cent of sowing machines and 93 per cent of total combines.

The present technical endowment of agriculture, therefore, if not presenting a complete barrier to the consolidation of a new agricultural model, at least causes inefficiencies in the agricultural sector. While in the past one of the problems of agriculture was the very low employment rate of agricultural equipment, today the extent of this problem is ever present. While the small peasant farms are tilled with incredibly archaic tools, the state-owned oversized machinery is more and more unemployed. Unfortunately, the supply of agricultural equipment remains to a large extent the same because of the limited restructuring of the state heavy industry.

Conclusions

As a result of the present steps being undertaken towards restructuring Romanian agriculture in accordance with the requirements of a market-oriented economy, three main results are most evident: (i) a drop in the overall agricultural output (about 30 per cent between 1989 and 1993); (ii) losses in the agricultural performance in terms of crop yield and animal productivity; (iii) decreases in the demand for food with the decline of purchasing power (which is a combined effect of increases in agricultural product prices and a drop in the average wages). It can be concluded that land reform tried to restore private property rather than to create a more efficient and productive agricultural pattern or development model. However, agricultural reform has contributed greatly to the social stability in the country. Agriculture served as an important unemployment buffer and ensured to a large extent the supply of foodstuffs, not only for the rural population but also for the urban population.

The newly formed small and fragmented private farms have rigid limitations on purchasing production factors such as fertilizers, seeds, pesticides and fuel. As a result, in view of the economic realities of transition to a market economy, these small farms and their farmers are not in a position to innovate and apply a more efficient factor mix. All the reform's elements represent important but insufficient steps towards a market economy in the agricultural sector. The absence of an appropriate structural policy could delay the agricultural recovery and implementation of a more efficient agricultural pattern. Among the complementary reforms needed, an effective land market is fundamental to a successful transition of the country to a market-oriented economy. At present there are serious constraints on the development of such a land market in Romania, despite the progress made in agrarian reform. Three main elements are missing from the implementation of such a policy: (i) clarifying the land ownership situation by formalizing ownership titles; (ii) establishing a land market which will facilitate the consolidation of highly fragmented land plots; (iii) instituting a mortgage-based credit system. Furthermore, a clear objective for structural development policy must be defined, regarding which is to be the main type of agricultural enterprise in accordance with the present-day realities and the aspirations of rural communities. Finally, in presenting this brief analysis of Romanian agrarian reform, there are some obvious elements missing that threaten the development and modernization of Romanian agriculture: (i) a non-discriminatory treatment by the state of all types of enterprise (family farms, family associations, agricultural associations, commercial companies) in its agricultural support services policy; (ii) adjustment of the upstream and downstream agricultural activities to the new realities of the present-day agrarian structure of Romania; (iii) privatization and de-monopolization of these services.

9 Agrarian reform in Russia: The case of Pskov, Orel and Rostov oblasts

PETER WEHRHEIM

Introduction

IN THE FIRST years of transition in Russia, the issues of farm privatization and agricultural market liberalization have received substantial attention. In fact, privatization of the farm sector has had top priority since 1991. However, when analysing the implementation and impact of land reform policies, it remains doubtful whether this process has proceeded very far. Furthermore, the origins of the dramatic changes in livestock inventories, production of cereals and trade of agricultural products were largely not induced from within the agricultural sector (USDA, 1995:4). Agrarian change was first and foremost brought about by macroeconomic reforms in Russia (Serova, 1994). Retail price liberalization of food products launched in 1992, the tightening of fiscal and monetary policies, and the increasing departure from a command economy type state regulation and the liberalization of foreign trade had a substantial impact on the agrarian structure and on sectoral production. Parallel to the macro-reforms and the agrarian transformation process, was a shift of policies from the federal to the regional level, i.e. the *oblast* took place, which presupposed an entirely new role for the regions,[1] increasing their influence over economic policy within the governmental structure (Melyukhina, 1994). However, in many cases the efforts of *oblast* governments to strengthen their power by implementing independent economic policies had as their objective merely to improve the region's income at the expense of other parts of the country or of the federal government in Moscow (Lücke, 1994:531).

In order to shed some light on the current stage of land reform, the degree of farm privatization will be considered in three Russian *oblasts*, as regional governments gained substantial policy-making power in the transition period. As a result of this, it is to be expected that the outcome of agrarian reform varies significantly across different *oblasts* within the Russian Federation. However, it can be questioned whether the regionalization of agricultural policy in Russia is indeed efficient from a macroeconomic point of view. As the regional distribution of agricultural production in Russia is still largely the result of many decades of central planning and administrative decisions, this 'forced' distribution during the transitional period has to be reconsidered. Therefore, while the impact of agrarian reform at the *oblast* level in Russia will be discussed, some general factors – decisive for the development of the regional production potential of agriculture – will be reviewed with respect to the transition period. This is done in the second part of this chapter.[2] In the next part some overall indicators relevant to three *oblasts* in the Russian Federation will be analysed, after which the focus is on the development and the impact of agrarian reform and its relation to the existing regional distribution of agricultural production. In the last part a summary and some concluding remarks are presented, in particular discussing existing market failures in the transition and a new, albeit different, role for the state. The empirical data on the three Russian *oblasts* of Pskov, Orel and Rostov are taken from a statistical survey done by researchers from the Institute for Economy in Transition and the Centre of Economic Analysis in Moscow (Serova *et al.*, 1995), unless otherwise stated. The data presented should, however, be considered with a view to the difficulties of data collection in this period due, for example, to the increasing variety of farm types, a growing importance of household plot and *dacha*-garden production, and shifts in crop mix. In this particular case there is a continuum in the study of agrarian transition, as these *oblasts* were also present in a World Bank study (Brooks and Lerman, 1994) that was carried out at the end of 1992.

Regional distribution of agricultural production in Russia

In the transition period the economic and political environment for agriculture in Russia deteriorated significantly. While the process of economic restructuring of the agricultural sector continues, an important question that needs to be considered is what will be the most efficient distribution of agricultural production in Russia in view of the rapidly changing economic conditions. Throwing some light on this question is relevant for policy-making as market failures in the agricultural sector might be due to non-matching regional production patterns with their comparative advantages, and the debate on regionalization of agricultural and food policies (also in the political field) is rather important. The theory of regional production patterns distinguishes several factors as being decisive in the development of the regional agricultural production potential (Weinschenk and Henrichsmeyer, 1966), namely (i) the distance between the location of production and the relevant market; (ii) the natural resource endowment (land and climatic conditions); (iii) agricultural policy; (iv) the level of economic development; (v) agricultural production technology; (vi) the entrepreneurial capability of farmers and farm managers.

In the process of economic transition these factors have contributed dynamically to the changes in the agricultural sector and their impact on regional distribution of agricultural production in Russia. The distance between a specific production region and the next consumer market itself might be stable, but during the transition period access to consumer markets has changed substantially. Pskov, an *oblast* close to St. Petersburg used to deliver large shares of its agricultural production to that metropolis. Since the old processing industry and the state procurement system collapsed, only a few farms have managed to develop new marketing channels, and sometimes barter trade prevails (Van Atta, 1993). Whereas beforehand transport costs were heavily subsidized, with trade liberalization the very long distances between many of the present production regions in Russia and its major cities are inhibiting the flow of commodities, an important factor in the current changes in regional distribution of agricultural production.

The natural resource endowment of specific production regions is equally fairly stable. However, during the socialist period regional self-sufficiency was often regarded as an important objective. As a result of such agricultural policies even marginal land with poor resource endowments was cultivated. The associated costs of such inefficient agricultural production were financed by government subsidies. In the current transition period government resources are becoming scarce and this support for agriculture in marginal production regions has to be critically reviewed. Agricultural policy itself has to be considered as another important factor in determining regional production potential and the outcome of the transition. To make the regional distribution of agriculture as efficient as possible it is also important that agricultural policies in the transition period avoid a regional segmentation of food markets within Russia, and instead contribute to the formation of integrated and efficient markets.

The regional level of economic development is also influencing the distribution of agricultural production in the transition period (and vice versa) for various reasons. First, the level and structure of food demand depends on the income level of the population. Population growth rates and age composition are affecting demand for food quantitatively. Income variations result in significant shifts in consumption patterns. In the transition period, food demand of the Russian population moved away from products with high income elasticities (such as meat) substituting them by foodstuffs with a lower income elasticity such as vegetables, potatoes and milk. Second, the level of economic development will also be a co-determinant for the production technology used in the agricultural sector, which is itself an important factor in the development of the regional production potential. In the transition period many farms experienced cash-flow problems due to decreasing government subsidies and the inability to sell their products at higher prices. At the same time price ratios between capital and labour (K/L) increased, with mostly only the private sector being able to adapt to this new situation. In the private farm sector, capital and hired labour was substituted by family labour, which is available in many peasant farms at low opportunity cost. In the collective sector traditional tendencies of overstaffing seem to continue in the transition period, even though liquidity problems of farms are cited as the cause of delays of wage payments by 70 per cent of farmers (Brooks and Lerman, 1994:66). Hence, it seems as if farms in the private sector react more flexible to the changing economic environment. Overall, there has been a drastic reduction in the use of fertilizer and pesticides, which interestingly enough did not translate in to a comparative drop in output (USDA, 1995:10; Liefert, Sedik and Foster, 1995). Since the regional distribution of agricultural production has changed and will continue to change in the transition period, this dramatic impact of price liberalization on production technology has important repercussions for regional labour markets. As agricultural productivity in Russia is likely to increase soon (as it is currently at a very low level), more and more labour will be released from this sector. Last, but not least, the capability of the farmer-entrepreneur and farm-manager is decisive in the development of the regional agricultural production potential. Particularly in the transition period, not only good production skills are needed but even more urgently managerial skills. An innovative entrepreneur will search for the most profitable new possibilities where to sell produce as old procurement systems have now collapsed. The farmer or farm-manager has also to decide on the product mix and marketed output given the resource endowment and production technology. Therefore one important conclusion can be drawn at this point: investments in economics and management training for farmers and farm-managers will prove to have high rates of return. Finally, in the transitional process an additional factor is of growing importance in the determination of regional comparative advantages for agricultural production and its future regional distribution, namely the regional existence (or absence) of support institutions for inputs and outputs of agricultural production. Institution-building is proving to be crucial, as marketing and rural financial institutions, educational and agricultural extension services, infrastructure and transport services are lacking or insufficient in many regions. To create a more positive environment for private agents who are willing to provide these services, the legal framework for institution-building has to be enhanced, and a coherent set of (tax, price and credit) policies should be implemented that actually promote market formation.

This primarily qualitative review of regional development, and the factors that will be influential during the transition, calls for a more quantitative assessment of the newly emerging comparative advantages of agricultural production regions in Russia, which has to be done on the basis of the new macroeconomic environment in order to improve the rationality of agricultural policies in the transitional period. This is not an easy task, however, as there are many different factors involved which are developing dynamically in the transition period. Models that capture the regional distribution of agricultural production have been developed most often for countries in which different regional demand and supply responses were estimated, significant costs were associated with shipping food products over long distances, or in which regional policies have influenced inter-regional trade in food products as, for instance, in Canada, Mexico or India (Henrichs-meyer, 1977:138). The structure of such models was mostly problem-specific (therefore not of a blueprint type), and based on substantial data inputs, which might be problematic in contemporary Russia.

Characteristics of the three oblasts

The *oblast* of Pskov is located along the north-western frontier of Russia adjacent to the republics of Estonia and Latvia. The *oblast* belongs to the so-called north-western economic region, which is one of 12 larger regional units of Russia. Its climate is moderate and the agricultural resource endowment in the *oblast* is close to the average Russian level. Pskov has an overall size of 55 000 km² and had 835 000 inhabitants in 1993. The *oblast* Orel is located in the southern part of the central economic region south of Moscow, the latter forming an important market for its agricultural production. The average agricultural resource endowment is better than the average for all Russian *oblasts*. With its 25 000 km² Orel is about half the size of Pskov *oblast*. Orel's population size of 912 000 is, however, similar. Finally, Rostov is the most southerly *oblast* discussed here. It is part of the North-Caucasian economic region and is located west of the Volgograd *oblast* and east of the Ukraine. It is the largest of the three *oblasts* in terms of size (100 000 km²) and population (4.4 million).

The relative importance of the agricultural sector in Pskov, Orel and Rostov (see Table 9.1) is shown by the relation of total agricultural output to total industrial output, which in all three *oblasts* reached levels between 15 and 23 per cent. The share of people employed in agriculture of the total EAP (again in 1993) ranged in the three *oblasts* between 17 and 21 per cent. These figures indicate that agriculture was still a major sector for employment in all three *oblasts* and was also important in terms of total output.

The contribution of the agricultural sector to both indicators would, however, be much higher if family labour spent on private farm land or in *dacha*-gardens and their respective output were taken into account. International trade of the *oblasts* reveals for 1993 some distinct features. In Pskov 45 per

Table 9.1: Agricultural indicators of Pskov, Orel and Rostov, 1992–3

	Pskov	Orel	Rostov
Population, × 1000 (1993)	838	911	4392
Total land area, × 1000 km²	55	25	100
Total agricultural land × 1000 Ha	1500	2059	8493
Total arable land (%)	59	80	71
Arable land with cereals (%)	32	59	57
Agric. prod./ind. prod. * (%)	22	23	15
Agricultural workforce (%)	19	21	17
Food imp./total imports *(%)	45	62	18

Source: Serova *et al.*, 1995.

cent of all imports from abroad were (raw and processed) food products. In Orel 62 per cent of all imports were food products, while this share was much lower in Rostov, with only 18 per cent.

Agrarian reform at oblast level

Agrarian structure

By a presidential decree of December 1991, farms were required to register by the end of 1992 as enterprises with limited liability, joint-stock companies, agricultural producer co-operatives, or associations of private farmers (Van Atta, 1993:79–80). A decree of March 1992 allowed *kolkhozi* and *sovkhozi* to re-register as collective farms. Individual members of collective farms could start a peasant farm, being allocated a plot of land and some capital assets (Brooks and Lerman, 1994:30). Even before reforms started, members of the *kolkhozi* and workers of *sovkhozi* were able to produce on small subsidiary plots of land. This group of smallholders is referred to as household-plot-farmers. Additionally, the urban population could always produce some agricultural commodities in their private *dacha*-garden. Under Gorbachev this possibility was expanded to the extent that most people applying for such a garden were granted one. They continue to have substantial importance in terms of subsistence production as well as in barter transactions between households. In Pskov, for example, the number of families having a *dacha*-garden increased between 1985 and 1993 from 40 100 to 139 300. In Orel in 1985 an estimated 52 700 families had a *dacha*-garden, while by 1993 this had trippled to 149 700 families (Serova *et al.*, 1995).

The former *kolkhozi* and *sovkhozi* received the option to maintain their legal status or to become farms of a new type. In addition, land and machinery were allocated to members of these farms and sometimes to other farming families, with the intention of promoting private peasant farms. In Pskov 30 per cent of the *kolkhozi* and 8 per cent of the *sovkhozi* decided to retain their status as collective units (as of 1 January 1993). The respective figures in Orel were 12 and 6 per cent, while in Rostov they were 29 and 23 per cent. This may be an indication that in Orel, where farming conditions are relatively favourable, the decision to assume a new legal structure, connected with higher transaction costs and potentially assuming more economic risk, was made more frequently.

The new farm structures in the three *oblasts* under review are shown in Table 9.2 for the beginning of 1993 and 1994. Former *kolkhozi* and *sovkhozi* most frequently chose to be registered as limited liability partnerships. In Rostov and Orel another attractive farm type was the closed joint-stock company, hidden in the figure of 'other collective structures'. In fact, out of 251 former *sovkhozi* that decided to re-register as collective units all over Russia, 137 were located in Rostov (Brooks and Lerman, 1994:34). In all three *oblasts* the total number of farms increased significantly between 1991 and

Table 9.2: New agrarian structure in Pskov, Orel and Rostov, 1993 and 1994

| | Pskov | | Orel | | Rostov | |
	1993	1994	1993	1994	1993	1994
Open joint-stock societies	1	1	3	1	15	14
Limited liability partnerships	210	244	60	302	234	357
Association of private farmers	5	4	5	4	21	32
Agricultural co-operatives	31	32	22	28	6	12
Farms of non-agricultural organ.	1	3	1	2	2	9
Other collective structures	n.a.	n.a.	238	n.a.	151	138
Private farms	723	n.a.	16	n.a.	4987	n.a.
Average farm size in *Oblast* (Ha)	25	n.a.	56	n.a.	42	n.a.

Note: As of 1 January 1993 and 1994.
Sources: Serova *et al.*, (1995); Brooks and Lerman (1994).

1994 (see Table 9.3). In July 1994, farms in Pskov had an average size of just over 18 hectares, in Orel the average farm size for 1993 was 51 hectares and in Rostov 42 hectares. The low average in Pskov can be explained partially by the restriction of land ownership which was set at a maximum of 22 ha of agricultural land for each peasant farm. Such relatively small farm sizes can be viable in the transition period due to the low opportunity costs of family labour. It has been estimated that the minimum viable size ranges from 10 to 15 ha per farm in southern Russia, and from 40 to 50 ha for farms in the non-*chernozem* (black soil) zone (World Bank, 1992:75). However, peasant farmers can rent additional land.

The increase in the total number of farms was most distinct in 1992, but in 1993 the trend was still continuing. The development in Pskov in 1994 indicates that the creation of individual farms must have slowed down, due to the

Table 9.3: Farm units in Pskov, Orel and Rostov: 1991–4

	1991	1992	1993	1994 1 Jan.	1994 1 July
Pskov					
Number of farms	54	574	2069	2903	3132
Average size (Ha)	33.1	25.1	21.9	18.8	18.3
Orel					
Number of farms	353	1283	1755	n.a.	n.a.
Average size (Ha)	56	57	51	n.a.	n.a.
Rostov					
Number of farms	1726	7817	12431	n.a.	n.a.
Average size (Ha)	42	42	42	n.a.	n.a.

Source: Serova *et al.* (1995).

deteriorating economic situation in 1994 and the decreasing chances to leave the collective farms after their legal reorganization. However, all former *kolkhozi* and *sovkhozi*, even after assuming their new legal status, are still referred to as the collective sector. The so-called individual farm sector includes only farms that are actually run by peasant farmers. Even though many of the former *kolkhozi* and *sovkhozi* were split up or reregistered under a new legal type of ownership, the dominance of the collective farm sector remains significant – at least in terms of land ownership – in all three regions. In 1993 in Pskov almost 90 per cent of all agricultural land was under the use of the collective farm sector. In Orel the collective farm sector had a share of almost 80 per cent, individual farms of 3.4 per cent and household-plot and *dacha*-producers had 3.5 per cent of the total agricultural land. In Rostov, the share of total agricultural land used by the collective farm sector was, at 85 per cent similarly as high as in the other two *oblasts*, while the share of individual farms, at 2.9 per cent, was equally low. In contrast, the share of household-plot and *dacha*-producers was, at 7.6 per cent, relatively high. Collective enterprises, which had re-registered, seem to behave much as did their predecessors. At least in 1992, subsidies helped to keep these farms alive in all three *oblasts* (Brooks and Lerman, 1994:8). Hence, agrarian reform in Russia has not proceeded very far yet. Despite numerous governmental *ukaz* (decrees) and a continued debate about land reform in Russia, the implementation of farm sector reforms has been much slower than was originally expected. This trend can be observed in most former socialist countries in Central Eastern Europe and the CIS (Czaki and Lerman, 1996:61). The number of new private farms, and the land available to them, remains limited. The stagnating 'real' privatization of former collective farms is still a severe obstacle to the creation of a viable, innovative and efficient private farm sector. One of the central issues in the reform process remains the free tradability of property rights for land, as land has to be used as collateral in credit allocation, and to promote an efficient process of restructuring the farm sector.

Production structure

In all three *oblasts* cereal production in 1993 was close to the average of 1986-90. By contrast, potato production went up significantly. In Pskov total vegetable output in 1993 had doubled in comparison with the 1986-90 average, indicating that peasant farmers (intensifying their production) became more important in this period. Another crop that was particularly important for Pskov's agriculture reveals severe bottlenecks in production: the total output of flax fibre in 1993 dropped in comparison to the 1986-90 level by more than 40 per cent, mainly due to the collapse of the local processing industry and coinciding low prices for the raw material. The dramatic drop in the output of feedcrops in Pskov is intimately related to the crisis of the livestock sector in this region (and generally in Russia). Silage production decreased in Pskov by 40 per cent, maize for feed use by almost 80 per cent and hay production by roughly 50 per cent. The situation in the livestock sector in the three Russian *oblasts* is similar to that in most other transitional economies, characterized by significant reductions of herds. Heads of beef-cattle in 1994 declined between 26 and 30 per cent. The decrease in the dairy-cow population was less severe, and varied in the three *oblasts* by between 11 and 18 per cent. However, the impact of the crisis is likely to be differential. A World Bank survey of 2600 farms in five Russian provinces (including the three *oblasts* under consideration here) revealed that milk yields achieved by private farms were significantly higher than milk yields in the collective sector (Brooks and Lerman, 1994:62). Due to the specific technology of dairy production, in particular represented by the high levels of labour that are used, peasant farms and household-plot or *dacha*-producers are specializing in dairy rather than cattle herds. Furthermore, it can be observed that in all three *oblasts* there was an important reduction in the number of pigs, which was even more severe, varying between 21 and 36 per cent (again related to demand contraction). Finally, the largest reductions in the herd size were registered for sheep and goats, while the poultry sector was less affected. Overall there are some differences to be noted in the degree of reduction and the resulting structure of livestock production. In Pskov the ratio of cattle to dairy cows is 2:1 and in Orel and Rostov it is 6:2 and 2.7:1, respectively, revealing the different resource endowments of the three regions. In Rostov, in particular, extensive cattle breeding, and goats and sheep on pastures still prevails.

The shift of production from collective farms (*kolkhozi* and *sovkhozi*) to household-plots, and to a lesser extent to peasant farms, was more significant in all three *oblasts* than the increase of land share of the private farm sector, indicating the relative efficiency of the private sector. Furthermore, the output of agricultural products in the different production spheres shows that the availability of production factors and the respective production technology is quite decisive. Household plot and *dacha*-producers, and individual peasant farmers, having a relative abundance of labour, and normally being confronted by capital and land rigidities, specialize in crops and animal husbandry that are best suited to their resource endowments: vegetables, potatoes, fruit, dairy production and poultry products. On the other hand, crops that need a high degree of mechanization, such as cereals, continued to be produced in all three *oblasts* largely by the remaining collective farm sector. A similar situation can be observed in the livestock sector. However, In Pskov the individual farmers' share of the total livestock population in the *oblast* in 1994 was still between 1 and 2 per cent, the share of pigs kept by household plot and *dacha*-producers had risen between 1986 and 1994 from 19 to 34 per cent, and the share of sheep and goats rose even more, to 92 per cent. In Orel the share of peasant farmers was less than 1 per cent of the animal husbandry stock; however, of dairy cows in the *oblast*, those held on household plots increased from 22 per cent in 1986 to 28 per cent in 1994, and the share of sheep and goats rose from 28 to 48 per cent. Nevertheless, the proportion of animals kept in the collective sector remained highest for beef-cattle in all three *oblasts*.

Impact on domestic marketing and international trade

Marketing food products has become one of the most challenging issues in the transitional period. Where many food processing industries and parastatal trading companies collapsed, the variety of – in particular informal – marketing channels increased significantly in all three *oblasts* although many products do not reach the consumer because of market fragmentation, inefficiency and 'missing markets'. From official statistics for collective farms a trend can be noted that barter trade transactions and food service outlets, including payment in kind, expanded for most agricultural commodities between 1992 and 1994, while retail outlets that sell directly to consumers (apart from other market outlets) also became very important marketing channels. In Pskov, the share of cereals sold during 1992 in farm shops and other free market outlets increased from 17 per cent in 1992 to 24 per cent in 1994. At the same time, the share of cereals marketed via barter trade deals increased significantly in all three *oblasts* (between 1992 and 1994 in Orel from 5.2 to 15.2 per cent, and in Rostov from 1.6 to 10.7 per cent). Much of the potato production from collective farms was sold on the free market, in own shops and kiosks (in Pskov 39 per cent, in Orel 53 per cent, and in Rostov 32 per cent), as were vegetables (in Pskov: 21 per cent, Orel 47 per cent and Rostov 42 per cent).

Figures on international trade for the three *oblasts* are available for 1991 and 1992 in quantity terms only.[3] In Rostov imports of unprocessed agricultural commodities such as potatoes and vegetables, as well as processed ones such as wheat flour, decreased significantly. This is probably due to increased subsistence production of 'consumables' in various forms. Exports of the same products decreased from 1991 to 1992 (vegetables by over 30 per cent, fruits and berries including grapes by over 60 per cent). Exports of processed products such as tinned fruits, which amounted to over 70 000 tons in 1991 were completely stopped in 1992. Both developments match the expected results of the transition process: after price liberalization, consumption of products with high income elasticity (e.g. meat, cheese) decreased significantly. Consumption shifted in turn to products with a lower income elasticity, such as potatoes, cereals and vegetables. As local and regional markets were lost, the surplus from an increased amount of meat and cattle produced in collective farms was exported. In Pskov a similar development took place with respect to imports of potatoes and vegetables as well as of fruits and berries, citrus fruits and melons, which decreased significantly. On the other hand, imports of some processed food products rose between 1991 and 1992 more than twofold such as for macaroni or tinned vegetables. However, many of these imported and processed food products are of fairly high quality and are most likely consumed by upper income groups. In this context it is expected that many of these imports are complements to rather than substitutes for domestic food items.

Agricultural policies

In 1992 *oblast* governments were entitled to regulate food prices at a decentralized level (Von Braun *et al.*, 1995:13). Hence, food prices have been regulated to varying extents and with different instruments in the Russian *oblasts*, determined primarily by local budget constraints and population composition. In Ulyanovsk, for example, strong controls over food prices along with substantial consumer price subsidies and rationing of some products had to be supplemented by the restriction of shipments of subsidized products out of the region (*ibid*). Such regionalization of agricultural policies will have adverse effects as the overall resource use for agricultural production will become suboptimal. However, only few specific data are available yet on the extent and impact of such food subsidies and taxes of the *oblast* government supplementing federal government policies. The share of government expenditures allocated to different kinds of agricultural subsidies in 1993 gives some means of comparing the structure of the *oblast*-level policies in this field. In Pskov, 92 per cent of all agricultural subsidies were used to stimulate production. This share was lower in Orel (72 per cent) and in Rostov (85 per cent), but it is still evident that in all three *oblasts* production subsidies were the major instrument to support the farm sector in 1993. Additionally, the data show that a very high proportion of all subsidies was allocated in all three *oblasts* to the livestock sector (Pskov: 90 per cent, Orel: 68 per cent, Rostov: 77 per cent). Another important agricultural policy instrument, was subsidies for mineral fertilizers which amounted to 4 per cent of the *oblast*-government budget for agriculture in Pskov, 7 per cent in Orel, and 10 per cent in Rostov. The overall shift of policy focus from the federal to the regional level is also underlined by the structure of capital investments in agriculture by source. At least in the case of Orel and Rostov the share of capital investment financed through federal sources decreased (respectively from 26.4 per cent to 21.4 and from 20.4 to 8.8 per cent), while the share of financial sources coming from the *oblast*-government rose (Serova *et al.*, 1995). In the case of Rostov the latter rose from 1.8 to 30.0 per cent.

Market failure and the role of government

The negative impact of macroeconomic and agrarian reform on the agricultural sector of the three Russian *oblasts* under review here obviously provide many arguments for government interventions in the agricultural sector. These have a long tradition in Russia, as well as in other countries of the northern hemisphere. The latter were legitimized as efficiency-oriented interventions, based on the policy-makers' perception that market failures result in sub-optimal use of resources for achieving maximum aggregate income, while regionalization of agricultural policies results in a sub-optimal distribution of resources. Regional and central governments have named externalities, economies of scale, and imperfect competition as well as insufficient information and related transaction costs, and the need to provide public goods, as main reasons for intervention. Non-efficiency-oriented arguments, such as income distribution (e.g. poverty reduction), inter-generational equity as well as food security are also frequently objectives of policy-makers. It has been argued that policies which are not based on efficiency considerations are most often implemented only in response to the demands of organized interest groups (De Janvry and Sadoulet, 1995:5), and one has to keep in mind that policies which might be advantageous for one interest group, such as farmers, could have disadvantages for other groups, such as urban consumers. To balance their conflicting interests (e.g. farmers demand high prices for food products, urban consumers demand low prices), it is important to have sufficient policy-making power at the federal level. Additionally, policy interventions must always be financially viable for government budgets. An equal distribution of resources between regions with different levels of average income is therefore a very important issue for countries with a federal structure.

Federal as well as regional governments can provide the legal framework and institutional support to private agents in the process of developing agricultural markets. Institutions, such as future-market systems, have to be established at the federal level to provide price information and to help maintain common quality standards. At the *oblast* level, local radio news and newspapers should be encouraged to publish market information for farmers, such as up-to-date prices paid for food products in different markets. Furthermore, the government has to ensure at a federal and regional level that markets do not become regionally separated or fragmented. *Oblast* governments can support marketing systems better by deregulating food prices and by reducing marketing barriers for private traders than by imposing price controls. To improve the quality of domestic products, the local government could introduce stricter quality standards and quality price incentives, particularly for products like meat, milk and associated products (De Haan *et al.*, 1992:ix). The support of basic rural infrastructure, such as well functioning transportation and communication services, can also enhance the development of a more viable private sector, upstream and downstream in the marketing chain.

The three *oblasts* discussed in this chapter are different in terms of location, population size and land area. However, the assumption that the regionalization of policy-making activities would result in distinct regional patterns of agrarian reform was not supported. This observation on the three different *oblasts* seems to hold true for the whole Russian Federation (Craumer, 1994:348). The influence of reform legislation on farm structure from the federal level was decisive in the emergence of similar new farm types in all three *oblasts*. Logically, as a result of this reform and shifts in marketing structures, the collective farm sector in all three *oblasts* declined in overall importance. The private farm sector not only gained in terms of subsistence farming but also in terms of marketed output, while a substitution process took place in food consumption from relatively superior to more inferior food products. Nevertheless, progress in agrarian reform has been shown to be not a linear process. The total number of farms increased dramatically in 1993 but this process nearly came to an end in 1994, while the largest shares of the land area under cultivation are still used by the collective sector. Although there seems to be a faster adjustment away from loss-making activities in the private sector, which would compensate for lost economies of scale, if any, (Brooks and Lerman, 1994:6), continuation of the agrarian reform process will depend on the future policy decisions of the federal government. To ensure private property rights for land and all the other production factors of farms will be one of the driving forces for farmers to realize profits. However, beside the provision of the respective legal framework for further reform, the federal government has to support the reforms by continuing macroeconomic stabilization policies. Macroeconomic distortions, such as inflationary pressures and budget constraints, have a negative impact on agriculture.

In order to promote the development of agricultural production in Russia, one of the most important objectives of government policy at all stages of the transition process should be to ensure the openness of regional markets. Competition among input suppliers, farmers and traders will result in more efficiency in the allocation of resources and higher productivity of all agents in the food chain. Competition will force individual agents to search for new marketing and transportation channels, new production technology and to lower transaction costs. At the same time, government should obstruct the emergence of regional oligopolistic or monopolistic market structures. If government is planning to intervene directly in markets, it is important to consider the different degrees of market distortions of various policy instruments. Income support through decoupled payments, for instance, may be more efficient than direct product or input subsidies, which further distort agricultural markets (USDA, 1995:11). Cutting these subsidies will most severely affect the collective farms. They will be pressured to change their production-mix and reduce employment, as a hard budget constraint is imposed on them. As long as diseconomies of scale exist in the collective sector, further shifts to the private farm sector can reduce the decline in production.

Government intervention in this period must be implemented extremely cautiously. The current regional distribution of agriculture is likely to be suboptimal and therefore a shift of agricultural policies from the federal to the regional level seems not to be the first best choice, as it might support regional production structures that are remainders of regional policies under the planned economy, not revealing the recent patterns of regional comparative advantages that have developed in the transition period. Although some indicators for the development of agrarian reform in the three *oblasts* and its implications for a policy division between regional and federal governments have been presented here, many questions remain. Policy-oriented research is necessary to identify sources of market distortions and bottlenecks, in support of the search for an optimal mix of policies (Timmer, 1991). Some of the most urgent issues to be addressed are: (i) what is the role of the rural credit institutions, and how can their strength be increased? (ii) which (public or private) institutions need to be set up to support agricultural input supply? (iii) how do prices differ for agricultural products across *oblasts* and across marketing institutions? (iv) what are successful new market channels for agricultural products and how can they be supported? (v) how has consumer behaviour adapted to the new economic conditions? Nevertheless, reliable information is necessary for policy-oriented research, although experience in Russia shows that this cannot always be provided in the current situation.

Notes

1. The Russian Federation has a three-tiered political system. Besides the federal government in Moscow, 89 sub-national governments (*oblast, krai, krug* and two major cities, Moscow and St. Petersburg); rural and communal municipalities also have administrative powers.
2. An earlier version of this chapter was presented at a Moscow Seminar of the European Association of the Agricultural Economists (EAAE) on 'International Issues of Land Reform in Russia' in October 1995.
3. International trade in this context refers to trade with companies outside the Russian Federation, including companies in other CIS countries.

10 The agrarian transition in Vietnam: institutional change, privatization and liberalization

DAO THE TUAN

Introduction

THIS CHAPTER DISCUSSES the agrarian transition that took place during the 1980s and the early 1990s in Vietnam. It analyses this process primarily as one of institutional change, focusing on the transformation from collective agriculture towards an agricultural sector dominated by the peasant household economy. After three consecutive changes in agrarian policies during the era under review the rights of allocation and use of labour, capital and land returned to the household, fully resuscitating the peasant economy. Results of peasant household surveys undertaken by the Vietnam Agricultural Science Institute (VASI), as presented in this chapter, show that a high percentage of households is still at the level of subsistence agriculture. Major constraints on commercial farming are the lack of capital and markets. However, the peasant economy has been changing very rapidly in the process of agricultural privatization.

The development of peasant households' income shows a rise in the average level and a reduction in the incidence of poverty. Income differentiation is increasing, although not yet leading to a high level of inequality. Taking into account the process of social change in rural areas of Vietnam over the last 60 years, as will be done in the last part of this chapter, it can be noted that in spite of rapidly rising population pressures, peasants' average incomes improved, and the level of inequity decreased relatively after many institutional changes. Nevertheless, at the present time the rural areas in Vietnam are at a stage of institutional crisis. Old institutions do not work any more and new ones are only at the initial stages of formation. We must therefore redefine the role of the state, to create more efficient market mechanisms and structures, and support the formation of farmer's associations of a new type in order to promote and assure rural development. Agricultural policies in contemporary Vietnam should support the dynamism of peasant households, stimulating them towards a transformation from home-consumption to production for the market by diversifying the production, creating more non-farm employment and raising their incomes.

The rural transition as a process of institutional change

The transition process in rural areas of Vietnam can be considered primarily as a series of consecutive transformations in search of more optimal institutions promoting development in this field. Since the early 1980s a transformation has taken place from collective agriculture to peasant farming. During the period of collective farming, particularly due to difficulties in the management of upland non-rice food crops and animal husbandry, these activities were gradually transferred to the household economy, in addition to the existing ownership of household plots and homestead gardens. Hence, income from the household economy increased and surpassed that derived from the co-operative. In some areas of Vietnam peasants practised the 'underground contract' (*khoan chui*), in which paddy land was leased to farmers for a fixed contribution to the co-operative. Generally, agricultural production increased in these villages. Therefore, decree No.100 of the Secretariat of the Vietnamese Communist Party (1981) was no more than the legalization of the *status quo*. Viewed from an institutional perspective this directive gave farmers the right to decide about the allocation of their labour and, more importantly, the returns for their efforts. *De facto*, in 1981, the household began to be reconstituted as the major unit of agricultural production instead of the co-operative. Since then, households have been allocated specific plots of land for management under a contract system (comparable with the 'household responsibility system' that was introduced in China, *Ed.*). Nevertheless, the co-operative still held monopoly power over the provision of inputs and the marketing of agricultural output, so the peasant household did not yet function as an autonomous unit.

Farmers were not yet fully satisfied with this new system. In many villages they practised the 'full contract' (*khoan trang*), in which paddy fields were leased to peasant households, without any responsibility on the part of the co-operative. This grassroots initiative is the foundation of the VCP-Decree No.10 (1988), which in reality legalized the right to decide on the use of capital. Together with the abolition of the state procurement and supply system, the peasant household economy was almost resuscitated. Nevertheless, in spite of this new policy, land was still controlled by the co-operatives. Property rights were indeed strengthened and households were allocated usufruct rights over land (in exchange for the payment of land tax), but the state still retained ownership of land. By 1992 a total of 6 million of the 7 million hectares of agricultural land were farmed under direct household usufruct rights, although the specific arrangements varied from place to place.

In spite of the existence of the 1987 Land Law that prohibits the selling and buying of land, an underground land market was forming. The new 1993 Land Law basically legalized (rather than initiated) this market, introducing the formal right to transfer usufruct rights. In July 1993, a revision of the Land Law allowed for the extension of tenurial rights to 20 years, more importantly making provision for the transfer (buying, selling, inheriting) of usufruct rights. Therefore, after three consecutive reforms, full rights regarding the main factors of production had been returned to the peasant household, while the collective farming system had been completely dismantled. This process occurred over a period of 12 years, and during this time the peasant household economy was gradually retaking full responsibility for agricultural production over the whole country.

The situation of the peasant household economy

In order to enhance further development of the rural areas an analysis of the existing institutions is necessary, indicating existing constraints and defining further institutional reforms for the near future. As the most important 'institution' in present-day Vietnam is the peasant household, it is during the last few years that the focus has shifted towards a better analysis of the role of this institution in rural development. Results of peasant household surveys in recent years allow us to design a broad typology of households in different regions of the country. In the period 1989-94, data were collected in 27 communes over 13 provinces representative of 7 regions, under the auspices of VASI, with other institutions participating – such as the National Research Programme on Rural Development – in order to ascertain an appropriate typology for the analysis of economic differentiation of peasant households.[1] After comparing various methods that had been previously used to categorize peasant households, we found that the typology based on the degree of insertion in markets provided the greatest explanatory value. Such a typology can show the stage at which households are in the process of their transformation from subsistence to commercial farming. There is a consistent relation with income differentiation: the self-sufficient farmers are generally poor, have less access to production factors, cannot diversify their economic activities, while commercial farmers can be normally described in the opposite manner. The above mentioned typology was constructed for the villages surveyed, distinguishing between different types of peasant households in seven regions of Vietnam. The households are categorized in the following way:

1. 'consumption only', i.e. directed to self-sufficiency; this may include:
   (a) food-deficient households (producing less food than family food requirements)
   (b) reproduction-deficient households (the financial balance is negative because expenditure is greater than gross annual income)
   (c) reproduction-sufficient households (the financial balance is positive but the objective is still home-consumption).
2. 'both consumption and the market' defined as peasant households, that are food- and reproduction-sufficient, but with additional surplus generated for the market.

3. 'only the market', with peasant families mainly engaged in the production of agricultural commodities for the market.

Survey results show that the richest villages are in the southern Mekong delta, followed by the south-eastern regions, both representing relatively the highest income inequality (Table 10.1), as in comparative terms it is still very low.

The Gini coefficients in these surveys are lower than in previous surveys, because they included only agricultural households. Poorest households are living in the mountains of the midlands and in the coastal regions, which coincides with the results of previous surveys. Medium income and highest equality are observed in the Red River delta. Although the percentage of households within each category varies from village to village, even within the same district, it is possible to draw some general conclusions from the data: (i) the percentage of commercial farmers is greater in the Mekong delta than in the Red River delta; (ii) more than 60 per cent of peasant households in the Red River delta produce only sufficient to satisfy home-consumption; (iii) nevertheless, in the Red River delta peasants are not deficient in food; those households are concentrated in the midlands, in the central coastal area and in the Mekong delta.

In northern Vietnam, although the proportion of self-sufficient households is very high, many households do not produce any surplus for the market. In contrast, in the Mekong delta nearly half the households of the villages surveyed were producing primarily for the market. Nevertheless, in this same region there is a high proportion of households that produce only for their own needs. In other words, a sharp differentiation appears in the Mekong delta between these two household types. The percentage of households with

Table 10.1: Typology of peasant households (1993)

Regions	Consumption 1a	1b	1c	Consumption and market	Market	Production (1000d/cap)	Gini* Coeff.
Northern mountains	6	4	21	48	21	1073	0.14
Red River delta	0	30	33	14	22	1621	0.13
South East	0	32	39	0	28	2389	0.21
Mekong delta	8	10	20	13	45	2564	0.20

Note: * The Gini coefficient or Gini concentration ratio is an aggregrate measure of inequality, which can vary anywhere from zero (perfect equality) to one (perfect inequality). In countries with highly unequal income distribution the Gini-coefficient lies between 0.50 and 0.70, while for countries with relatively equitable distribution, it is in order of 0.20 to 0.35.

Source: VASI Survey Data.

dual objectives, suggesting a transitional stage from self-sufficiency to commercialization is highest in the mountainous areas of the north and central coast.

In summary, the majority of Vietnamese farmers are very poor and still at the stage of subsistence farming. Commercial farming has only relatively higher importance in the south; hence, this region represents higher income levels. Under these conditions the differentiation among households is still very limited. In the mountainous areas, high population increase is the main cause of deforestation. Food production is still mostly done through shifting (and sometimes 'slash and burn') cultivation, where development of industrial crops, cattle husbandry and reforestation demand high investment to which poor farmers have no access. However, in many areas where forests have already been destroyed farmers are in a difficult situation, and can try to survive only by producing food crops with poor yields and supplementing their income from the forest. In the midland and coastal areas, the problem of food deficiency is also severe, mostly due to difficult ecological conditions, so the percentage of food-deficient farmers is relatively high. As in the mountains, development of industrial crops and cattle husbandry is limited because these need substantial investments and market access.

In the north the development of commercial rice production is limited by the lack of land, and the expansion of cash crops and animal husbandry by the lack of inputs and market outlets. In the south commercial rice farming is developed, but low rice prices cause substantial difficulties, while the trend towards agricultural diversification is limited because of inefficient market structures. The main constraint for self-sufficient peasants is often (the non-availability of) credit, as the existing rural financial system is not accessible to the poor. The major constraint for commercial farmers is the lack of markets. Credit and market institutions in the country are not yet sufficiently developed to support the now predominant household economy. This situation explains why in recent years the Mekong Delta developed more rapidly than other regions of the country. We cannot expect a rapid development of agriculture in areas where self-sufficient peasants are the majority.

The first step towards rural development is therefore the change from the subsistence economy to commercial farming. This change is, among others, determined by the availability of a credit system for the poor. Since the structural adjustment of the agricultural sector the banks are now working as commercial banks, so credit is mostly unavailable to the poor. In this situation it is rather difficult to expect change in the rural area merely by introducing the principle of market liberalization. In order to show the dynamic change in the peasant household economy we repeated surveys in the Northern Red River delta, with the same samples, before and five years after the 1988 land reform.

Between 1988 and 1993 the number of households producing basically for home consumption rose, but there was an even larger increase in the number

Table 10.2: Peasant household income (1988–93)

Types	Households (%)	Gross Income (×1000 Dong/cap) (1993 Constant)	Category
1988:			
1	39	706	Consumption
2	26	896	Consumption + Market
3	13	1096	Consumption + Market
4	21	1690	Market
1993:			
1	48	1041	Consumption
2	10	1698	Consumption + Market
3	27	1653	Market
4	15	2373	Market

Source: VASI Survey Data.

of peasant households producing solely or mostly for the market. Although the income gap between strata was not widening from the lowest to the highest end in average terms, the difference between the subsistence-oriented households and those producing both for home consumption and the market had grown substantially.

Regional differentiation of average household income

In terms of regional spread the peasant household income surveys present another picture. Vietnam is divided into seven economic regions. Of these, only two regions (of the Red River and the Mekong River deltas) are plains. Other regions have mostly mountainous areas, especially the northern mountains and midlands, and finally, the central highlands. Table 10.3 presents net per capita income data from household surveys conducted in 1990 and 1993 by the General Statistical Office of Vietnam in various provinces of five regions in Vietnam (excluding the northern central coast and the south east). Comparing with data from the World Bank Vietnam Living Standards Survey (1994), the data from the General Statistical Office (1994) are on average 12 per cent higher, because the VLSS data cannot be used for computing net income, as the World Bank uses per capita real expenditure for computing the Gini-coefficient. Table 10.3 indicates that average net per capita income increased in all regions over four years following the 1988 land reform, although faster in some regions than in others. Provinces that have lower population densities, with commodity production and opportunities for

Table 10.3: Peasant household income and poverty

Region	Province	Year	Income Cap/Mnth (1000 dong) 1992 Prices	Gini Coeff.	Households under poverty line (%)	Food poverty line (%)
Northern mountains	Yen Bai	1989	62.0	0.287	31.9	
		1992	75.9	0.254	13.2	35.5
Red River delta	Nam Ha	1989	63.3	0.202	25.4	
		1992	89.7	0.307	13.1	24.3
South-central coast	Binh Dinh	1989	61.4	0.217	27.0	
		1992	91.1	0.314	12.9	22.6
Central highlands	Dac Lac	1989	69.6	0.343	30.1	
		1992	76.9	0.325	12.6	25.2
Mekong delta	Can Tho	1989	90.0	0.267	12.1	
		1992	113.0	0.291	8.6	16.5
Average		1989	69.3	0.263	25.3	
		1992	89.3	0.298	12.1	

Source: VASI Survey Data; World Bank (1995a: 142).

alternative employment in the non-agricultural and service sectors, had higher average per capita incomes. Clearly, in 1989 net per capita income was highest in the Mekong delta region and lowest in the southern central coastal regions, with 68 per cent of the former. Within three years incomes had increased, with the Mekong delta still representing the highest per capita income region, while the lowest average incomes were found in the northern mountainous region, at a level of 67 per cent of the former. Abstracting from intra-regional variation and using average incomes per region, this indicates that the regional income gap did not change during the last few years. Per capita incomes of the plains had improved faster, while peasant incomes in mountainous regions are increasing at a slower rate. The coefficient of variation between regions in 1989 is 16.6 per cent and that of 1992 is 16.8 per cent. In summary, regional differentiation did not change after the introduction of the 1988 land reform.

Data on net per capita incomes were used in conjunction with quintile calculations from these surveys in order to calculate the Gini-coefficient between income groups of the different regions. The percentage of people under the poverty line is also calculated, which is defined as the income equivalent of 20 kg of rice per month per capita (Centre for Population and Labour Resource Research, 1993). The data presented in Table 10.3 indicate that in 1989, inequality between individual net incomes was least in the Red River delta with income below the national average, while most in the central highlands with above-average income and in the northern mountainous region which had below-average income. The Mekong delta had clearly the highest average income and a low percentage of poor, but inequality was only just above average, perhaps because the market economy in this region is the most developed of the country, where richer households that had access to factors of production (i.e. land labour and capital), engaged in intensive agriculture together with a variety of activities such as gardening, perennial crop cultivation (such as tea, rubber and coffee), aquaculture, forestry, processing, service (inputs, transportation, marketing), and handicraft activities.

Data for 1992 indicate that although average incomes were highest in the Mekong delta, inequality is also one of the highest, but the percentage of poor households is relatively low. The Northern mountains have the lowest income, a relatively high equality and the highest percentage of poor households. The southern central coastal region shows a higher than average income together with increased level of inequality and a medium percentage of the poor. Comparing the Gini-coefficient of regions from 1989 to 1992, it appears that the degree of income differentiation has increased on average for the country from 0.258 (1989) to 0.298 (1992) but the percentage of the poor decreased from 25.3 to 12.1 (Table 10.3). There are substantial differences with data presented in the VLSS, because of a broader definition of the food poverty line, although regional differences tend to be similar. Since the introduction of the 1988 land reform, inequality increased in all regions with the exception of the mountainous areas, but absolute poverty decreased. Furthermore, income differentiation between peasant households in the north and the centre increased faster than that of the south.

Long-term agrarian change

In order to understand social changes in the rural areas, processes must be monitored over longer periods of time. Over the past six decades, population in the rural areas grew substantially, even though Vietnam was at war for half this period and suffered heavy casualties. In the Mekong delta the population annual growth rate was 2.2 per cent, due both to natural increase and net inward-migration that was over twice that of the Red River delta, which was subject to net outward-migration (Table 10.4).

Land available for agriculture diminished by one-third in the Red River delta (-0.6 per cent per annum) due to the use of land for activities such as housing, roads, and the construction of irrigation systems. It increased only slowly in the Mekong delta (0.2 per cent per annum) with the reclamation of land, especially in the Plain of Reeds and Long Xuyen. Arable land available per capita has declined in both deltas, and more rapidly in the Mekong caused by the rapid population growth. In 1990, agricultural land per capita was little more than one-third of what it was in 1930 in the Red River delta (-1.6 per cent per annum) and less than one-third in the Mekong delta (-2.0 per cent per annum). Nevertheless, land availability for agriculture per person in the Mekong delta is more than three times that of the Red River delta. As paddy yields improved, total output expanded dramatically in net terms by approximately 150 per cent over six decades. Currently the paddy yield is higher in the Red River delta than in the Mekong River delta. Nevertheless, in the Red

Table 10.4: Evolution of agrarian systems in Vietnam

	Year	Rural population (million)	Arab. land per. crops (×1000 ha)	Land density (m²/cap)	Food crops production (thous.tons)	Food yield (t/m)	Food/ capita (kg.)
Red River delta	1930	6.5	1.2	1846	1.8	1.5	277
	1990	11.9	0.8	689	4.9	5.9	411
Growth rate (%)		1.0	(0.6)	(1.6)	1.7	2.3	0.6
Mekong delta	1930	3.2	2.0	6250	2.6	1.3	812
	1990	11.8	2.3	1949	9.6	4.2	816
Growth rate (%)		2.2	0.2	(2.0)	2.2	2.0	(0.01)

Source: see Table 10.5.

River delta an individual person produces less than in the Mekong delta, i.e. gross income per capita from paddy production in the north is substantially less than in the south.

A history of institutional reforms

Rural areas in Vietnam have been affected by many institutional changes since World War II: in 1946–7, in the north and the south, land which previously belonged to the French and their collaborators was confiscated and redistributed, while land rent was reduced. In the north in 1953–5 a radical land reform occurred, followed in 1958–60 by a process of rapid collectivization. In the south, in 1955–6 land reform was implemented under the Ngo Dinh Diem regime, which restricted rent and limited land ownership to 100 hectares. Again, in the 1970s, land reform occurred both in territories controlled by the Provisional Revolutionary Government and by the Nguyen Van Thieu regime. Following the liberation of South Vietnam collectivization was also introduced to the south in 1978, but had little time to take root as de-collectivization began in 1981 with the issuing of Decree No. 100.

Using the sporadically available data, an attempt is made in Table 10.5 to establish the course of social change through an examination of net peasant incomes and social equity represented by the Gini coefficient for the two most important regions in the country over the period from 1930 to 1990. Average income is used, together with data on income distribution, to calculate the Gini coefficient in this case. However, a number of caveats affecting the interpretation of data need to be given at the outset: (i) for comparative purposes, the average net annual income is calculated as kilograms of paddy per capita. Admittedly, the use of paddy as a deflator has some imperfections as the real prices for paddy have changed, and vary from north to south; (ii) in the north, the Gini coefficient for the collective period was based on the average income and income distribution data from some provincial statistics offices; (iii) due to the lack of data on income distribution during the French period and in South Vietnam, distribution of land was used as the equity criterion.

With these limitations in mind, it is clear that average net incomes increased in both regions over the 60 year period, with some fluctuations due to major disruptions such as wars. Furthermore, the rate of increase has been higher in the south. By 1990 the regional income differential was 2:1, although the costs of living are also relatively greater in the south. Table 10.5 also illustrates that social equity improved in both regions over the period, although the more detailed data available for the north indicates fluctuations, with strong improvement of equity following institutional reforms, first after the indepenedence of Vietnam in 1945, and thereafter since 1954, when the Democratic Republic of Vietnam was firmly established in the north. Two

The 'Market Panacea'

Table 10.5: Income and social equity in Vietnam (1930–90)

Area	Year	Average net income (kg/cap)	Gini coeff.	Sources
Red River Delta	1930	584	0.43*	Gourou (1936, 1940)
	1945	370	0.59*	Gen. Stat. Office (1982)
	1954	501	0.35	Gen. Stat. Office (1971, 1979, 1982)
	1957	568	0.07	and Data from Provincial Statistical Offices
	1965	596	0.15	
	1970	570	0.26	
	1978	680	0.25	
	1990	69ƶ	0.25	Gen. Stat. Office (1992)
Mekong Delta	1930	782	0.87*	Gourou (1940)
	1955	600	0.84*	Callison (1983)
	1966	866	0.80*	USDA (1973)
	1972	863	0.55*	Nishimura (1975)
	1981	1009	0.30	Gen. Stat. Office (1982)
	1990	1259	0.35	Gen. Stat. Office (1992)

Note: *Gini-coefficient of land ownership (not of income).

general conclusions can be drawn from Table 10.5. First, it appears that in the north the process of social differentiation of the household proceeded even of the period of collectivization of the 1960s.

Households had the opportunity to generate private income within the co-operative structure and it is estimated that household plots contributed 40–60 per cent of all agricultural output, while 60–70 per cent of peasant income came from the household economy (General Statistics Office, 1979, 1982). Furthermore, access of peasant families to the collective share was not fully equitable, which exacerbated the process of differentiation. Second, social differentiation was alleviated both in the north and the south following institutional reforms which frequently took the form of land redistribution (in 1988 and 1993). Other studies in Asia note that the process of social differentiation occurs in areas that are subjected to population pressure and production intensification (Hayami and Kikuchi, 1981), although institutional reform can influence the differential access to production factors of the peasantry. However, after the privatization of the agricultural sector, the social differentiation of peasants increased. This is a normal process in market economies. However, experiences of many countries show that a policy emphasis on rural development, employment creation and investment in human capital will actually increase the equity.

Conclusions

The 1993 Land Law will undoubtedly have an impact on future social differentiation, although the outcome is not clear at this stage. This institutional agrarian reform, unlike those which preceded it, did not require the reallocation of unevenly distributed land. Rather, it appears that the most important component is that land 'use-rights' can now be transferred, leased, inherited and used as collateral. In other words, it sanctions the emerging land market. During the debates before the adoption of this law some economists argued that the situation will necessarily lead to the concentration of land in the hands of some farmers, while others will either engage in non-agricultural activities or move to the urban areas. However, this outcome is not obvious. In fact Hayami and Kikuchi (1981) found that for other agricultural countries in Asia the return to land increased much faster than the return to labour, so peasants were reluctant to give up their land. In Vietnam now, as in other southeast Asian countries, the increasingly active population cannot be fully absorbed by industrial and service sectors, so the agriculturally active population continues to increase. In this situation the land concentration will occur only with difficulty.

The socioeconomic changes induced by the 1993 Land Law need to be examined in the context of the rapidly emerging market economy. On the one hand, privatization of agricultural services in the provision of inputs and the marketing of output may provide income generating opportunities in the countryside which would alleviate the negative impact of landlessness. However, private trading and the extension of financial markets may also promote differentiation. It appears that the most important constraint on rural development is the lack of alternative employment opportunities in order to increase rural incomes. The diversification of agriculture and the development of non-agricultural activities are limited by the lack of market outlets and the low purchasing power of peasants.

There is currently in Vietnam a rural institutional crisis with the following characteristics:

- the state is withdrawing from many activities in rural areas with the elimination of subsidies and the bankruptcy of state enterprises in services and commerce
- the slow development of the private sector in services, trade and rural industrial activities within a framework of highly imperfect markets
- the lack of collective action in order to support the household economy. The old type of co-operative is changing into the new type only with great difficulty (only 10 to 20 per cent of them are transforming into service

co-operatives). New forms of peasant associations appear only very timidly.

The process of institutional restructuring that occurs in the rural areas cannot do without support from the state (and of civil society). Therefore there is a need to:

(1) redefine the role of the state in rural development: the state must invest in infrastructure, work out appropriate policies and legal frameworks for the development of markets, and should finance rural development projects, especially in marginal areas;

(2) support the development of new types of co-operation which will replace state organizations and the old types of co-operatives, in particular in delivering agricultural services to peasant households;

(3) reinforce market institutions in order to create more efficient markets. In this context we can observe in rural areas the formation of new types of peasant organizations. This process is mostly determined by local initiatives, without any guidance from above. The following organizational trends can be distinguished:

a) The change from the old form of co-operation to a new one. The old type was a production co-operative. When control over production returned to the hands of the household economy, the old co-operatives did not have any further reason to exist. State policies should encourage these old institutions to transform into new forms of service co-operative. But this process of change is complex because many of old co-operatives do not have capital. They cannot obtain more credit from the bank as most of them are indebted. For the few service co-operatives it is difficult to be involved in all forms of service to peasant households, and they often focus mainly on input procurement. Many other services are left to the private sector.

b) Old types of peasant organizations, which in the past had political characters such as Peasant's Union, Women's Union, Youth Union or Veterans' Unions, are changing into socio-political organizations, involving themselves in the provision of services to peasant households such as the supply of credit and extension of technology. Again, the contribution of these activities is limited because these organizations do not have enough funds and experience in this field. Only the activities of the association of gardeners have had some impact.

c) New types of co-operatives are emerging from local initiatives. From a survey to identify different types, the following have been noted: credit, irrigation, crop production extension, animal husbandry, fishery, agro-processing, forestry, gardening and construction. They are still absent from input marketing. However, these newly emerged associations meet many difficulties, and there is no agency to support them, nor a legislation framework for the development of this form of co-operation. Although these are the beginning of the development of a civil society in Vietnam, particularly in the rural areas, providing the foundations of a new institutional framework, many state officials do not take them seriously.

Note

1. Some parts of the current research work performed by the VASI have been published by the author in: Benedict J.T.Kerkvliet and D.J.Potter. 1995. (Eds) *Vietnam's Rural Transformation*, Westview Press/Institute of Southeast Asian Studies, Boulder, Colorado, pp.139-64.

References

ADAI. 1990. 'La Tenencia de la Tierra: Analísis y Opciones', Preliminary Version, Tegucigalpa.

Appleton, S. and J. Mackinnon. 1995. 'Poverty in Uganda: Characteristics, Causes and Constraints', Centre for the Study of African Economies, Oxford.

Appendini, K. and D. Liverman. 1994. 'Agricultural Policy, Climate Change and Food Security in Mexico', *Food Policy*, Vol. 19 (2), pp. 149–64.

Aragón, E.M. 1994. 'El Salvador: El Contenido y Alcance de las Políticas Agrícolas de los Ultimos Años', in: Noé Pino, H., P. Jímenez, A.Thorpe (Eds.), *¿Estado o Mercado? Perspectivas para el Desarrollo Agrícola Centroamericano hacia el Año 2000*, POSCAE-UNAH, Tegucigalpa.

Arias Peñate, S. 1988. *Los Subsistemas de Agroexportación en El Salvador: el Café, el Algodon y el Azúcar*, UCA Editores, San Salvador.

Arrivillaga, E.D. 1993. 'Militares y Sociedad Civil', *Puntos de Vista*, No.7, Tegucigalpa.

Baumeister, E. 1991a. 'Desarrollo Agropecuario, Participación Campesina y Diversificación Agrícola', in: Ruben, R., G. Van Oord (Eds.), *Más Alla del Ajuste*, DEI, San José.

Baumeister, E. 1991b. 'Elementos para Actualizar la Caracterización de la Agricultura Centroamericana', Mimeo, Managua.

Bentley, J.W. 1990. 'Conocimiento y Experimentos Espontáneos de Campesinos Hondureños sobre el Maíz Muerto', *Manejo Integrado de Plagas*, Vol. 17, pp. 16–26.

Bentley, J.W. 1991. 'The Epistemology of Plant Protection: Honduran Campesino Knowledge of Pests and Natural Enemies', in: Gibson, R.W., A. Sweetmore (Eds), *Proceedings of a Seminar on Crop Protection for Resource Poor Farmers*, CTA-NRI, Chatham.

Bentley, J.W. and K.L. Andrews. 1991. 'Pests, Peasants and Publications: Anthropological and Entomological Views of an Integrated Pest Management Program for Small-Scale Honduran Farmers', *Human Organisation*, Vol. 50 (2), pp.113-24.

BCRA (Banco Central de la República de Argentina). 1988. *Síntesis Estadística*, Buenos Aires.

Bishop, C., K.S. Howe, D. Kopeva and Mishev, P. 1994. 'Land Markets and Tenure', in: Buckwell, A., S. Davidova, K.Moulton, A.Schmitz (Eds.), *Privatisation of Agriculture in New Market Economies: Lessons From Bulgaria*, Kluwer Academic Publishers, New York, pp. 75–85.

Brandao, A.S.P. and G.C. de Rezende. 1989. 'The Behaviour of Land Prices and Land Rents in Brazil', in: *Agriculture and Governments in an Interde-*

pendent World, Proceedings of the Twentieth International Conference of Agricultural Economists, Dartmouth Publishers, Aldershot.

Braun, von J., E. Serova, H.Seeth and O. Melyukhina. 1995. 'Russia's Food Economy in Transition: Current Issues and Long-Term Consumption and Production Perspectives'. Discussion paper, IFPRI, Washington.

Brett, E.A. 1996. 'Uganda 1987-94', Country Case-Study in: Engberg-Pedersen *et al.* (Eds.), *Limits to Adjustment in Africa*, James Currey & Portsmouth N.H., Heinemann, London.

Brooks, Karen and Zvi Lerman. 1994. *Land Reform and Farm Restructuring in Russia*, World Bank Discussion Paper, nr.233, Washington.

Buainain, A.M. and G.C. de Rezende. 1995. 'Structural Adjustment and Agricultural Policies: The Brazilian Experience since the 1980s', in: J.Weeks (Ed.), *Structural Adjustment and the Agricultural Sector in Latin America and the Caribbean*, MacMillan/ILAS, Basingstoke.

Buckwell, A. 1994. 'Restructuring of Agriculture in Central and Eastern Europe: Progress, Problems and Policies'. Paper presented at OECD meeting of the *ad hoc* Group of Experts in East-West Relations in Agriculture, 12–15 September.

Buhl J. 1996. 'Cotton is the Engine of Growth', MA Minor Thesis, Centre of African Studies, Copenhagen University, June (in Danish).

Bulmer-Thomas, V. 1989. *La Economía Política de Centroamérica desde 1920*, BCIE, San José.

Bulmer-Thomas, V. 1996. *The New Economic Model and its Impact on Poverty and Income Distribution in Latin America*, MacMillan/ILAS, Basingstoke.

Byerlee, D. and G. Sain. 1991. 'Relative Food Prices under Structural Adjustment', *Food Policy*, February, pp.74–87.

Callison, C.S. 1983. *Land-to-the-tiller in the Mekong delta*, University Press of America, Lanham, New York and London.

Calva, J.L. 1991. 'The Agrarian Disaster in Mexico, 1982–9', in: M.J. Twomey, A. Helwege (Eds.), *Modernisation and Stagnation: Latin American Agriculture in the 1990s*, Greenwood Press, Westport, pp. 101–20.

Cambar Custodio, M. 1990. Estructura de la Tenencia de Tierras en Honduras, Paper presented at the Conference 'Impacto del Proyecto de Titulación de Tierras sobre el Mercado de Tierras en Comunidades Rurales', Tegucigalpa.

Carter, M.R. and D. Mesbah. 1991. 'Enlisting the Land Market to Relink Agrarian Growth with Poverty Reduction: Will it Work?', Land Tenure Centre, University of Wisconsin, Mimeo.

Carter, M.R. and E. Alvarez. 1990a. 'Changing Paths: The Decollectivisation of Agrarian Reform Agriculture in Coastal Peru', in: W.Thiesenhusen (Ed), *Searching for Agrarian Reform in Latin America*, Allen and Unwin, New York, pp.156-87.

Carter, M.R. and D. Mesbah. 1990b. 'Economic Theory of Land Markets and its Implications for the Land Access of the Rural Poor', Land Tenure Centre, University of Wisconsin, Mimeo.

CENPAP. 1993. 'Aportes para la Estrategia de Desarrollo Agropecuario en Nicaragua', in: *Por la Busqueda de una Estrategia de Desarrollo para Nicaragua*, Escuela de Economía Agrícola-UNAN, Managua.

Censo Nacional Agropecuario (IV). 1993. Secretaria de Planificación, Coordinación y Presupuesto, Tegucigalpa.

Centre for Population and Labour Resource Research. 1993. *Doi va ngheo o Vietnam* (Hunger and Poverty in Vietnam), Hanoi.

CEPAL. 1990. *Magnitud de la Pobreza en América Latina en los Años Ochenta*, CEPAL, Santiago.

Clemens, H. 1993. 'La Estrategia de Desarrollo Agropecuario en Nicaragua: Una Visión desde la Universidad', in: *Por la Busqueda de una Estrategia de Desarrollo para Nicaragua*, Escuela de Economía Agrícola-UNAN, Managua, pp. 11–30.

Coles, A. 1988. 'Transacciones de Parcelas y el Proyecto de Titulación de Tierras en Honduras', University of Wisconsin LTC, Mimeo, Tegucigalpa.

Collier, P. 1994. 'Economic Aspects of the Ugandan Transition to Peace', Mimeo, Centre for the Study of African Economies, Oxford.

Collier, P. and J.W.Gunning. 1992. 'Aid and Exchange Rate Adjustment in African Trade Liberalisation', in: *Economic Journal*, July pp. 925–39.

ComStat, 1990. *Romanian Statistical Yearbook*, National Committee for Statistics, Bucharest.

ComStat, 1994. *Romanian Statistical Yearbook*, National Committee for Statistics, Bucharest.

Coulomb, P. 1991. 'Politique Foncieres-Notes de Cours', Volume Nrs. 3–4, CIHEAM-IAM, Montellier.

Cox, M. 1988. 'Efectos de Ajuste Macroeconómico sobre el Sector Agroalimentario Chileno', *Ajuste Macroeconómico y Sector Agropecuario en América Latina*, IICA, Buenos Aires, pp. 1–21.

CPSS. 1996. *Perspectives on Central Asia*, Sovetbek J. Toktomyshev and Vyachelav I. Shapovalov, 'Fergana Valley, My Native Kyrgyz South.', *Internet Journal*, Vol.1 (2), February, Pittsburg.

Craumer, P. 1994. 'Regional Patterns of Agricultural Reform in Russia', *Post-Soviet Geography*, 1994, Vol. 35 (6), pp. 329–51.

Czaki, C. and Z. Lerman, 1996. 'Agricultural Transition Revisited. Issues of Land Reforms and Farm Restructuring in East Central Europe and the Former USSR', Plenary Papers VIIIth EAAE Conference, 'Redefining the Roles for European Agriculture', Edinburgh, pp. 61–96.

Davidova, S., D.Kopeva and A.Buckwell. 1996. 'Bulgaria: economics and politic of post-reform farm structures'. Paper presented to the COST Final Workshop, Romania, 15–16 June.

De Haan, C., T. Schillhorn van Veen and K. Brooks. 1992. 'The Livestock Sector in Eastern Europe'. World Bank Discussion Paper No. 173, Washington.

Demery, L. 1994. 'Structural Adjustment: Its Origins, Rationale and Achievements', in: G.A. Cornia, G.Helleiner (Eds.), *From Adjustment to Development in Africa*, MacMillan, Basingstoke.

Department of Policy and Management, Ministry of Agriculture. 1993. *Giau va ngheo o nong thon hien nay* (The rich and the poor in the countryside today), Hanoi.

——. 1991. *Thuc trang kinh te ho nong dan Viet nam sau doi moi co che quan li kinh te trong nong nghiep* (Situation of the peasant household economy after the renovation), Hanoi.

Dumitru, M. 1994. *Land Structure Evolution; An essay of Land Policy Analysis*, Master's Thesis, CIHEAM-IAM, Chania.

Dorner, P. 1972. *Land Reform and Economic Development*, Penguin, Harmondsworth.

Duncan, A. 1994. 'Report: Agricultural and economic reform issues in Kyrgyzstan, former Soviet Central Asia', *Food Policy*, Vol.19 (1), pp. 85–87.

EIU. 1993. *Country Report: Georgia, Armenia, Azerbaijan, Central Asian Republics*, The Economist Intelligence Unit, No.1, London.

EIU. 1995. *Country Report: Central Asian Republics: Kazakhstan, Kyrgyz Republic, Tajikistan, Turkmenistan, Uzbekistan*, The Economist Intelligence Unit, 1st Quarter, London.

Ellis, F. 1988. *Peasant Economics: Farm Households and Agrarian Development*, CUP, Cambridge, UK.

Engberg-Pedersen P., P. Gibbon, P.Raikes and L. Udsholt (Eds.). 1996. *Limits to Adjustment in Africa*, James Currey & Portsmouth N.H., Heinemann, London.

Euroconsult/CWFS. 1995. *Farm Restructuring and Land Tenure in Reforming Socialist Economies: A Comparative Analysis of Eastern and Central Europe*, World Bank Discussion Paper No. 268, World Bank, Washington.

Faaland, J. and J.Parkinson. 1991. 'The Nature of the State and the Role of Government in Agricultural Development', in: C.P.Timmer (Ed.), *Agriculture and the State*, Cornell University Press, Ithaca, London, pp. 247–74.

Faber, M. 1993. 'Project Rehabilitation: Getting the Issues Right', in: C.Kirkpatrick (Ed.), *Project Rehabilitation in Developing Countries*, Routledge, London and New York.

Fallas Venegas, H. and Rivera Urrutia, E., 1988, *Agricultura y Cambio Estructural en Centroamérica*, IICA Series Documentos de Programas No. 8.

FAO. 1988. *Potencialidades del Desarrollo Agrícola y Rural en América Latina y el Caribe: Informe Principal*, Rome.

FAO. 1989. 'Efectos de los Programas de Estabilización y Ajuste Estructural sobre la Seguridad Alimentaria', Comité de Seguridad Alimentaria Mundial, CFS:89/3, Rome, Mimeo.

FAO. 1990. *Efectos de los Programas de Estabilización y Ajuste Estructural en la Seguridad Alimentaria*, Estudio Desarrollo Económico y Social No. 89, Rome.

FAO. 1995. *FAO Production Yearbook 1994*, FAO, Rome.

Ferreira L. 1994. 'Poverty and inequality during structural adjustment in rural Tanzania' World Bank Transitional Economics Department, Research Paper No.8, Washington.

Ferroni, M. and Valdés, A. 1991. 'Agriculture in the Latin American Open Economy', *Food Policy*, February, pp. 2–9.

Furtado, C. 1981. *Economic Development of Latin America: Historical Background and Contemporary Problems*, Cambridge University Press, Cambridge.

General Statistical Office, 1971, 1979, 1982, 1992. *Nien giam thong ke* (Statistical Yearbooks), Hanoi.

——. 1991. *Nhung van de kinh te va doi song qua ba cuoc dieu tra nong nghiep cong nghiep va nha o* (Economic and living problems through three surveys on agriculture, industry and housing), Hanoi.

Ghura, D. and T.J. Grennes. 'The real exchange rate and macro-economic performance in sub-Saharan Africa', *Journal of Development Economics*, Vol. 42, pp. 155–74.

Gibbon P. 1996. 'Zimbabwe 1991–94', Country Case-Study in: Engberg-Pedersen *et al.* (Eds.), *Limits to Adjustment in Africa*, James Currey & Portsmouth N.H., Heinemann, London, pp. 349–97.

Glewwe, P. and D. de Tray. 1991. 'The Poor in Latin America During Adjustment: A Case Study of Peru', Mimeo.

Goitia, A. 1991. 'Reforma Agraria con Orientación de Mercado', in: R.Ruben, G. Van Oord (Eds.), *Más Alla del Ajuste*, DEI, San José.

Goldin, I. and G.C. de Rezende, 1990, *Agriculture and Economic Crisis: Lessons from Brazil*, Development Centre Studies, OECD, Paris.

González, B.R. 1993. *El Régimen de Tenencia de la Tierra en Costa Rica*, UNA, Heredia.

Gourou, P. 1936. *Les paysans du delta tonkinois*, Editions d'art et d'histoire, Paris.

Gourou, P. 1940. *Utilization du sol en Indochine Francaise*, P. Hartman, Paris.

Green, R.H. 1989. 'Articulating Stabilisation Programmes and Structural Adjustment: Sub-Saharan Africa', in: S. Commander (Ed.), *Structural Adjustment and Agriculture: Theory and Practice in Africa and Latin America*, ODI, London, pp. 35–54.

Grupo Esquel. 1989. 'Las Políticas de Desarrollo Rural en América Latina: Balance y Perspectivas', in: F. Jordan (Ed.), *La Económia Campesina: Crisis, Reactivación y Desarrollo*, IICA, San José, pp. 5–90.

Harris, B. 1990, 'Another Awkward Class: Merchants and Agrarian Change in India', in: N. Bernstein, *et al.* (Eds.), *The Food Question: Profits versus People?*, Earthscan, London.

Hayami Y. and Kikuchi M. 1981. *Asian Village Economy at the Cross-roads*, University of Tokyo Press, Tokyo.

Helleiner, G.K. 1992. 'The IMF, the World Bank and Africa's Adjustment and External Debt Problems: An Unofficial View', *World Development*, Vol 20(6).

Henrichsmeyer, W. 1977. 'Zum Interregionalen Wettbewerb und Strukturellen Wandel der Landwirtschaftlichen Produktion', in: *Schriften der Gesellschaft für Wirtschaft- und Sozialwissenschaften des Landbaues*, Vol. 14, 'Standortprobleme der Agrarproduktion', München, pp. 129–41.

Heredia, C.A. and M.E. Purcell. 1994. *La Polarización de la Sociedad Mexicana: Una Visión desde de la Base de las Políticas de Ajuste Económico del Banco Mundial*, Equipo Pueblo/Development Gap, México.

Herrero, A.F. and S. Trejos. 1992. 'El Impacto de las Reformas Políticas Macroeconómicas y Sectoriales en los Pobres Rurales de Siete Paises Latinoamericanos', in: R.A. Trejos (Ed.), *Ajuste Macroeconómico y Pobreza Rural en América Latina*, IICA, San José, pp. 401–33.

Hutchful, E. 1996. 'Ghana 1983–94, Country Case-Study in: Engberg-Pedersen *et al.* (Eds.), *Limits to Adjustment in Africa*, James Currey & Portsmouth N.H., Heinemann, London, pp. 143–214.

IDB (Inter-american Development Bank). 1995. *Economic and Social Progress in Latin America*, 1995 Report, Washington.

IDRC. 1987. *Economic Adjustment and Long-Term Development in Uganda*, Manuscript Report 116e, International Development Research Centre, Ottawa.

IICA. 1989. *Plan of Joint Action for Agricultural Reactivation in Latin America and the Caribbean*, Principal Document, San José.

IMF. 1995. 'Uganda: Back from the Brink and on the Path to Sustained Growth', *Survey*, December 11th.

IMF. 1996. 'Uganda: ESAF', *Survey*, January 8th.

INA. 1992. 'Evolución e las Acciones de Reforma Agraria durante el Período 1986-91', Paper presented by the Executive Director at the PRACA Reunion, San José, 5-6 March.

INA. 1994. Various internal documents on co-operatives.

INRA. 1993. 'El INRA, La Reforma Agraria y la Titulación en el Proceso de Estabilización, Consolidación y Desarrollo del Sector Reformado', *Por la Busqueda de una Estrategia de Desarrollo para Nicaragua*, ESECA-UNAN, Managua, pp. 45–58.

International Development Research Centre. 1987. *Economic Adjustment and Long-Term Development in Uganda*, Ottawa.

Ivanova, N. 1993. 'Measuring and Analysis of Government Protection to Bulgarian Agriculture during the Transition Period'. Working Paper No. 2, PHARE/APAU, Sofia, Bulgaria.

Ivanova, N. 1995. 'Impact of Price and Time: Policy on Bulgarian Agriculture'. Paper presented at the Seminar. 'Bulgarian Agriculture Problems and Perspectives', December, Sofia, Bulgaria.

de Janvry, A. and E. Sadoulet. 1989. 'Investment Strategies to Combat Rural Poverty: A Proposal for Latin America', *World Development*, Vol. 17 (8), pp. 1203–21.

de Janvry, A. and E. Sadoulet. 1995. *Quantitative Development Analysis*, Baltimore.

de Janvry, A., D. Runsten and E. Sadoulet. 1987. *Technological Innovations in Latin American Agriculture*, Program Series Papers No. 4., IICA, San José.

Jansen, K. and E. Roquas. 1996. Modernizing Insecurity: The Land Titling Project in Honduras, Paper presented at the SLAS Conference, Leeds, 28–30 March.

Jonakin, J. 1995. 'Agrarian Policy and Crisis in Nicaragua's Political Transition', Paper presented at the XIX International LASA Conference, Washington, September 28–30.

Katorobo, J. 1995. 'Reforming the Export Marketing System: Monopoly versus Competition in Export Marketing', in: P. Langseth, *et al. Uganda: Landmarks in Rebuilding a Nation*, Fountain, Kampala.

Kay, C. 1995. 'Rural Development and Agrarian Issues in Contemporary Latin America', in: J. Weeks (Ed.), *Structural Adjustment and the Agri-*

cultural Sector in Latin America and the Caribbean, MacMillan/ILAS, Basingstoke, pp. 9–44.

Kekic, Laza. 1996. 'Assessing and Measuring Progress in the Transition', Paper presented at the DSA Conference, 18–20 September, University of Reading, UK.

Kerkvliet, Benedict J.T. and D.J. Potter. (Eds.) 1995. *Vietnam's Rural Transformation*, Westview Press/Institute of Southeast Asian Studies, Boulder, Colorado.

Khan, Azizur R. 1996. 'The Transition to a Market Economy in Agriculture', in: K.Griffin (Ed.), *Social Policy and Economic Transformation in Uzbekistan*, ILO, Geneva, pp. 65–92.

Kirmse, R.D., L.F. Constantino and G.M. Guess. 1993. *Prospects for Improved Management of Natural Forests in Latin America*, LATEN Dissemination Note No. 9, World Bank, Washington.

Kopeva, D., P. Mishev and M. Jackson. 1995. 'Formation of Land Market Institutions and Impacts on Agricultural Activity', *Journal of Rural Studies*, Vol.10 (4), pp. 377-85.

Kopeva, D., K.Howe and P.Mishev. 1994. 'Land Reform and Liquidation of Collective Farm Assets in Bulgarian Agriculture: Progress and Prospects', *Communist Economies and Economic Transformation*, Vol.6, pp. 203–17.

Krissoff, B. and P. Trapido. 1991. 'Food and Agricultural Policy Reform: The Case of Venezuela', *Food Policy*, April, pp. 140–51.

Kyle, S. 1992. 'Pitfalls in the Measurement of Real Exchange Rate Effects on Agriculture', in: *World Development*, Vol.2 (7).

Larsen, J. 1995. 'The Land Titling Project in Santa Bárbara, 1983-93', Draft PhD Notes, University of Oxford.

Lavigne, M. 1995. *The Economics of Transition: From Socialist Economy to Market Economy*, MacMillan, UK.

Lewis, J.D. and S.D. Younger. 1994. 'Exchange Rate Management in Uganda', in: J.S. Duesenberry, *et al.*, *Improving Exchange Rate Management in Sub-Saharan Africa*, CAER Discussion Paper No. 31, November, HIID, Cambridge Ma.

Liefert, William M. 1995. 'Grain Sector Reform and Food Security in the Countries of the former USSR', Paper presented at Policy Workshop in Kiev, Ukraine, 6–8 December.

Liefert, W., D. Sedik and C. Foster. 1995. 'Russia: Progress in Agricultural Reform', *Transition*, OMRI, Vol.1 (16), 8 September, pp. 50–52, 60.

Lipton, M. 1968. 'The Theory of the Optimising Peasant', *Journal of Development Studies*, Vol. 4 (3), pp. 327–51.

López, M. and Spoor, M. 1992. Cambios Estructurales en el Mercado de Granos Básicos en Nicaragua, Escuela de Economía Agrícola-UNAN, Managua, Mimeo.

López Cordovez, L. 1990. 'Crisis, Políticas de Ajuste y Agricultura', in: O. Nuñez (Ed.), *Lo Agrario*, EDUCA, San José.

Loxley, J. 1989. 'The IMF, the World Bank and Reconstruction Uganda', in: B. Campbell and J. Loxley (Eds), *Structural Adjustment in Africa*, MacMillan, Basingstoke, pp. 67–91.

Lücke, M. 1994. 'Wirtschaftliche Grundlagen des Regionalismus in der Russischen Föderation', in: *Zeitschrift für Wirtschafts- und Sozialwissenschaften*, Vol. 114 (4), pp. 532–45.

Luiselli, C. 1988. 'Las Politicas de Ajuste Estructural sobre el Sector Agroalimentario de México, *Ajuste Macroeconómico y Sector Agropecuario en América Latina*, IICA, Buenos Aires.

Mackintosh, M. 1987. 'Agricultural Marketing and Socialist Accumulation: A Case Study of Maize Marketing in Mozambique', *Journal of Peasant Studies*, Vol.14, pp. 243–67.

Maletta, H. 1995. 'Argentine Agriculture and Economic Reform in the 1990s', in: J.Weeks (Ed.), *Structural Adjustment and the Agricultural Sector in Latin America and the Caribbean*, MacMillan/ILAS, Basingstoke.

Martínez, J.R. 1994. 'Los Militares, Su Peso Especifico en la Vida Política Hondureña', *Tiempos Nuevos*, March, pp. 16–28.

Martin, Keith. 1994. 'Central Asia's Forgotten Tragedy', *RFE/RL Research Report*, Vol.3 (30), 29 July, pp. 35–48.

Matus, J.G. and D. Vega V. 1992. 'Política Macroeconómica y Sectorial, sus Reformas y la Pobreza Rural en México', in: R.A Trejos (Ed.) *Ajuste Macroeconómico y Pobreza Rural en América Latina*, IICA, San José, 309–35.

Maurel, M-C. 1993. 'Recurrence de la question agraire en Europe Centrale, ou la rivalité des modeles', *Revue Geographique des Pirenée et de Sud-Ouest*, No. 63. (2).

Melyukhina, O. 1994. 'Regional Issues of Russia's Economic and Agricultural Development', Mimeo, Institute for the Economy in Transition, Moscow.

Mishev, P. 1995. 'Price and Trade Policy in the Grain Sector and Food Security'. Working Paper No. 1, PHARE/ALAU, Sofia, Bulgaria.

MOAF, 1995. *Information Bulletin*, Various Issues, Ministry of Agriculture and Food, Bucharest.

Morales, J.A. 1991a. 'Structural Adjustment and Peasant Agriculture in Bolivia', *Food Policy*, February, pp. 58–66.

Mosley, P., T. Subasat and J. Weeks. 1995. 'Assessing Adjustment in Africa', *World Development*, Vol.23 (9).

Mosley, P. 1996. 'The Failure of Aid and Adjustment Policies in Sub-Saharan Africa: Counter Examples and Policy Proposals', *Journal of African Economics*, vol. 5(3) pp. 406–43.

Muchnik, E. and M. Allue. 1991. 'The Chilean Experience with Agricultural Price Bands', *Food Policy*, February, pp. 67–73.

Mundlak, Y., D. Cavallo and R. Domenech. 1991. 'Agriculture and Growth in Argentina', *Food Policy*, February, vol. 16(1) pp. 10–16.

Muñoz, O., H. and Ortega. 1991. 'Chilean Agriculture and Economic Policy, 1974–86', in: M.J. Twomey and A. Helwege (Eds), *Modernisation and Stagnation: Latin American Agriculture in the 1990s*, Greenwood Press, Westport, pp. 161–88.

National Statistical Institute. 1996. *Statisticheski godishnik 1995*, Sofia, Bulgaria.

Nishimura, H. 1975. 'Farm management analysis and its problem of rice farming in the Mekong delta', *South-East Asian Studies*, Vol.13, No 1, 127–145.

Noé Pino, H., A. Thorpe, R. Sandoval Corea. 1992. *El Sector Agricola y la Modernización en Honduras*, CEDOH-POSCAE, Tegucigalpa.

Noé Pino, H. and P. Jímenez, A. Thorpe (Eds). 1994. *¿Estado o Mercado? Perspectivas para el Desarrollo Agrícola Centroamericano hacia el Año 2000*, POSCAE-UNAH, Tegucigalpa.

Norton, R. 1987. *Agricultural Issues in SAP*, Economic and Social Development Paper 66, FAO, Rome.

Pánuco-Laguette, H., M. Székely. 1996. Income Distribution and Poverty in Mexico', in: V.Bulmer-Thomas (Ed.), *The New Economic Model and its Impact on Poverty and Income Distribution in Latin America*, MacMillan/ILAS, Basingstoke.

Paz-Cafferata, J. and J.F. Larios. 1988. 'Impacto de las Politicas de Ajuste Macroeconómico sobre el Sector Agrario en el Perú', *Ajuste Macroeconómico y Sector Agropecuario en América Latina*, IICA, Buenos Aires, pp. 1–17.

Piñeiro, M. 1985. Agricultural Research in the Private Sector: Issues and Analytical Perspectives, ISNAR Working Paper, The Hague.

PNUD. 1994. *Informe sobre el Desarrollo Humano 1994*, Fondo de Cultura Económica, México.

Pomareda, C., R. Norton, L. Reca, J. Torres Zorilla. 1989. *Las Políticas Macroeconómicas y la Agricultura*, Series Documentos de Programas 14, IICA, San José.

Posas, M. 1992. La Autogestión en el Agro Hondureño: in: *El Caso de la Empresa Asociativa Campesina 'ISLETAS'*, Colección Realidad Nacional No.36, Editorial Universitaria, Tegucigalpa.

POSCAE-OXFAM. 1993. 'Los Campesinos ante los Retos de los Noventas', Mimeo, Tegucigalpa.

POSCAE-WISCONSIN. 1994. 'El Mercado de Tierras en Honduras', Mimeo, Tegucigalpa.

de Rezende, G.C. 1989. 'Brazil 1981–6', in: S. Commander (Ed.), *Structural Adjustment and Agriculture: Theory and Practice in Africa and Latin America*, ODI, London.

Raikes P. 1986. 'Eating the Carrot and Wielding the Stick: the Agricultural Sector in Tanzania' in: Boesen J., K. Havnevik, J.Koponen and R. Odgaard (Eds) *Tanzania: Crisis and Struggle for Recovery*, Scandinavian Institute of African Studies, Uppsala.

Raikes P. and Gibbon P. 1996. 'Tanzania 1986–94', Country Case-Study in: Engberg-Pedersen *et al.* (Eds), *Limits to Adjustment in Africa*, James Currey & Portsmouth N.H., Heinemann, London, pp. 217–307.

Reca, L.G. and C.J. Garramon. 1989. 'Argentine Interactions between the Adjustment Programme and the Agricultural Sector', in: *Agriculture and Governments in an Interdependent World*, Proceedings of the Twentieth International Conference of Agricultural Economists, Dartmouth Publishers, Aldershot.

Republic of Uganda. 1992. *Rehabilitation and Development Plan 1991/92–1994/95*, Vol.1, p. 71, MFEP, Kampala.

Republic of Uganda. 1993-1996. *Background to the Budget, 1993–94, 1994–95, 1995–96, 1996–97*, MFEP, Kampala.

Republic of Uzbekistan. 1994. *Decrees and Resolutions: On Measures for Intensification of Economic Reforms, Protection of Private Property and Promotion of Entrepreneurship*, Uzbekistan Publishing House, Tashkent.

Ruben, R. and F. Fúnez. 1993. *La Compra-Venta de Tierras de la Reforma Agraria*, Guaymuras, Tegucigalpa.

Rumer, B.Z. 1989. *Soviet Central Asia: 'A Tragic Experiment'*, Unwin Hyman, Boston.

Salgado, R., P. Jiménez, H. Chávez, H. Noé Pino, J. Melmed-Sanjak, A-L. Restrepo, A.Thorpe. 1994. *El Mercado de Tierras en Honduras*, CEDOH-POSCAE-WISCONSIN, Tegucigalpa.

Schiff, M., A.Valdés. 1992. *A Synthesis of the Economics of the Political Economy in Developing Countries, Volume 4: The Political Economy of Agricultural Pricing Policy*, Johns Hopkins Univ. Press, Baltimore.

Schultz, Th.W. 1964. *Transforming Traditional Agriculture*, Lyall Books, London.

Sepehri, A. 1994. 'Back to the Future? A Critical Review of *Adjustment in Africa*: *Reforms, Penalty and the Road Ahead*, *Review of African Political Economy*, No. 62, pp. 559–68.

Serova, E. 1994. 'Agrarian Reform and Reinstatement of Collectivism, Cooperatives and Self management in the Countryside'. Paper prepared for the Conference on 'Institutionen in Transformationsprozeß der Landwirtschaft', Bielefeld, September.

Serova, E., A. Mannellya, A. Korbut, O. Melyukhina, S. Shashnov and A.Surinov, 1995. 'Annotated Statistics of Pskov, Orel and Rostov Oblasts', Mimeo, February, Institute for the Economy in Transition, Centre of Economic Analysis, Moscow.

Sharer, R. *et al.* 1994. 'Uganda's Sustained Structural Reforms Yield Broad Gains', *IMF Survey*, 24th January.

Sivignon, M. 1992. 'La diffusion des modeles agricoles: essay d'interpretation des agricultures de l'Est et de Sud de l'Europe', *Revue Geographique des Pirenée et de Sud-Ouest*, Vol. 63 (2).

Speirs M. 1996. 'Burkina Faso 1983–94', Country Case-Study in: Engberg-Pedersen *et al.* (Eds.), *Limits to Adjustment in Africa*, James Currey & Portsmouth N.H., Heinemann, London, pp. 81–139.

Spoor, M. 1994. 'Issues of State and Market: From Interventionism to Deregulation of Food Markets in Nicaragua', *World Development*, Vol. 22 (4), pp. 517–532.

Spoor, M. 1995a. 'Agrarian Transition in Former Soviet Central Asia: A Comparative Study of Uzbekistan and Kyrgyzstan', *The Journal of Peasant Studies*, Vol. 23 (1), September, pp. 46–63.

Spoor, M. 1995b. *The State and Domestic Agricultural Markets in Nicaragua: From Interventionism to Neo-Liberalism*, MacMillan/ISS, Basingstoke; St.Martin's Press, New York.

Spoor, M. 1996a. 'Upheaval along the Silk Route: The Dynamics of Economic Transition in FSU Central Asia', Working Paper Nr. 216, April, Institute of Social Studies, The Hague.

Spoor, M. 1996b. 'Mongolia: Agrarian Crisis in the Transition to a Market Economy', *Europe-Asia Studies*, Vol.48 (4), June, pp. 615–28.

Spoor, M. and M. López. 1993. 'Cambios Estructurales en el Mercado de Granos Básicos en Nicaragua', DEA/UNAN, Managua.

State Planning Committee, 1994. *Khao Muc Song Dan Cu Viet Nam* (Vietnam Living Standards Survey 1992-1993), General Statistical Office, Hanoi.

Stat Kom KR. 1996. *Kyrgyzstan v Tsifrakh 1995* (Kyrgyzstan in Figures 1995), National Statistical Committee of the Republic of Kyrgyzstan, Bishkek.

StatKom SNG. 1995. *Statisticheskii Ezhegodnik* (Statistical Yearbook), CIS Statistical Committee, May, Moscow.

StatKom SNG. 1996. *Sodruzhestvo Nezavisimykh Gosudarstv v 1995 Godu* (The CIS in 1995), CIS Statistical Committee, January, Moscow.

Stoneman C. 1993. 'The World Bank: Some lessons for South Africa', *Review of African Political Economy,* No. 58, November, pp. 87–98.

Thorpe, A.T. 1991. 'Las Politicas de la Reforma Agraria y la Necessidad de Planificación Agrícola', in: H. Noé Pino, A.Thorpe (Eds.), *La Reforma Agraria y el Ajuste Estructural,* CEDOH, Tegucigalpa.

Thorpe, A.T. 1992. 'Caminos Políticos y Económicos hacia la Reactivación y Modernización del Sector Agrícola: Una Vez entendido el Ajuste', in: H. Noé Pino, A.Thorpe, S. Sandoval Corea, *El Sector Agrícola y la Modernización en Honduras,* CEDOH-POSCAE, Tegucigalpa.

Thorpe, A.T. 1993. 'El Mercado de Tierras en Honduras: Panorama y Perspectivas', POSCAE Mimeo, Tegucigalpa.

Thorpe, A.T. 1995a. 'Adjusting to Reality: The Impact of Structural Adjustment on Honduran Agriculture', *Structural Adjustment and the Agriculture Sector in Latin America and the Caribbean,* Weeks, J. (Ed.), MacMillan/ILAS, Basingstoke.

Thorpe, A.T. 1995b. Macro-Economic Conditions for a Sustainable Agriculture in Central America, University of Portsmouth Department of Economics Working Paper No.65.

Thorpe, A.T. 1996. 'Honduras, The New Economic Model and Poverty', *The New Economic model in Latin America and its Impact on Income Distribution and Poverty,* V. Bulmer-Thomas (Ed.), MacMillan/ILAS, Basingstoke.

Thorpe, A.T., A-L. Restrepo. 1995a. 'Algunas Consideraciones sobre el Crédito Agrícola', in: H. Noé Pino, A.Thorpe, A-L. Restrepo (Eds.), *El Crédito Agrícola en el Ambiente Centroamericano,* POSCAE-UNAH, Guaymuras, Tegucigalpa, pp. 21–70.

Thorpe, A. and A-L. Restrepo. 1995b. *El Sector Agricola y la Modernización en Honduras,* CEDOH-POSCAE, Tegucigalpa.

Timmer, P.C. 1986. *Getting Prices Right: The Scope and Limits of Agricultural Price Policy,* Cornell University Press, New York, London.

Timmer, P.C. 1991. *Agriculture and the State,* Cornell University Press, New York, London.

Tomich, T.P. 1991. 'Land Reform: Comments in Politics and Policy Making', in: G. Meier, (Ed.), *Developing Countries,* ICEG, ICS Press, San Francisco.

UE (Unión Europea). 1995. Honduras: Country Strategy Paper, Mimeo, Brussels.

University of Wisconsin, LTC. 1985. 'Evaluación de Punto Medio del Proyecto de Titulación de Tierras en Honduras', Project No. 522–0173, Mimeo, Tegucigalpa.

University of Wisconsin, LTC. 1990. 'Case Study of Rural Land Markets in Ecuador', Mimeo, April.

USDA. 1973. *Agriculture in the Vietnam economy*, US Department of Agriculture, Washington.

USDA. 1993a. *Agricultural Statistics of the Former USSR Republics and the Baltic States,* Economic Research Service, US Department of Agriculture, Washington.

USDA. 1993b. 'Former USSR', Situation and Outlook Series, Economic Research Service, US Department of Agriculture, May, Washington.

USDA. 1995. 'Former USSR Update: Agriculture and Trade Report', Economic Research Service, US Department of Agriculture, September, Washington.

Valdés, A. 1992. 'Agricultural Trade and Pricing Policies in Developing Countries: Implications for Policy Reform', *Sustainable Agricultural Development, The Role of International Cooperation, Proceedings of the Twenty-First International Conference of Agricultural Economists*, Dartmouth Press, Aldershot.

Valdés, A. 1993. 'The Macroeconomic Environment Necessary for Agricultural Trade and Price Policy Reforms', *Food Policy*, August, pp. 272–82.

Van Atta, Don. 1993. *The 'Farmer Threat', The Political Economy of Agrarian Reform in Post-Soviet Russia*, Westview Press, Boulder, Colorado.

Wachter, D. 1992. 'Die Bedeutung des Landtitelbesitzes fur eine nachhaltige landwirstchaftliche Bodennutzung. Eine empirisiche Fallstudie in Honduras', *Geografische Zeitschrift*, Vol. 80 (3), pp. 174–83.

Weeks, J. 1995a. 'Introduction', in: J. Weeks (Ed.), *Structural Adjustment and the Agricultural Sector in Latin America and the Caribbean*, MacMillan/ILAS, Basingstoke, pp. 1–8.

Weeks, J. 1995b. 'Macroeconomic Adjustment and Latin American Agriculture since 1980', in: J. Weeks (Ed.), *Structural Adjustment and the Agricultural Sector in Latin America and the Caribbean*, MacMillan/ILAS, Basingstoke, pp. 61–92.

Weiner D., S. Moyo, B. Munslow and P. O'Keefe. 1985. 'Land Use and Agricultural Productivity in Zimbabwe', *Journal of Modern African Studies*, Vol. 23 (2), pp. 251–86.

Weinschenk, G. and W. Henrichsmeyer. 1966. 'Zur Theorie und Entwicklung des Räumlichen Gleichgewichts der Landwirtsschaftlichen Produktion', *Berichte über Landwirtschaft*, Hamburg, pp. 201–42.

White, H. 1992. 'The Macroeconomic Impact of Development Aid: A Critical Survey', *Journal of Development Studies*, Vol.28 (2).

White, H. and G. Wignaraja. 1992. 'Exchange Rates, Trade Liberalisation and Aid: The Sri Lankan Experience', *World Development*, Vol 20(10), pp. 1471–80.

Williams, R.G. 1986. *Export Agriculture and the Crisis in Central America*, University of North Carolina Press, Chapel Hill.

World Bank. 1981. *Accelerated Development in Sub-Saharan Africa: An Agenda for Action*, World Bank, Washington.

World Bank. 1986. *Poverty and Hunger*, World Bank, Washington.

World Bank 1989. *African Adjustment and Growth in the 1980s*. World Bank, Washington.

World Bank. 1992. *Food and Agricultural Policy Reforms in the Former USSR: An Agenda for the Transition*, World Bank, Washington.

World Bank. 1993a. *Kyrgyzstan, The Transition to a Market Economy*, World Bank Country Study, Washington.

World Bank. 1993b. *Latin America and the Caribbean: A Decade after the Debt Crisis*, World Bank, Washington.

World Bank. 1993c. *Uzbekistan: An Agenda for Reform*, World Bank Country Study, World Bank, Washington.

World Bank. 1994a. *A Continent in Transition: Sub-Saharan Africa in the mid-1990s*, Internal Document, World Bank, December.

World Bank. 1994b. *Honduras: Country Economic Memorandum/Poverty Assessment*, World Bank, Washington.

World Bank. 1994c. *Kazakhstan, Agricultural Sector Review*, Internal Report, December, World Bank, Washington.

World Bank. 1994d. *Statistical Handbook 1993, States of the Former USSR* (*Statistichekii Sbornik, 1993 god*), World Bank, Washington.

World Bank. 1994e. *Uzbekistan, Economic Memorandum: Subsidies and Transfers*, Official Document, World Bank, Washington.

World Bank. 1994f. *Adjustment in Africa: Reforms, Results, and the Road Ahead*, Oxford University Press for the World Bank, Oxford.

World Bank, 1995a. *Vietnam, Poverty Assessment and Strategy*, World Bank, Washington.

World Bank. 1995b. *World Debt Tables 1994-95*, World Bank, Washington.

World Bank. 1996. *World Development Report: From Plan to Market*, Oxford University Press, published for the World Bank, Washington.

Wuyts M. 1994. 'Accumulation, Industrialization and the Peasantry: A Reinterpretation of the Tanzanian Experience', *Journal of Peasant Studies*, Vol. 21 (2), pp. 159–93.

Zhukov, S.V. 1995. 'Tendentsii Ekonomicheskogo Rasvitiia Gosudarstv Tsentralnoi Azii' (Economic Development Trends of the Central Asian States), Mimeo, November, Tashkent.